NEW YORK
&
NEW JERSEY
GOLF GUIDE

YOUR PASSPORT TO GREAT GOLF!

ABOUT THE AUTHOR

Jimmy Shacky is the author of *Florida Golf Guide* and *Golf Courses of the Southwest*, both published by Open Road Publishing. He lives in Ft. Lauderdale, Florida, with his wife Suzanne.

Each Open Road golf guide gives you complete coverage of the courses that best suit your game. Detailed information is given on everything from course difficulty, total yards, greens fees, pro shops, club rentals, facilities, and much more! New guides also offer places to stay and fun excursions for individuals and families!

NEW YORK

&

NEW JERSEY

GOLF GUIDE

YOUR PASSPORT TO GREAT GOLF!

JIMMY SHACKY

OPEN ROAD PUBLISHING

OPEN ROAD PUBLISHING

Open Road publishes golf guides to your favorite destinations, as well as travel guides to American and foreign locales. Write for your *free* catalog of all our titles.

Catalog Department, Open Road Publishing
P.O. Box 11249, Cleveland Park Station, Washington, DC 20008

1st Edition

Copyright © 1994 by Jimmy Shacky
- All Rights Reserved -
ISBN 1-883323-10-X
Library of Congress Catalog No. 94-66038

Front Cover photo courtesy of Omni Sagamore Resort
Back Cover photo courtesy of Marriott's Seaview Resort

TABLE OF CONTENTS

INTRODUCTION

You'll find some of the world's finest and most respected golfing establishments in New York and New Jersey. Every important architect has been drawn to this part of America. If ever a Hall of Fame devoted to the art of golf course architecture is built, the Empire State and the Garden State would undoubtedly reap more than their fair share of awards.

Every type of golf course imaginable has been scrutinized from top to bottom, making it easy for you to choose a series of courses that will best complement your style of play. I've included course type, year built, architect, local pro, amount of holes per locale, yardage, rating and slope, how many days in advance to place a tee-time, price differences from high-to-low, amenities, credit cards, driving ranges, practice greens, locker rooms, rental clubs, walkers, snack bars, restaurants, lounges, meeting rooms, and more!

In addition, the following types of courses have been listed in multiple sections for the sake of making the book truly complete: 9-hole, Executive, Par-3, Military, and those much coveted private establishments. You'll also find an excursion section devoted to pointing out the most compelling attractions for you and your family to enjoy, as well as a listing of places to stay.

Don't leave home without this book, because without it you may never know if you're close to an exciting golfing venue! The **NEW YORK / NEW JERSEY GOLF GUIDE** was written to save you time as you plan your next golf outing, by pulling together all this critical information to help guide you to a huge variety of courses, or perhaps help you discover a hidden gem you've never heard of before.

You won't find a more straightforward, informative golf guide. My hope is that you'll discover a special course that you'll want to play again and again, and when you arrive home, you'll have a great story to share with your friends.

May your life be one filled with a never-ending string of Pars, Birdies, Eagles, and Albatrosses. Happy golfing!

2. HOW TO USE THIS BOOK

When I first looked at New York, I wasn't quite sure of how I wanted to represent it. I looked at it from various angles, broke it down into individual counties, and finally reassembled them into their distinct regions. After much deliberation, I decided to divide the state into the following four regions: North, Central, South, and West.

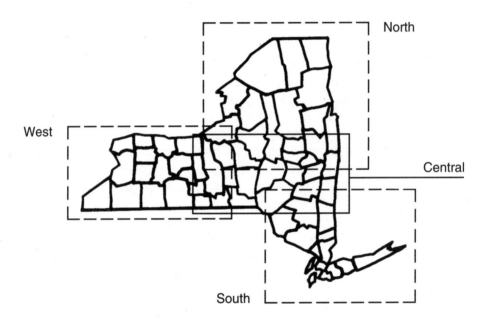

I wanted each section to feature an even amount of courses to choose from, and as you'll see in the pages that follow, I came close to achieving that goal. I didn't want one section noticeably smaller or bigger than the other, and that is why I divided the New York map in its present form, without having to add a fifth region (East).

For the sake of simplicity, and because of its relatively small size, the New Jersey map was divided into two respective regions: North and South.

Note: *The cities selected in the New York "Where to Stay" section coincide with the cities that are listed in this book (those that are near the golf courses selected).*

HOW TO USE THIS BOOK

Look up the state that interests you the most in the Table of Contents and turn to the beginning of that section. You'll be introduced to the general location of each featured golf course, the city or town that it's in, and its county borders.

Example: New York - North Map

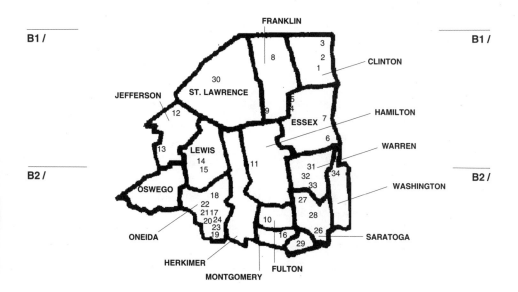

Below each map is an alphabetical listing of all the counties and a numerical directive to a golf course location within a representative city. Before I break down the first county listing for the state of New York (North), take a look at both the left and right side of the map located above this paragraph. You should easily find two primary directives written as: B1 (Block 1) and B2. They serve to breakdown the area map into two distinct sections, making it twice as easy to locate both the county and city of your choice,

The following is an example of the first county listing in this particular section of the book. To the right you'll find an explanation for each one of its sections.

Clinton

B1 / Peru ... 1

Clinton : This is the name of the first county listing.

B1 /   : This indicates which block of the map
                 the county is located in.

Peru ... 1   : This is the numerical directive assigned to
                 the city of Peru.

This example tells us that Clinton county is located on the first block (B1) of the map above. Take a look at the example map once again and scan the first block (B1).

HOW TO USE THIS BOOK

from either left-to-right or right-to-left, while searching for Clinton County. You'll find it on the northeast corner of the map. Now go back to the example that showcases the first county listing. Following the forward slash after the B1 section, we can see that the city of Peru has a golf course location, represented with the number 1, that you can play on. When you go back to the map you'll notice its location below two additional courses (2 & 3) in Clinton County.

FINDING THE RIGHT COURSE

Each course listing can be found in one of three ways:

1) Region: Region names and their following page numbers are listed in the Table Of Contents.

2) County: County names and their following page numbers are listed in the Table Of Contents. The following title bar illustrates how each county is represented throughout the book:

CLINTON COUNTY

County names are listed at the top section of every page, in alphabetical order. Keep in mind that each page covers two independent courses. If the second course listing is located in the following county, the following county will be written after the preceding county by a forward slash on the title bar as follows:

CLINTON / ESSEX COUNTIES

The title bar above indicates the county location of the two courses on that particular page. The first is located in Clinton County, and the second is located in Essex county.

3) Name: If you already know the name of a particular course that you'll want to play, you can look it up quickly in the Index.

Below the county title, you'll find the corresponding courses with their detailed information in alphabetical order. Look at the example on the following page (**ADIRONDACK GOLF & COUNTRY CLUB**); it's the first section directly below the title that you will see.

COURSE LISTINGS

The following is a breakdown of the format used for each course listing:

ADIRONDACK GOLF & COUNTRY CLUB
RR3 Rock Rd., Box 96, Peru, NY 12972 / (518) 643-8403

The **ADIRONDACK GOLF & COUNTRY CLUB** is the name of the establishment and is followed by its address, city, state, zip, area code and phone number. The phone numbers listed are for the pro shop of each establishment (when made available). It is by far the quickest way to place your tee time or make an appointment with a golfing professional for a private lesson.

This is the **BASIC INFORMATION** box that is included with every course description. Let's have a look below at all of the individual sections.

BASIC INFORMATION

Course Type: Public
Year Built: 1980's
Architect: B. Silva, M. Mungeam, J. Cornnish
Local Pro: Bruce Fry

Course: N/A
Holes: 18 / Par 72

Back : 6,851 yds. Rating: 71.9 Slope: 123
Middle: 6,359 yds. Rating: 69.6 Slope: 117
Ladies: 5,069 yds. Rating: 71.0 Slope: 116

Tee Time: 4-5 days in advance.
Price: $18 - $28

Credit Cards:	■	Restaurant:	■
Driving Range:	■	Lounge:	■
Practice Green:	■	Meeting Rooms:	■
Locker Room:		Tennis:	
Rental Clubs:	■	Swimming:	
Walkers:	■	Jogging Trails:	
Snack Bar:	■	Boating:	■

Course Type: Most area golfers play on public courses, and this book's coverage of public courses is extensive. Many other types of courses allow non-members to play, too. Here is a listing and a definition for each title:

A **Municipal** course is one that is owned and operated by a local governing body. These courses are open to the general public without membership.

A **Public** course is privately owned by a single owner or a corporation. Play is open to the general public. Many of these courses cater to local players by offering inviting memberships at discount rates. These memberships will usually allow advance tee-time privileges as an added bonus.

A **Semi-private** course is one that is also owned privately or by a corporation. Like municipal and public courses, these courses are open to the general public. Many of these courses will offer a higher priority to their members in booking reservations.

HOW TO USE THIS BOOK

A **Private** course is one that is reserved for membership play only. These courses are frequently called **country clubs** and are meticulously kept. Private courses have a code of ethics that is strictly followed by golfers throughout America. Please adhere to the following principles and practices.

If you happen to be a member of a private course, you may have the opportunity of playing other private courses too. The first thing you'll need to find out is whether the course you want to play will reciprocate with the course that you are a member of. Some courses will only reciprocate with courses in their immediate area and others will only reciprocate with courses out of state. There is no rule with whom they must reciprocate. The proper method of communication is to have your golf professional set up an appointment with the pro at the course that you'll want to play.

One of the most popular ways of getting onto a private course is to become a friend with one of its members. They have the luxury of setting up an invitation for you to play the course at your leisure. It's a great way of getting to know people and hopefully being in a position to extend your gratitude by inviting them to play on your private course in the near future. If you're not a member of a private course, you can certainly invite them to a course you've enjoyed playing in the past.

A **Resort** course is one that is owned and operated by a resort-hotel. These courses offer excellent vacation packages for people both in and out of the states of New York and New Jersey. Some of these courses are privately run for the guests of the resort only. Don't despair, the majority of them do allow public play.

Course Type: Public
Year Built: 1980's
Architect: Bill Silva
Local Pro: Bruce Fry

This is the first section within the Basic Information box. Let's have a look at all of the individual subsections:

Course Type: Public

Course Type will tell you the type of play that each course allows.

Year Built: 1980's

The **Year Built** corresponds to the year the course was opened. Over a certain period of time, courses lose their shape through the forces of nature. If any additional work had been done to the course by anyone after the original architect, a following date after a forward slash will indicate the year the change took place. Remember that there will be times when you'll see N/A following the colon marks, indicating that no one is quite sure of the exact dates.

Architect: Bill Silva

The original **Architect's** name will be the first name listed. If any additional work had been done to the course by anyone after the original architect, the secondary architect's name will be listed after the forward slash. An **N/A** suggests that the architect's name is unknown to the golfing establishment.

Local Pro: Bruce Fry

Local Pro: These are the people that you'll want to contact to book lessons. They often have the expertise on how the course should be played and the elements that you should watch out for.

Course: N/A
Holes: 18 / Par 72

This is the second section in the Basic Information box. The following will explain both sub-headings:

Course: N/A

Course: Some establishments have more than just one course for you to choose from. Each course is assigned a different name for people to identify it with. Many courses simply choose the location of each course from a certain starting point and end up calling their courses "East" or "West."

Whenever I was confronted with a two course situation, I chose the course that was most sought after. In this particular example, the N/A appears because the establishment only has one course, and thus does not need another name to differentiate it from another course. It simply goes by the title name of the establishment: **ADIRONDACK GOLF & COUNTRY CLUB.**

Holes: 1

Holes: This number is the amount of holes for that particular course. If more than one course is featured, the hole number and par move into parenthesis under the sub-heading **Course**. The new number in the sub-heading **Holes** indicates the amount of holes available to play.

HOW TO USE THIS BOOK

Course: East (18 / Par 72)
Holes: 36

Looking at the top example tothe left, we now know that the main body of the course description will be based on the **East** course. The numbers in the parenthesis tells us that it's an 18 hole / Par 72 layout. We also know that the establishment offers an additional course by the number 36 indicated in the sub-heading: **Holes**.

Note: Some courses offer 27 holes of golf. In most instances they'll tie two courses together to get a total of three layouts for the public to choose from. Others may have as many as 99 holes to play. Resort establishments are usually the ones that feature the greatest variety of courses within a single location.

Back: 6,851 yds. Rating: 71.9 Slope: 123
Middle: 6,359 yds. Rating: 69.6 Slope: 117
Ladies: 5,069 yds. Rating: 71.0 Slope: 116

As you work your way down the **Basic Information** box, these three sets of numbers will be the next section to appear. They are the most important and informative listings in the book. These numbers indicate the length and severity of the course from a number of different starting positions called tee-markers.

The order of difficulty for these tee-markers are as follows: Back-tees, Middle-tees, and the Ladies-tees. Knowing how to read and interpret the numbers in this section will help you make an educated choice as to the best course suited for your individual game.

Back: 6,851 yds.
Middle: 6,359 yds.
Ladies: 5,069 yds.

This sub-section indicates the total yardage from each of the individual tees. I chose to represent each course with these three sub-sections because it breaks down the entire playing field to its simplest form. Many of the newer courses offer additional tees for a wider spectrum of players. Most courses color-code their tee-markers, from back to front in the following way: Blue, White, and Red.

HOW TO USE THIS BOOK

Rating: 71.9
Rating: 69.6
Rating: 71.0

Course ratings are an indication of how difficult a course is for a scratch golfer (a golfer who shoots par or better). This book includes the U.S.G.A. (United States Golf Association) ratings to the extent available. The best way to judge a course sight-unseen is to evaluate both the course rating and the slope rating. Each tee marker will have a different course rating that will judge the difficulty from the distance that the course is to be played from that marker.

Here is an example that will help you understand the system. If course #1 and #2 are rated at 71.4, would it be safe to assume that these courses are equally difficult? Can a person judge the severity of play without ever seeing the courses in the first place? Yes! Use this approach: When comparing two different courses, always look at the par rating for both courses. If course #1 is a par 72 at 6,624 yards, and course #2 is a par 70 at 6,515 yards, we can assume that both of these courses are relatively the same. The biggest difference between the two is that course #1 is 109 yards longer than course #2. A possible one stroke difference. The shorter course is harder to play because it is a Par 70 course rather than a Par 72. With a two-stroke difference minus the one-stroke given to the first course, the shorter course is still one stroke harder than the first.

You can also picture it this way. If you could take that 109 yard difference and place it on any random hole on course #1, that hole will automatically change to a one-stroke par difference. Say we placed that 109 yard difference on a Par 4 hole that measures 408 yards. It can now be considered a Par 5 at 517 yards. Course #2 still has a one-stroke difference to make up despite its relative length. It is unquestionably the harder of the two.

Slope: 123
Slope: 117
Slope: 116

High handicap players (players that shoot well above par 72) can rely on this secondary system developed by the United States Golf Association (U.S.G.A.).

When comparing two or more courses, the one with the highest slope rating will be the most difficult to play. The U.S.G.A. considers a slope rating of 113 to be of average difficulty. The only way you'll get a full understanding of how this number relates to your personal game would be to write down your final score along with the course ratings for the next 10 courses you play in the future.

HOW TO USE THIS BOOK

When you look back at these numbers, pick the courses that you had posted similar numbers on. If their slope ratings are about even or closely related, the average number between them is the number best suited for your game. Always play from the tees that post the closest slope rating to the one you now consider your personal average. This will bring the course down to your playing style and will allow you to have the most amount of fun on a level that is challenging but not over-bearing. If your game has been improving, start playing from the back tees. If you find playing from the back tees too lengthy, search for a course that offers a higher slope rating from the middle tees.

Tee Time: 4 days in advance.
Price: $18 - $28

This is the fourth section in the **Basic Information** box. The following will explain both sub-headings:

Tee Time: 4 days in advance.

The numbers in this sub-heading indicate how many days the course will allow you to book a tee time (a reservation to play) in advance.

Note: The numbers used in this book are based on a walk-in scenario. Keep in mind that most of the Resort courses listed in this book will allow you to book a tee-time well in advance if you plan to stay at their establishment. It isn't unusual to post a tee-time as far back as six months to a year.

Price: $18 - $28

Price: The numbers in this sub-heading indicate the price variance for the entire year based on the lowest to highest price. Prices are subject to change without notice. Please call to confirm.

Credit Cards:	■	Restaurant:	■
Driving Range:	■	Lounge:	■
Practice Green:	■	Meeting Rooms:	■
Locker Room:		Tennis:	
Rental Clubs:	■	Swimming:	
Walkers:	■	Jogging Trails:	
Snack Bar:	■	Boating:	■

This is the fifth and last section in the **Basic Information** box. Any listing with a black box next to it indicates that the course offers that subject or amenity.

A Black box by *Boating* indicates that the course is a half-hour away from the ocean or any other body of water by automobile.

Some courses only allow walking during certain hours of the day. If that happens to be an objective of yours, please call the course to confirm the proper time of the day.

COURSE DESCRIPTION

You'll find a concise course description for every listing with information that will help you choose the course to play. The following is a sample piece:

*"**Adirondack Golf & Country Club** will challenge all types of players despite their handicaps. You'll find interesting holes throughout its rolling terrain — holes that will force you to think about club selection and your chances of pulling off certain types of shots. The 9th hole, a par-4 measuring 433 yards from the back-tees, is the hardest design on the course. You'll need to stay on the left side of the fairway to avoid the diagonal brook that comes into play at around 160 to 230 yards from the tees."*

Golf courses, or their particular holes, may be defined in one of three architectural terms: **Strategic**, **Penal,** and **Heroic**.

Strategic: Strategic holes allow a golfer two driving options off the tee. Think of a dog-leg left hole with water coming into play along the entire left side. Your first option would be to flirt with the water by playing your ball over the water, cutting off as much length from the hole as possible, and having the ball spin back and onto the fairway, leaving you with a simple short length shot to the green. If you're not successful and the ball ends up in the water, you'll be penalized two strokes.

The next option would be to eliminate the water completely and play to the safest part of the fairway known as the "bailout" area. From this point you'll have a long and difficult approach shot.

Penal: Penal holes are the most demanding. You can only play them one way or you'll end up in a lot of trouble. An island par-3 hole with water dividing the teeing area from the green is a great example. You're forced to hit the ball over water and land it on the green to be successful.

Heroic: Heroic holes are a matter of expression. The basic premise is based on the nature of the terrain that the course features. Mountain courses with high elevation changes, desert courses secluded among hundreds of cacti and ocean-side courses with par-3's playing over ocean water fit into this category perfectly.

You'll even find courses that feature all three of these examples within one championship layout.

DIRECTIONS

Directions to the course can be found directly below each course description. They start from a major highway en route to the course. If you're visiting an area for the first time, please make sure you take along a concise map of the area with you.

It always helps to be prepared in case you venture off in the wrong direction and end up in an unfamiliar area. Nothing is more frustrating than waking up early in the morning and arriving at the course long after your reservation time.

3. N.Y. NORTH/COUNTIES AND CITIES

Clinton
B1 / Peru ... 1
B1 / Plattsburgh ... 2
B1 / Rouses Point ... 3

Jefferson
B1 / Alexandria Bay ...12
B1 / Watertown ...13

Oswego
B2 / Fulton ... 25

Saratoga
B2 / Clifton Park ... 26
B2 / Corinth ... 27
B2 / Saratoga Springs ... 28

Essex
B1 / Lake Placid ... 4
B1 / Saranac ... 5

Lewis
B1 / Lowville ... 14
B2 / Turin ...15

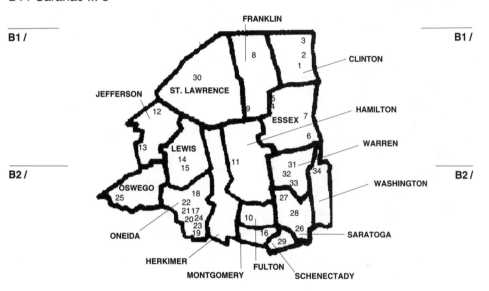

B1 /   B1 /

B2 /   B2 /

B1 / Ticonderogta ... 6
B1 / Westport ... 7

Montgomery
B1 / Amsterdam ... 16

Schenectady
B2 / Schenectady ... 29

Franklin
B1 / Malone ... 8
B1 / Tupper Lake ... 9

Oneida
B2 / Marcy ... 17
B2 / McConellsville ... 18
B2 / New Hartford ... 19
B2 / New York Mills ... 20
B2 / Oriskany ... 21
B2 / Rome ... 22
B2 / Utica ... 23
B2 / Whiteboro ... 24

St. Lawrence
B1 / Canton ... 30

Fulton
B2 / Johnstown ... 10

Warren
B2 / Bolton Landing ... 31
B2 / Lake George ... 32
B2 / Queensbury ... 33

Hamilton
B1 / Inlet ... 11

Washington
B2 / Whitehall ... 34

ADIRONDACK GOLF & COUNTRY CLUB

RR3 Rock Rd., Box 96, Peru, NY 12972 / (518) 643-8403

BASIC INFORMATION

Course Type: Public
Year Built: 1980's
Architect: B. Silva, M. Mungeam, J. Cornnish
Local Pro: Bruce Fry

Course: N/A
Holes: 18 / Par 72

Back : 6,851 yds. Rating: 71.9 Slope: 123
Middle: 6,359 yds. Rating: 69.6 Slope: 117
Ladies: 5,069 yds. Rating: 71.0 Slope: 116

Tee Time: 4-5 days in advance.
Price: $18 - $28

Credit Cards: ■   Restaurant: ■
Driving Range: ■   Lounge: ■
Practice Green: ■   Meeting Rooms: ■
Locker Room: Tennis:
Rental Clubs: ■   Swimming:
Walkers: ■   Jogging Trails:
Snack Bar: ■   Boating: ■

COURSE DESCRIPTION

Adirondack Golf & Country Club will challenge all types of players despite their handicaps. You'll find interesting holes throughout its rolling terrain — holes that will force you to think about club selection and your chances of pulling off certain types of shots. The 9th hole, a par-4 measuring 433 yards from the back-tees, is the hardest design on the course. You'll need to stay on the left side of the fairway to avoid the diagonal brook that comes into play at around 160 to 230 yards from the tees.

DIRECTIONS

Take I-87 to Exit 36 and make a left towards Rt. 22. Make your first left on Rt. 22 to South Junction Rd. Make another right onto Lyons Rd. towards the end, and make a right onto Rock Rd. Look for the course on your right.

BLUFF POINT GOLF & COUNTRY CLUB

75 Bluff Point Drive, Plattsburgh, NY 12901 / (518) 563-3420 / 3172

BASIC INFORMATION

Course Type: Semi-private
Year Built: 1890
Architect: A.W. Tillinghast
Local Pro: N/A

Course: N/A
Holes: 18 / Par 72

Back: 6,309 yds. Rating: 71.2 Slope: 123
Middle: N/A   Rating: N/A Slope: N/A
Ladies: 5,478 yds. Rating: 71.6 Slope: 125

Tee Time: 5-7 days in advance.
Price: $15 - $29

Credit Cards: ■   Restaurant: ■
Driving Range: ■   Lounge: ■
Practice Green: ■   Meeting Rooms: ■
Locker Room: ■   Tennis:
Rental Clubs: ■   Swimming:
Walkers: ■   Jogging Trails:
Snack Bar: ■   Boating: ■

COURSE DESCRIPTION

Bluff Point Golf & Country Club is the oldest resort course in the United States and is the 3rd oldest overall. It has a rich and valued history of entertaining some of the most influential people in America's political and industrial past. The course is situated on beautiful Lake Champlain and offers spectacular views of the Adirondack Mountains and the Green Mountains of Vermont.

Golfers enjoy the many panoramic views that the course has to offer through its lushly landscaped design.

DIRECTIONS

Take I-87 to Exit 36 and turn left. Make another left when you get to South Junction Rd. Go to the end and make a left at Lakeshore Rd. The course will be approximately 1-mile further on the right. Turn down Bluff Point Dr.

NORTH COUNTRY GOLF CLUB

Hayford Rd., P.O. Box 186, Rouses Point, NY 12979 / (518) 297-5814

BASIC INFORMATION

Course Type: Public
Year Built: 1934
Architect: N/A
Local Pro: Jim Daily

Course: N/A
Holes: 18 / Par 72

Back: 6,268 yds. Rating: 69.0 Slope: N/A
Middle: N/A Rating: N/A Slope: N/A
Ladies: 5,718 yds. Rating: N/A Slope: N/A

Tee Time: 2 days in advance.
Price: $22 - $24

Credit Cards:	■	Restaurant:	■
Driving Range:	■	Lounge:	■
Practice Green:	■	Meeting Rooms:	■
Locker Room:		Tennis:	
Rental Clubs:	■	Swimming:	
Walkers:	■	Jogging Trails:	
Snack Bar:	■	Boating:	■

COURSE DESCRIPTION

North Country Golf Club is a classically built course that requires accuracy above distance to play well. The course is presently being reevaluated for both rating and slope.

This country club has over 500 players that enjoy playing the course each opening season, mostly because the course is short enough to walk comfortably and long enough to be challenging for more than one type of player. Single digit handicappers will find the layout an easy spread to conquer but should note that there are locations that are quite challenging and competitive to a wide spectrum of handicappers.

DIRECTIONS

The course is about a 1/4-mile off Rt. 11 between Champlain and Rouses Point.

CRAIG WOOD GOLF COURSE

Rd. 73, Lake Placid, NY 12946 / (518) 523-9811

BASIC INFORMATION

Course Type: Municipal
Year Built: 1920's / 1930's
Architect: Semour Dunn
Local Pro: Brian Halpenny

Course: N/A
Holes: 18 / Par 72

Back: 6,554 yds. Rating: 69.8 Slope: 116
Middle: N/A Rating: N/A Slope: N/A
Ladies: N/A Rating: N/A Slope: N/A

Tee Time: Two weeks in advance.
Price: $10 - $17

Credit Cards:	■	Restaurant:	■
Driving Range:	■	Lounge:	■
Practice Green:	■	Meeting Rooms:	■
Locker Room:	■	Tennis:	
Rental Clubs:	■	Swimming:	
Walkers:	■	Jogging Trails:	■
Snack Bar:	■	Boating:	■

COURSE DESCRIPTION

Craig Wood Golf Course is a fun adventure enjoyed by amateurs and high-handicappers alike. The rolling terrain of the playing field runs along the entire length of the course — and if you're going to play it aggressively, you'll need to do it on the easier front-nine, half the course. This part of the course features open fairways, allowing you to hit your drives with all the might you can muster. The back-nine is a completely different story. Here, the fairways converge on both ends, leading up to elevated greens with undulating surfaces.

DIRECTIONS

Take Rt. 17 north or south to Century Rd. and go west for approximately 2.5 miles until you get to Paramus Rd. Make a right at Paramus Rd. and you'll find the course a half-mile further on your right.

SARANAC INN GOLF & COUNTRY CLUB
Rt. 30, Saranac Inn, Saranac Lake, NY 12983 / (518) 891-1402

BASIC INFORMATION

Course Type: Semi-private
Year Built: 1904
Architect: Seymour Dunn
Local Pro: N/A

Course: N/A
Holes: 18 / Par 72

Back : 6,631 yds. Rating: 73.1 Slope: 124
Middle: 6,453 yds. Rating: 72.6 Slope: 121
Ladies: 5,263 yds. Rating: N/A Slope: N/A

Tee Time: 14 days in advance.
Price: $45 - $45 (includes cart)

Credit Cards:	■	Restaurant:	■
Driving Range:	■	Lounge:	■
Practice Green:	■	Meeting Rooms:	■
Locker Room:		Tennis:	
Rental Clubs:	■	Swimming:	
Walkers:		Jogging Trails:	
Snack Bar:	■	Boating:	■

COURSE DESCRIPTION

Saranac Inn Golf & Country Club is not an unduly difficult course to play. From the start, the motivating factor of the design was to build a course that would complement many different players within the scope of their individual abilities. The few hazards along the course have been carefully selected to make the layout a much more competitive attraction for low-handicap players.

Seymour Dunn built over 300 courses around the world before he designed this one for a select clientele during the turn of the century. His strategic hole configurations are truly inspirational.

DIRECTIONS
Five miles from Saranac Lake Placid Airport on left side of Hwy. 30, midway between Saranac lake and Tupper Lake.

TICONDEROGA COUNTRY CLUB
Hague Rd., P.O. Box 27, Ticonderoga, NY 12883 / (518) 585-2801

BASIC INFORMATION

Course Type: Semi-private
Year Built: 1927
Architect: Semour Dunn
Local Pro: George Mackey

Course:N/A
Holes: 18 / Par 71

Back : 6,287 yds. Rating: 70.1 Slope: 120
Middle: N/A yds. Rating: N/A Slope: N/A
Ladies: 5,022 yds. Rating: 69.6 Slope: 119

Tee Time: First come, first serve.
Price: $11 - $25

Credit Cards:	■	Restaurant:	■
Driving Range:		Lounge:	■
Practice Green:	■	Meeting Rooms:	
Locker Room:	■	Tennis:	■
Rental Clubs:	■	Swimming:	
Walkers:	■	Jogging Trails:	
Snack Bar:	■	Boating:	■

COURSE DESCRIPTION

Ticonderoga Country Club features a generous playing field that's slightly harder than the numbers indicated in the information box, due to the many undulations and mounds throughout the playing field. It isn't unusual for your ball to end up on an uneven lie after a well-struck drive.

Get to the course early and practice hitting balls above and below your stance. Your ability to finesse the ball and work it from different angles is much more important than brute strength for a successful score. You should find the front-nine rather unusual in its configuration, as it features four par-5's, two par-4's, and two par-3's.

DIRECTIONS
Go north on I-87 to Exit 28. At Rt. 74E you'll need to go south to Rt. 9N. The course will be 5-miles south on the right side.

ESSEX COUNTY

WESTPORT COUNTRY CLUB
Liberty St., Westport, NY 12993 / (518) 962-4470

BASIC INFORMATION

Course Type: Public
Year Built: 1890's
Architect: N/A
Local Pro: Tim Salerno

Course:N/A
Holes: 18 / par 72

Back : 6,544 yds. Rating: 71.5 Slope: 120
Middle: 6,203 yds. Rating: 70.0 Slope: 118
Ladies: 5,256 yds. Rating: 70.5 Slope: 112

Tee Time: 3 days in advance.
Price: $25 - $30

Credit Cards:	■	Restaurant:	■
Driving Range:	■	Lounge:	■
Practice Green:	■	Meeting Rooms:	■
Locker Room:		Tennis:	
Rental Clubs:	■	Swimming:	
Walkers:	■	Jogging Trails:	
Snack Bar:		Boating:	■

COURSE DESCRIPTION
Westport Country Club is one of those courses you're not quite sure of at first, but tend to like more and more as you play through each succeeding hole. The 8th-hole is one of the most interesting and most demanding of all. This par-4 measures 440 yards in length and requires a nice long drive, straight down the middle of the fairway. A gully sits in the middle of the fairway at about 280 yards from the championship tees. From the middle-tees beware; if you end up in it, you'll be facing a difficult blind shot to a two-tier green protected by sand bunkers both left and right.

DIRECTIONS
Take I-87 to Exit 31 and go east when you get to Rt. 9 N 22. The course will be about three miles into the Village of Westport. Follow the signs to the course.

WHITEFACE INN RESORT GOLF COURSE
P.O. Box 231, Lake Placid., NY 12946 / (518) 523-2551

BASIC INFORMATION

Course Type: Semi-private
Year Built: Late 1880's
Architect: John Van Kleek
Local Pro: J. Peter Martin

Course: N/A
Holes: 18 / Par 72

Back : 6,490 yds. Rating: 71.5 Slope: N/A
Middle: 6,293 yds. Rating: 70.6 Slope: N/A
Ladies: 5,035 yds. Rating: 73.9 Slope: N/A

Tee Time: 7 days in advance.
Price: $20 - $29

Credit Cards:	■	Restaurant:	■
Driving Range:		Lounge:	■
Practice Green:	■	Meeting Rooms:	■
Locker Room:	■	Tennis:	■
Rental Clubs:	■	Swimming:	■
Walkers:	■	Jogging Trails:	■
Snack Bar:	■	Boating:	■

COURSE DESCRIPTION
The great Walter Hagen, one of the legends of early American golf history, was a contributing consultant to John Van Kleek's admirable work. The *Whiteface Inn Resort Golf Course* still holds a certain inspirational charm that brings in golfers' from all over the state. It's not a difficult course, but it does have its moments where you'll be questioning your club selection.

Mid-to-low handicappers and senior citizens who have trouble hitting their balls long will enjoy this layout the most.

DIRECTIONS
From I-87 north to Exit 30 (Keene), follow Rt. 9 north for 2-miles to Rt. 73 and continue on for about 28-miles to Lake Placid. Take Rt. 86 west to Whiteface Inn Rd. and make a right to the course. It will be on your right about 2.5-miles further.

26

FRANKLIN COUNTY

MALONE GOLF CLUB

Duane Stage Rd., Box 26, Malone, NY 12953 / (518) 483-2926

BASIC INFORMATION

Course Type: Semi-private
Year Built: 1939 / 1987
Architect: Donald Ross / Robert Trent Jones
Local Pro: Derek Sprague

Course: East (18 / Par 72)
Holes: 36

Back : 6,688 yds. Rating: 71.9 Slope: 124
Middle: 6,256 yds. Rating: 69.8 Slope: 128
Ladies: 5,408 yds. Rating: 70.1 Slope: N/A

Tee Time: 7 days in advance.
Price: $26

Credit Cards: ■   Restaurant: ■
Driving Range: Lounge: ■
Practice Green: ■   Meeting Rooms:
Locker Room: ■   Tennis:
Rental Clubs: ■   Swimming:
Walkers: ■   Jogging Trails:
Snack Bar: ■   Boating:

COURSE DESCRIPTION

The *Malone Golf Club* offers 36 Championship golf holes divided into two great golf courses, each a challenge to both the beginner and advanced golfer. Both courses have been designed in part by Robert Trent Jones. The East Course is a traditional style layout with rolling hills and diverse terrain. The front-nine was rated " Best Pure Classic Nine" in the world by **Golf Week** (Oct. 91), according to the staff at the course. Beautiful scenery is provided by the foothills of the Adirondack mountains.

DIRECTIONS

From I-87, go north to Exit 30 (Keene), follow Rt. 9 north for 2-miles to Rt. 73 and continue for about 28-miles to Lake Placid. Take Rt. 86 west to Whiteface Inn Rd. and make a right toward the course. It will be on your right another 2.5-miles further.

TUPPER LAKE GOLF COURSE

P.O. Box 629, Tupper Lake, NY 12986 / (518) 359-3701

BASIC INFORMATION

Course Type: Public
Year Built: 1932 / 1941
Architect: Williard Wilkenson / Donald Ross
Local Pro: Brent Smith

Course: N/A
Holes: 18 / Par 71

Back : 6,254 yds. Rating: N/A Slope: N/A
Middle: 6,003 yds. Rating: N/A Slope: N/A
Ladies: 5,389 yds. Rating: N/A Slope: N/A

Tee Time: 3 days in advance.
Price: $42

Credit Cards: Restaurant: ■
Driving Range: ■   Lounge: ■
Practice Green: ■   Meeting Rooms: ■
Locker Room: ■   Tennis:
Rental Clubs: ■   Swimming:
Walkers: ■   Jogging Trails:
Snack Bar: ■   Boating: ■

COURSE DESCRIPTION

Tupper Lake Golf Course opens up both its sides to a completely different layout. The front-nine features a much flatter playing field with narrow fairways that make it difficult to drive the ball aggressively.

The back-nine moves along a much more wooded area. The fairways are a little wider here, but still demand a certain amount of accuracy to drive your ball onto them. If you've never experienced playing golf at a high altitude, you're going to delight at the extra yardage that your ball will travel in the thin air. The course features an incredible array of beautiful mountain vistas.

DIRECTIONS

Take I-97 from Albany to Rt. 28 and follow that to Rt. 30 into Tupper Lake. Follow the signs to the course that show the way to the *Ski Center*.

ALBAN HILLS COUNTRY CLUB
129 Alban Hills Dr., Johnstown, NY 12095 / (518) 762-3717

BASIC INFORMATION

Course Type: Semi-private
Year Built: 1982
Architect: N/A
Local Pro: Till Albanese

Course: N/A
Holes: 18 / Par 72

Back : 5,819 yds. Rating: 66.3 Slope: 103
Middle: N/A   Rating: N/A   Slope: N/A
Ladies: 5,015 yds. Rating: 67.6 Slope: 105

Tee Time: 1 day in advance.
Price: $12 - $14

Credit Cards:	Restaurant: ■
Driving Range:	Lounge: ■
Practice Green: ■	Meeting Rooms:
Locker Room: ■	Tennis:
Rental Clubs: ■	Swimming:
Walkers: ■	Jogging Trails:
Snack Bar: ■	Boating: ■

COURSE DESCRIPTION

Alban Hills Country Club is the type of course that will suit a beginner or any other type of player short on distance.

The overall length of the course is only 5,819 yards from their back-tees. That should be a comfortable distance for any type of player to take advantage of. It makes for a good venue to build confidence by making your pars, and hopefully a large selection of birdies.

If you need to work on your short game, you'll find the course to be a constructive exercise, one that can replace the arduous repetition of hitting balls from a driving range.

DIRECTIONS

Take the New York State Thruway to Exit 28 (Fonda Fulton) and go north at Rt. 30 A to Rt. 67 and make a right. Follow the signs to the course.

INLET GOLF CLUB
Rt. 28, Inlet, NY 13360 / (315) 357-3503

BASIC INFORMATION

Course Type: Public
Year Built: 1989 (Back-nine)
Architect: N/A
Local Pro: Roland Christy

Course: N/A
Holes: 18 / Par 70 (Ladies Par 74)

Back : 6,130 yds. Rating: N/A Slope: N/A
Middle: N/A yds. Rating: N/A Slope: N/A
Ladies: 5,544 yds. Rating: N/A Slope: N/A

Tee Time: First come, first serve.
Price: N/A

Credit Cards:	Restaurant: ■
Driving Range:	Lounge: ■
Practice Green: ■	Meeting Rooms:
Locker Room: ■	Tennis:
Rental Clubs: ■	Swimming:
Walkers:	Jogging Trails:
Snack Bar:	Boating: ■

COURSE DESCRIPTION

Inlet Golf Club is a short test of golf that will be appreciated by high-handicap players the most. The layout is straightforward and offers many good opportunities for par or better through its scenic playing field. You'll find rolling terrain running along a beautiful wooded area, enhancing the appearance of the course and the overall fulfillment of a given round.

If you're a better than average golfer, you can use the course to sharpen your short game for future challenges.

DIRECTIONS

North of Utica, 52 miles to Old Forge Rt. 28 to Inlet. Go through village of Inlet and look for the course on your left.

GOLF CLUB OF NEWPORT, THE
Honey Hill Rd., Box 512, NY 13416 / (315) 845-8333

BASIC INFORMATION

Course Type: Public
Year Built: 1969
Architect: Jeffrey Cornish
Local Pro: Pete Grygiel

Course: N/A
Holes: 18 / Par 72

Back : 7,039 yds. Rating: 73.7 Slope: 120
Middle: 6,269 yds. Rating: 68.8 Slope: 113
Ladies: 5,350 yds. Rating: 69.1 Slope: 115

Tee Time: 7 days in advance.
Price: $12 - $24

Credit Cards:		Restaurant:	■
Driving Range:	■	Lounge:	■
Practice Green:	■	Meeting Rooms:	■
Locker Room:	■	Tennis:	
Rental Clubs:	■	Swimming:	
Walkers:	■	Jogging Trails:	
Snack Bar:	■	Boating:	■

COURSE DESCRIPTION

The *Golf Club of Newport* is an enjoyable, demanding layout designed by Jeffrey Cornish. The fine series of holes that he designed will challenge any type of golfer at every level the game has to offer.

You'll find a good mixture of lively play throughout this colorful course, especially on the 9th hole, the most demanding of the par-4's at 470 yards – which incidentally is the longest allowable length for a par-4 written in the "Rules of Golf" by the U.S.G.A. A solid tee shot is needed for good position, for the strong prevailing winds that are typically found on this hole will often stretch it the length of a par-5.

DIRECTIONS

Take Rt. 12 north to Rt. 8 and make a right to Steuben Rd. Proceed left and make a right at Honey Hill Rd. The course will be on your right side.

THENDARA GOLF CLUB
P.O. Box 153, Fifth Avenue, Thendora, NY 13472 / (315) 369-3136

BASIC INFORMATION

Course Type: Semi-private
Year Built: 1923 / 1956
Architect: Donald Ross
Local Pro: Dave Geiger

Course: N/A
Holes: 18 / Par 72

Back: 6,435 yds. Rating: 70.2 Slope: 124
Middle: 6,213 yds. Rating: 69.1 Slope: 121
Ladies: 5,757 yds. Rating: 72.8 Slope: 121

Tee Time: 1-7 days in advance
Price: $20 - $30

Credit Cards:		Restaurant:	■
Driving Range:	■	Lounge:	■
Practice Green:	■	Meeting Rooms:	■
Locker Room:	■	Tennis:	
Rental Clubs:	■	Swimming:	
Walkers:	■	Jogging Trails:	
Snack Bar:		Boating:	■

COURSE DESCRIPTION

Thendara Golf Club will entertain all types of players despite their individual handicaps; each hole features three teeing distances to choose from.

The front-nine is very much the same as it was when it was first constructed in 1923. The design is filled with old time architectural traditions, such as small undulating greens, flat fairways, and an open playing field reminiscent of a linksland course. The back-nine, built in 1956, takes an unexpected complete turnaround. You'll be hitting your drives towards tree-lined narrow fairways that are rolling and unpredictable, of which four play into water.

DIRECTIONS

From Utica: Take Rt. 12 N to Rt. 28 N and follow the signs to the course.

THOUSAND ISLAND GOLF CLUB
340 Rt. 1, Box W, Alexandria Bay, NY 13607 / (315) 482-9454

BASIC INFORMATION
Course Type: Public Resort
Year Built: 1906
Architect: Seth Rayner
Local Pro: Frank Picone

Course: N/A
Holes: 18 / Par 72

Back : 6,302 yds. Rating: 69.2 Slope: 118
Middle: 6,051 yds. Rating: 68.0 Slope: 116
Ladies: 5,240 yds. Rating: 68.5 Slope: 114

Tee Time: 1 day in advance.
Price: $29 - $35

Credit Cards:	■	Restaurant:	■
Driving Range:	■	Lounge:	■
Practice Green:	■	Meeting Rooms:	
Locker Room:	■	Tennis:	
Rental Clubs:	■	Swimming:	
Walkers:	■	Jogging Trails:	
Snack Bar:	■	Boating:	■

COURSE DESCRIPTION
The *Thousand Island Golf Club* is an easy course to take control of for most mid-to-high handicappers. It's a links course that features undulations both on the fairways and on the greens.

Holes 1 through 9 play wide open and allow aggressive play off their tees. Holes 9 through 16 feature trees that come into play making ball placement a little more important. And the remaining two finishing holes offer an open environment that are equal to the starting holes.

This is a straightforward course that isn't too hard to play well on.

DIRECTIONS
Take Rt. 18 to Exit 51 and make a right at the first stop sign. Make a left at Coury Rd. 100 to the east end of Wellesey Island.

WATERTOWN GOLF CLUB
P.O. Box 927, Thompson Park, Watertown, NY 13601 / (315) 782-4040

BASIC INFORMATION
Course Type: Public
Year Built: 1926
Architect: N/A
Local Pro: Stu Jamieson

Course: N/A
Holes: 18 / Par 72

Back : 6,309 yds. Rating: 69.5 Slope: N/A
Middle: 5,944 yds. Rating: 68.1 Slope: N/A
Ladies: 5,492 yds. Rating: 71.0 Slope: N/A

Tee Time: 4 days in advance.
Price: $20

Credit Cards:		Restaurant:	■
Driving Range:	■	Lounge:	
Practice Green:	■	Meeting Rooms:	■
Locker Room:	■	Tennis:	■
Rental Clubs:	■	Swimming:	■
Walkers:	■	Jogging Trails:	
Snack Bar:		Boating:	■

COURSE DESCRIPTION
Watertown Golf Club is a community-type venue that gets a lot of play by high-handicappers in general. It's not a difficult course, and thus allows many good scoring opportunities from a variety of areas on each given hole.

The open playing field is easy to walk and is best enjoyed in this manner.

DIRECTIONS
Take Rt. 81 to Exit 44 and make a left. You'll see a stop sign about 300 yards away. Once there, make a right on Rt. 11 and a left at the upcoming set of lights (Thompson Blvd.). Make another right and follow the street to the second stop sign, where you'll make another right onto Gotham St. Enter the park, which will be about 400 yards further on your left, to get to the course. Once there, simply follow the signs.

30

WILLOWBROOK GOLF COURSE

RR 5 RT. 37, Watertown, NY 13601 / (315) 782-8192

BASIC INFORMATION

Course Type: Public
Year Built: 1950's
Architect: N/A
Local Pro: Douglas McDavitt

Course: Red & Yellow (18 / Par 72)
Holes: 27

Back : 6,250 yds. Rating: N/A Slope: N/A
Middle: 5,992 yds. Rating: N/A Slope: N/A
Ladies: 5,908 yds. Rating: N/A Slope: N/A

Tee Time: 7 days in advance.
Price: $9 - $23

Credit Cards:	■	Restaurant:	■
Driving Range:	■	Lounge:	■
Practice Green:	■	Meeting Rooms:	■
Locker Room:	■	Tennis:	
Rental Clubs:	■	Swimming:	
Walkers:	■	Jogging Trails:	
Snack Bar:	■	Boating:	■

COURSE DESCRIPTION

Willowbrook Golf Course is a traditional links style layout that features both undulating and rolling fairways, thick rough, small greens, no bunkers and lots of wind.

One of the unique features that makes this course stand out is the fact that it doesn't have a single sand-bunker incorporated into its design; instead, they opted to grow high-rough areas that are next to impossible to play out of.

The #3-hole is the toughest test on the course. It's a short par-3 that measures only 110 yards from the back-tees. You'll need to hit your ball to a small elevated green that is surrounded by a rock ledge.

DIRECTIONS

Take Rt. 81 to Exit 48. At Hwy. 342, go east bound to Rt. 37 and south towards the course. It will be on your right.

CARLOWDEN COUNTRY CLUB

Box 245, Lowville, NY 13367 / (315) 493-9893

BASIC INFORMATION

Course Type: Public
Year Built: 1920's
Architect: N/A
Local Pro: Bill Marilley

Course: N/A
Holes: 18 / Par 72

Back : 6,157 yds. Rating: N/A Slope: N/A
Middle: 5,763 yds. Rating: N/A Slope: 110
Ladies: 4,866 yds. Rating: N/A Slope: N/A

Tee Time: 1 day in advance.
Price: $10 - $16

Credit Cards:		Restaurant:	■
Driving Range:	■	Lounge:	■
Practice Green:	■	Meeting Rooms:	■
Locker Room:	■	Tennis:	
Rental Clubs:	■	Swimming:	
Walkers:	■	Jogging Trails:	
Snack Bar:	■	Boating:	■

COURSE DESCRIPTION

Although primarily a strong test for iron play, *Carlowden Country Club* offers a comfortable playing field that will complement different playing styles along its 6,157-yard distance from its championship tees.

One of the most exciting holes on the course is the 12th, a par-5 that extends out to 486 yards, and is a double-dogleg. You'll need to hit a straight drive about 150 yards out to take the first dogleg out of play. If you're a strong hitter, you can hit over the trees that run along the left side to set yourself up for an Eagle.

DIRECTIONS

From Watertown: Take Rt. 26 to the Junction of Rt. 26 & 126 in the Village of W. Carthage. Continue on Rt. 26 S to the town of Denmark. Make your first right and the course will be on your left.

TURIN HIGHLANDS GOLF COURSE
East Rd., Turin, NY 13473 / (315) 348-9912

BASIC INFORMATION

Course Type: Public
Year Built: 1970's
Architect: N/A
Local Pro: Jeannie Rubadue

Course: N/A
Holes: 18 / Par 72

Back : 6,852 yds. Rating: 72.0 Slope: N/A
Middle: 6,080 yds. Rating: 67.0 Slope: N/A
Ladies: 5,639 yds. Rating: N/A Slope: N/A

Tee Time: 1 day in advance.
Price: $15 - $23

Credit Cards:		Restaurant:	■
Driving Range:	■	Lounge:	■
Practice Green:	■	Meeting Rooms:	■
Locker Room:		Tennis:	
Rental Clubs:	■	Swimming:	
Walkers:	■	Jogging Trails:	
Snack Bar:	■	Boating:	■

COURSE DESCRIPTION
The *Turin Highlands Golf Course* offers a traditional design layout with trees running along many interesting holes, with the 11th hole playing the hardest. This well designed par-4 hole stretches 373 yards from the back-tees. You'll be facing a tight fairway that features trees both left and right of the fairway. You'll need to play the ball to the middle of the fairway for a clear approach shot to the pin.

The green is rather large —like most of the other greens — and features concave grass bunkers that are difficult to play out of. The safest shot would be to land the ball dead center regardless of the pin position.

DIRECTIONS
Take the New York Thruway to Utica Exit 31 and head north to Rt. 12. You can follow the signs to the course from Rt. 12.

ARTHUR CARTER AMSTERDAM MUNICIPAL GOLF COURSE
Van Dyke Ave., Amsterdam, NY 12010 / (518) 842-6480

BASIC INFORMATION

Course Type: Municipal
Year Built: 1938
Architect: Robert Trent Jones
Local Pro: Joe Merendo

Course: N/A
Holes: 18 / Par 71

Back : 6,370 yds. Rating: 70.2 Slope: 120
Middle: N/A Rating: N/A Slope: N/A
Ladies: 5,352 yds. Rating: 70.2 Slope: 110

Tee Time: 2 days in advance.
Price: $4 - $17

Credit Cards:		Restaurant:	■
Driving Range:		Lounge:	■
Practice Green:	■	Meeting Rooms:	
Locker Room:	■	Tennis:	
Rental Clubs:		Swimming:	
Walkers:	■	Jogging Trails:	
Snack Bar:		Boating:	

COURSE DESCRIPTION
Arthur Carter Amsterdam Municipal Golf Course offers beautiful views of the Mohawk Valley. It's a Robert Trent Jones design that features a variety of flat and rolling terrains. Most of the fairways are generously wide, allowing aggressive play from the tees, yet you do have to be careful of the many trees along the course. They can easily come into the play of action.

The course is a fun challenge for mid-to-high handicappers who have been searching for a layout that will allow them to take chances.

DIRECTIONS
Take the New State Thruway Exit 27 to Rt. 30 north to Van Dyke Ave. (6th traffic light) and turn left. Stay on Van Dyke for about a mile and look for the course on your left.

32

BARKER BROOK GOLF CLUB
Rogers Rd., Oriskany, NY 13425 / (315) 821-6438

BASIC INFORMATION
Course Type: Public
Year Built: 1964 / 1992
Architect: Charles Miner / David Keshler
Local Pro: N/A

Course: N/A
Holes: 18 / Par 72

Back : 6,257 yds. Rating: N/A Slope: N/A
Middle: 6,057 yds. Rating: N/A Slope: N/A
Ladies: 5,501 yds. Rating: N/A Slope: N/A

Tee Time: 7 days in advance.
Price: $8 - $14

Credit Cards:	■	Restaurant:	■
Driving Range:		Lounge:	■
Practice Green:	■	Meeting Rooms:	■
Locker Room:		Tennis:	
Rental Clubs:	■	Swimming:	
Walkers:	■	Jogging Trails:	
Snack Bar:	■	Boating:	

COURSE DESCRIPTION
Barker Brook Golf Club runs along a hilly surface and features a whopping twelve holes that play into water. The course was mainly designed to challenge mid-to-high handicappers; and that's exactly what it does, quite well.

The layout is situated in a picturesque country setting, far away from the bustling noises that characterize city life. It makes playing the game much more fun and peaceful, allowing you to concentrate on your following shot, without being bothered by untimely disturbances.

It's a well manicured course that's fun to play.

DIRECTIONS
Take Rt. 20 to Oriskany Falls along to the Village and make a left on Main St. Follow the signs to the course.

CRESTWOOD GOLF CLUB
P.O. Box 379, Rt. 291, Marcy, NY 13403 / (315) 736-0478

BASIC INFORMATION
Course Type: Public
Year Built: 1956 / 1960's
Architect: N/A
Local Pro: Skip Cerminaro

Course: N/A
Holes: 18 / Par 72

Back : 6,952 yds. Rating: N/A Slope: N/A
Middle: 6,643 yds. Rating: 70.7 Slope: 121
Ladies: 5,913 yds. Rating: N/A Slope: N/A

Tee Time: 1 day in advance.
Price: $12 - $15

Credit Cards:	■	Restaurant:	■
Driving Range:		Lounge:	■
Practice Green:	■	Meeting Rooms:	■
Locker Room:	■	Tennis:	
Rental Clubs:		Swimming:	
Walkers:	■	Jogging Trails:	
Snack Bar:	■	Boating:	■

COURSE DESCRIPTION
Crestwood Golf Club was built specifically for the enjoyment of a unique staff of doctors working at the Marcy Psychiatric Center, a government building which is presently used as a prison and has since changed its name. David Berkowitz and Charles Manson were evaluated here before they were sentenced to prison.

Legend has it that eighteen Doctors' chose to replicate their favorite holes from across America. No one can identify the replications, but what you will find is a very exciting collection of holes that are fun to play. The challenge is definitely one that every golfer will enjoy.

DIRECTIONS
Take the New York State Thruway onto the Exit 31 (Utica) and follow that to Rt. 49 W and onwards to Rt. 291 N. Look for the course on your right.

ONEIDA COUNTY

DOMENICO'S GOLF COURSE

13 Church Rd., Whiteboro, NY 13492 / (315) 736-9812

BASIC INFORMATION

Course Type: Public
Year Built: 1982
Architect: Joseph Spinella
Local Pro: N/A

Course: N/A
Holes: 18 / Par 72

Back : 6,715 yds. Rating: 70.5 Slope: 118
Middle: 6,257 yds. Rating: 67.9 Slope: 108
Ladies: 5,458 yds. Rating: 71.5 Slope: N/A

Tee Time: 2 days in advance.
Price: $12 - $14

Credit Cards: Restaurant:
Driving Range: Lounge: ■
Practice Green: ■   Meeting Rooms:
Locker Room: Tennis:
Rental Clubs: ■   Swimming:
Walkers: ■   Jogging Trails:
Snack Bar: ■   Boating:

COURSE DESCRIPTION

Domenico's Golf Course is a no-non-sense layout located in the suburbs of Utica, New York. The course features only 12 bunkers, two ponds and several small creeks that meander around 14 holes.

Built on 150 acres of farmland, the design features three par-5's (longest: 541 yards), twelve par-4's, and three par-3's. Most of the greens are on the small side and de-mand high-flying fade-shots for best results.

DIRECTIONS

Located on east side of Judd Rd. where the New York State Thruway crosses over-head. Take Exit 32 at West Moreland, N.Y. It'll be approximately 3-miles before you see the first stop sign. Make a right onto Judd Rd. Look for the course about 2-miles fur-ther on your left.

HIDDEN VALLEY GOLF CLUB

189 Castle Rd., Whiteboro, NY 13492 / (315) 736-9953

BASIC INFORMATION

Course Type: Public
Year Built: 1962
Architect: N/A
Local Pro: N/A

Course: N/A
Holes: 18 / Par 71

Back : 6,456 yds. Rating: N/A Slope: N/A
Middle: 6,067 yds. Rating: N/A Slope: N/A
Ladies: 5,517 yds. Rating: N/A Slope: N/A

Tee Time: 1 day in advance.
Price: $12 - $14

Credit Cards: Restaurant: ■
Driving Range: ■   Lounge: ■
Practice Green: ■   Meeting Rooms: ■
Locker Room: ■   Tennis:
Rental Clubs: ■   Swimming:
Walkers: ■   Jogging Trails:
Snack Bar: ■   Boating: ■

COURSE DESCRIPTION

Hidden Valley Golf Club offers an easy layout that will mostly challenge high-handi-cappers in general.

Rolling fairways make driving the ball an interesting guess, but the rest of the course is quite simple to understand and play through. You won't need much direction to play well here, just keep the ball on the fairway and play as aggressively as you possibly can!

The total yardage is only 6,456 yards from the back-tees, which is easily in reach for most amateur golfers.

DIRECTIONS

Take the New State Thruway to Rt. 5 and go west to Woods Rd. and make a left. When you get to Castle Rd., make a left towards the course.

ONEIDA COUNTY

M<Connellsville Golf Club

Box 58, McConnellsville, NY 13401 / (315) 245-1157

BASIC INFORMATION

Course Type: Semi-private
Year Built: 1942
Architect: N/A
Local Pro: Michael Bertlesman

Course: N/A
Holes: 18 / Par 70

Back : 6,313 yds. Rating: 70.2 Slope: 119
Middle: 6,087 yds. Rating: 69.2 Slope: 116
Ladies: 5,539 yds. Rating: N/A Slope: N/A

Tee Time: 1 day in advance.
Price: $22

Credit Cards:	■	Restaurant:	■
Driving Range:	■	Lounge:	■
Practice Green:	■	Meeting Rooms:	■
Locker Room:	■	Tennis:	
Rental Clubs:	■	Swimming:	
Walkers:	■	Jogging Trails:	
Snack Bar:	■	Boating:	■

COURSE DESCRIPTION

McConellsville Golf Club offers an impressive array of golf experiences for mid-to-high handicappers. You'll need to hit your drives accurately to be successful on most of the narrow fairways. With the course playing only 6,313 yards from the back-tees, you may prefer hitting your drives with a 3-wood for control. Setting yourself up for a good follow-through approach shot makes all the difference in the world.

You should find this layout a great place to perfect your short-game.

DIRECTIONS

Take Exit 34 to Rt. 13 and go north to McConnellsville. Follow the signs to the course.

Rome Country Club

Rd. 6 P.O. Box 376, Rome, NY 13440 / (315) 336-6464

BASIC INFORMATION

Course Type: Semi-private
Year Built: 1929
Architect: N/A
Local Pro: Jonathan Cupp

Course: N/A
Holes: 18 / Par 72

Back : 6,775 yds. Rating: 72.4 Slope: 125
Middle: 6,391 yds. Rating: 70.8 Slope: 122
Ladies: 5,505 yds. Rating: N/A Slope: N/A

Tee Time: 7 days in advance.
Price: $10 - $20

Credit Cards:	■	Restaurant:	■
Driving Range:	■	Lounge:	■
Practice Green:	■	Meeting Rooms:	
Locker Room:	■	Tennis:	
Rental Clubs:	■	Swimming:	
Walkers:	■	Jogging Trails:	
Snack Bar:	■	Boating:	

COURSE DESCRIPTION

Carved from the foothills of the Adirondacks, this splendid course offers a stunning playing field at a very affordable price. The lush fairways and superbly maintained tees and greens are fully irrigated and well known throughout the state. The front-nine is relatively open and appeals to the true power hitter. The back-nine, by contrast, is much tighter and requires pinpoint accuracy towards well-defined landing areas. One thing is certain: you'll use every club in your bag by the end of a given round. This exceptional course is the type you'll want to play more than just once!

DIRECTIONS

From the New York State Thruway, take Exit 33 to Rt. 365 and go north to Rome. Take Rt. 69 west for about 6-miles and look for the course on your left.

STONEBRIDGE GOLF & COUNTRY CLUB

Graffenburg Rd., New Hartfort, NY 13413/ (315) 733-5662

BASIC INFORMATION

Course Type: Public
Year Built: 1950's
Architect: Geoffrey Cornish
Local Pro: Steven Shrader

Course: N/A
Holes: 18 / Par 72

Back : 6,835 yds. Rating: N/A Slope: N/A
Middle: 6,415 yds. Rating: 70.3 Slope: N/A
Ladies: 5,775 yds. Rating: 71.2 Slope: 121

Tee Time: 1 day in advance.
Price: $11 - $15

Credit Cards:		Restaurant:	■
Driving Range:		Lounge:	■
Practice Green:	■	Meeting Rooms:	■
Locker Room:	■	Tennis:	
Rental Clubs:		Swimming:	
Walkers:	■	Jogging Trails:	
Snack Bar:	■	Boating:	

COURSE DESCRIPTION

Stonebridge Golf & Country Club seems to have been carved right inside of a dense forest. You'll need to play a proficient game of golf to score well here. The fairways are narrow and demanding. Distance takes second place to accuracy on this shotmakers course, but if you can hit a ball long and straight, you'll be at a definite advantage on many of the long par-4's.

You'll want to play this course more than just once.

DIRECTIONS

Take the New York State Thruway to the Utica Exit and follow that to Rt. 12 S. Go to Rt. 8 S and get off at the Washington Mills Exit and make a left. Take your second right onto Higley Rd. and follow that to Graffenberg, where you'll need to make a right. The course will be on your left.

TWIN PONDS GOLF & COUNTRY CLUB

169 Main St., New York Mills, NY 13417 / (315) 736-0550

BASIC INFORMATION

Course Type: Public
Year Built: N/A
Architect: N/A
Local Pro: Frank Girmonde

Course: N/A
Holes: 18 / Par 70

Back : 6,170 yds. Rating: 67.4 Slope: 106
Middle: 6,025 yds. Rating: 66.7 Slope: 104
Ladies: 5,765 yds. Rating: 70.7 Slope: 112

Tee Time: 1 day in advance.
Price: $11 - $30

Credit Cards:	■	Restaurant:	■
Driving Range:		Lounge:	■
Practice Green:	■	Meeting Rooms:	■
Locker Room:	■	Tennis:	
Rental Clubs:	■	Swimming:	
Walkers:	■	Jogging Trails:	
Snack Bar:	■	Boating:	■

COURSE DESCRIPTION

Twin Ponds Golf & Country Club is a shotmakers course first and foremost. At 6,170 yards from the championship tees, the course is easy enough for most mid-to-high handicappers to play well on, but perhaps too easy for a single-digit handicapper.

You'll need to chip and putt well to score low numbers on this course. The greens are extremely small, undulating, quick, and hard to hold onto. You'll need to practice a high-flying fade that lands softly to take command of them. A trusty putting stroke will get you a long way.

DIRECTIONS

Please call the course for exact directions from whichever location you'll be coming from.

ONEIDA / OSWEGO COUNTY

VALLEY VIEW GOLF COURSE
Memorial Pkwy., Utica, NY 13501 / (315) 732-8755

BASIC INFORMATION

Course Type: Municial
Year Built: 1941
Architect: Robert Trent Jones
Local Pro: Hank Furgol

Course: N/A
Holes: 18 / Par 71

Back : 6,651 yds. Rating: 69.2 Slope: N/A
Middle: N/A   Rating: N/A Slope: N/A
Ladies: 5,942 yds. Rating: N/A Slope: N/A

Tee Time: First come, first serve.
Price: $10 - $12

Credit Cards:	Restaurant:	■
Driving Range:	Lounge:	
Practice Green: ■	Meeting Rooms:	
Locker Room: ■	Tennis:	
Rental Clubs: ■	Swimming:	
Walkers: ■	Jogging Trails:	
Snack Bar: ■	Boating:	

COURSE DESCRIPTION

No matter how long or how short a course may be, if it was designed by the great Robert Trent Jones, it deserves to be played just to see how this great designer made use of the surrounding land structures. This course is no exception to the rule, and will appeal to many different types of players, both new and accomplished.

If you're a single digit handicapper, don't expect anything better than a chance to improve your short game.

DIRECTIONS

The course is located a 1/2-mile from Genesee St. on Memorial Pkwy. Look for it on your right.

BATTLE ISLAND STATE GOLF COURSE
Rd. 1, Fulton, NY 13069 / (315) 593-3408

BASIC INFORMATION

Course Type: Public
Year Built: 1902
Architect: N/A
Local Pro: Bill Grigiel

Course: N/A
Holes: 18 / Par 72

Back : 5,973 yds. Rating: 67.9 Slope: 109
Middle: 5,798 yds. Rating: 67.1 Slope: 107
Ladies: 5,531 yds. Rating: 68.7 Slope: N/A

Tee Time: 1 day in advance.
Price: $12 - $14

Credit Cards:	Restaurant:	■
Driving Range:	Lounge:	■
Practice Green: ■	Meeting Rooms:	■
Locker Room: ■	Tennis:	
Rental Clubs: ■	Swimming:	
Walkers: ■	Jogging Trails:	
Snack Bar: ■	Boating:	■

COURSE DESCRIPTION

Battle Island State Golf Course is a great attraction for ammeters who are having problems hitting the ball a long distance. It measures just below 6,000 yards from the back-tees and features a hilly terrain, many mature trees, high rough at strategic landing areas, great landscaping, and many scenic holes.

Good course management and one' ability to hit a ball accurately are the magical ingredients to getting pars and birdies. You can drive most of the holes with a 3-wood for added control.

DIRECTIONS

Take Rt. 690 W from Syracuse and follow it to Rt. 48 N, which will take you into Fulton. Look for the course on your right, it will be about 3-miles further.

OSWEGO COUNTY

ELMS GOLF CLUB, THE

9613 Elms Rd. North, Sandy Creek, NY 13145 / (315) 387-5297

BASIC INFORMATION

Course Type: Public
Year Built: 1931 / 1972
Architect: N/A
Local Pro: N/A

Course: N/A
Holes: 18 / Par 70

Back : 6,087 yds. Rating: 68.0 Slope: 110
Middle: 5,713 yds. Rating: 66.0 Slope: 108
Ladies: 5,170 yds. Rating: 72.0 Slope: 114

Tee Time: 1 day in advance.
Price: $13 - $15

Credit Cards:	■	Restaurant:	■
Driving Range:		Lounge:	■
Practice Green:	■	Meeting Rooms:	
Locker Room:		Tennis:	
Rental Clubs:	■	Swimming:	
Walkers:	■	Jogging Trails:	
Snack Bar:	■	Boating:	■

COURSE DESCRIPTION

The *Elms Golf Club* offers a lush natural setting atop a country plateau filled with mature trees and beautiful sights. At a distance of only 6,087 yards from the back-tees, many golfers will feel comfortable taking their stance atop the many wonderful tees. The layout is a set-up for strategic play, so be forewarned that many of the greens are rather small and demanding, making tee-shot placements important for clear approach shots. The back-nine is unquestionably the harder half, featuring a greater number of narrow fairways, and two holes with the appearance of having been carved right out of a forest.

DIRECTIONS

Take I-81 to Exit 36 (Pulaski) and go west on Rt. 13 to Rt. 3. Proceed northbound for about 9-miles. The club will be on your left.

GREENVIEW COUNTRY CLUB

Whig Hill Rd., West Monroe, NY 13167 / (315) 668-2244

BASIC INFORMATION

Course Type: Public
Year Built: 1960's
Architect: N/A
Local Pro: N/A

Course: N/A
Holes: 18 / Par 71

Back : 6,299 yds. Rating: 69.5 Slope: 116
Middle: 6,065 yds. Rating: 66.9 Slope: 116
Ladies: 5,864 yds. Rating: 68.3 Slope: 114

Tee Time: 1 day in advance.
Price: $12 - $16

Credit Cards:		Restaurant:	■
Driving Range:	■	Lounge:	■
Practice Green:	■	Meeting Rooms:	■
Locker Room:		Tennis:	
Rental Clubs:	■	Swimming:	
Walkers:	■	Jogging Trails:	
Snack Bar:	■	Boating:	■

COURSE DESCRIPTION

Greenview Country Club is a simple course from beginning to end. You needn't worry about making mistakes here; all of the holes features ample room to drive the ball in either direction without much trouble — in the form of hazards — to stop your ball from advancing on its way. Most of your approach shots will be played with high-lofted clubs; giving you the desired spin to hold the ball on many of the courses large greens. The fairways are rolling in nature, and you'll find seven holes that play into water.

Keep your eyes open for deer, geese, cranes, and other wildlife.

DIRECTIONS

Take I-81 N to Exit 32 and make a right onto Rt. 49 E. The course will be on your left.

38

SARATOGA COUNTY

BROOKHAVEN GOLF CLUB
25 Hamilton Ave., Corinth, NY 12822 / (518) 893-7458

BASIC INFORMATION
Course Type: Semi-private
Year Built: 1963
Architect: George Pulver
Local Pro: Jim Farley

Course: N/A
Holes: 18 / Par 72

Back : 6,527 yds. Rating: 71.3 Slope: 125
Middle: 6,141 yds. Rating: 69.5 Slope: 121
Ladies: 4,806 yds. Rating: N/A Slope: N/A

Tee Time: 3 days in advance.
Price: $8 - $10

Credit Cards:		Restaurant:	■
Driving Range:		Lounge:	
Practice Green:	■	Meeting Rooms:	
Locker Room:	■	Tennis:	
Rental Clubs:	■	Swimming:	
Walkers:		Jogging Trails:	
Snack Bar:	■	Boating:	

COURSE DESCRIPTION
When you can play a course that stretches out to 6,527 yards in length for only $10, you simply can't go wrong.

Brookhaven Golf Club is in a rural setting, which adds to the overall experience of playing golf in an undisturbed area. It's not a very difficult course, but it does have its elements to contend with: a hilly terrain and tight fairways will force you to think carefully about club selections.

You'll find water coming into play on six holes. The club is located in the Kayaderosseras range of the Adirondack mountains.

DIRECTIONS
Take Exit 15 off I-87, go south on Rt. 50 and north on Rt. 9N for approximately 12-miles. Follow the signs to the course which will take you to Alpine Meadows Rd.

EAGLE CREST GOLF CLUB
Rt. 146A, Clifton Park, NY 12065 / (518) 877-7082

BASIC INFORMATION
Course Type: Public
Year Built: 1964
Architect: Gino Turchi
Local Pro: Jim Jeffers

Course: N/A
Holes: 18 / Par 72

Back : 6,884 yds. Rating: 72.1 Slope: 123
Middle: 6,263 yds. Rating: 68.8 Slope: 118
Ladies: 5,350 yds. Rating: 69.9 Slope: 115

Tee Time: 2 days in advance.
Price: $15 - $20

Credit Cards:	■	Restaurant:	■
Driving Range:	■	Lounge:	■
Practice Green:	■	Meeting Rooms:	■
Locker Room:	■	Tennis:	
Rental Clubs:	■	Swimming:	
Walkers:	■	Jogging Trails:	
Snack Bar:	■	Boating:	■

COURSE DESCRIPTION
Eagle Crest Golf Club is an imaginative layout that presents a very difficult challenge from its championship tees.

Although the course favors a fade on most of the holes, you'll need to play a good variety of shots to bring in a respectable number at the end of a given round. You'll also need to play your approach shots close to the pin to have a successful putting day. Many of the greens feature difficult undulations, the type that will chip away at your putting abilities severely if you're not prepared for them. Get to the course early to practice your putting stroke.

The course record to this day is par-69.

DIRECTIONS
Take Rt. 87 to Exit 9 and go west on Rt. 146 to Rt. 146A. Proceed for 2 1/2 miles further and look for the course on your right.

SARATOGA SPA STATE PARK

Saratoga Spa Championship, Saratoga Springs, NY 12866 / (518) 584-2006

BASIC INFORMATION

Course Type: Public
Year Built: 1960
Architect: N/A
Local Pro: Jack Polanski

Course: Saratoga Spa (18 / Par 72)
Holes: 27

Back : 7,025 yds. Rating: 74.0 Slope: 127
Middle: 6,344 yds. Rating: 70.0 Slope: 115
Ladies: 5,663 yds. Rating: 72.0 Slope: N/A

Tee Time: 2 days on weekends only.
Price: $12 - $14

Credit Cards:	■	Restaurant:	■
Driving Range:	■	Lounge:	■
Practice Green:	■	Meeting Rooms:	■
Locker Room:	■	Tennis:	■
Rental Clubs:	■	Swimming:	■
Walkers:	■	Jogging Trails:	■
Snack Bar:	■	Boating:	

COURSE DESCRIPTION

All of the great luxuries of life come together at the *Saratoga Spa State Park* golf course. This fabulous establishment features a remarkable course with many fascinating holes. If you weren't aware of your location, you'd swear this was Pine Hurst #2. The price of admission is simply remarkable for the type of golf you'll be treated to. The terrain is mostly flat and fairly wide around the fairways, allowing aggressive play off the tees, despite the fact that the course features many mature Pine trees — not to worry, they rarely come into the course of play.

DIRECTIONS

Take Exit 13N off the Northway (Rt. 87) . The course will be about 2-miles further on the left hand side of Rt. 9. Follow the signs to Saratoga State Park.

SCHENECTADY MUNICIPAL GOL F COURSE

400 Oregon Avenue, Schenectady, NY 12309 / (518) 382-5155

BASIC INFORMATION

Course Type: Municipal
Year Built: 1934
Architect: Jim Thompson
Local Pro: Bob Haggerty

Course: N/A
Holes: 18 / Par 72

Back : 6,570 yds. Rating: 71.1 Slope: 123
Middle: 6,255 yds. Rating: 69.4 Slope: 118
Ladies: 5,275 yds. Rating: 68.1 Slope: 115

Tee Time: 2 days in advance.
Price: $11 - $16

Credit Cards:		Restaurant:	■
Driving Range:	■	Lounge:	■
Practice Green:	■	Meeting Rooms:	
Locker Room:	■	Tennis:	
Rental Clubs:	■	Swimming:	
Walkers:	■	Jogging Trails:	
Snack Bar:	■	Boating:	

COURSE DESCRIPTION

Schenectady Municipal Golf Course allows golfers of all abilities a fun platform to play golf on. It's cut through a heavily wooded area and is designed for accuracy above distance, especially through the many narrow fairways that the course features.

If you're a low-to-mid handicapper, the course will offer you many good chances at par or better, but if you're a high handicapper, be prepared for a formidable challenge.

Most of the tees and greens are set on an elevated piece of real estate.

DIRECTIONS

Take the New York State Thruway to Exit 25 and follow that to Rt. 7. That will take you to "Golf Road." Look for the road and the course on your right.

STADIUM GOLF CLUB
333 Jackson Avenue, Schenectady, NY 12304 / (518) 374-9104

BASIC INFORMATION

Course Type: Public
Year Built: 1961
Architect: Doug Hennel
Local Pro: Mike Klimtzak

Course: N/A
Holes: 18 / Par 71

Back : 6,316 yds. Rating: 69.5 Slope: 113
Middle: 5,959 yds. Rating: 67.7 Slope: 110
Ladies: 5,406 yds. Rating: 67.0 Slope: 109

Tee Time: 3 days in advance.
Price: $15 - $18

Credit Cards:	■	Restaurant:	■
Driving Range:	■	Lounge:	■
Practice Green:	■	Meeting Rooms:	■
Locker Room:	■	Tennis:	
Rental Clubs:	■	Swimming:	
Walkers:	■	Jogging Trails:	
Snack Bar:	■	Boating:	

COURSE DESCRIPTION
Stadium Golf Club is a privately-owned public facility located in the Pine Bush section of the Capital District region. The course is built around the existing structure of an old 6,000 seat baseball stadium that housed the AA Schenectady Blue Jays of the New York -Penn Baseball League (a farm club of the Philadelphia Phillies). The course designer opted to place huge greens (some in excess of 40,000 sq. ft.) instead of sand-bunkers throughout the course. If you're not on top of your game, you may end up three-putting a lot of these greens.

DIRECTIONS
From the New York State Thruway, take Exit 25 to I-90 and proceed to I-890 going west to Exit 7. At Rt. 7, you'll need to go east at the first set of lights (Watt St.). Make a right there, and look for Jackson Ave. up ahead and make a right to the pro-shop.

ST. LAWRENCE UNIVERSITY GOLF COURSE
Rt 11, Canton, NY 13617 / (315) 386-4600

BASIC INFORMATION

Course Type: Public
Year Built: N/A
Architect: N/A
Local Pro: Renie Calkin

Course: N/A
Holes: 18 / Par 72

Back : 6,694 yds. Rating: 72.1 Slope: 122
Middle: 6,310 yds. Rating: 70.5 Slope: 119
Ladies: 5,430 yds. Rating: 73.1 Slope: 120

Tee Time: 3 days in advance.
Price: $17 - $20

Credit Cards:	■	Restaurant:	■
Driving Range:	■	Lounge:	■
Practice Green:	■	Meeting Rooms:	■
Locker Room:	■	Tennis:	
Rental Clubs:	■	Swimming:	
Walkers:	■	Jogging Trails:	
Snack Bar:	■	Boating:	

COURSE DESCRIPTION
The ***St. Lawrence University Golf Course*** is an exceptional layout for a relatively flat course. You'll find plenty of room to work your drives along the wonderful views that this course has to offer.

The overall distance, rating, and slope should feel comfortable for most golfers, but don't underestimate the course; it does have its places where you'll be questioning your position in relation to the pin placements on the mostly undulating greens, making club selection a very important ingredient towards hitting successful shots that will allow you a fair chance at par.

DIRECTIONS
At the Village of Canton, Rt.11, adjacent to the Best Western University Inn.

HILAND GOLF CLUB
73 Haviland Rd., Queensbury, NY 12804 / (518) 761-4653

BASIC INFORMATION

Course Type: Semi-private (Resort Style)
Year Built: 1987
Architect: Stephen Kay
Local Pro: Mark Jorgensen

Course: N/A
Holes: 18 / Par 72

Back : 6,843 yds. Rating: 73.0 Slope: 135
Middle: 6,373 yds. Rating: 71.5 Slope: 132
Ladies: 5,677 yds. Rating: 71.8 Slope: 123

Tee Time: 7 days in advance.
Price: $18 - $36

Credit Cards:	■	Restaurant:	■
Driving Range:	■	Lounge:	■
Practice Green:	■	Meeting Rooms:	■
Locker Room:	■	Tennis:	■
Rental Clubs:	■	Swimming:	
Walkers:	■	Jogging Trails:	
Snack Bar:	■	Boating:	■

COURSE DESCRIPTION

Hiland Golf Club is truly one of the most spectacular clubs in New York. This wonderful course hosted the 1992 Michelob New York State Championship. The course is meticulously kept up to "tour" standards and features 13 water holes throughout it's inventive design.

It's a great test of golf for better than average golfers in search of an inspiring country layout. Accurate approach shots are critical to a good score. You'll find bent grass on the tees, fairways, and bunkers.

DIRECTIONS

Take I-87 to Exit 19, go 1.7 miles east on Rt. 254, go left on Bay Rd. past the Adirondack College. At first traffic light, turn right on to Haviland Rd. for 1 mile. The course will be on your left.

QUEENSBURY GOLF COURSE
RR 3 Rt. 149, Box 3262, Lake George, NY 12845 / (518) 793-3711

BASIC INFORMATION

Course Type: Public
Year Built: 1954
Architect: Cassidy
Local Pro: N/A

Course: N/A
Holes: 18 / Par 70

Back : 6,067 yds. Rating: 67.4 Slope: 112
Middle: 5,536 yds. Rating: 67.4 Slope: 105
Ladies: 4,755 yds. Rating: 66.5 Slope: 106

Tee Time: 3-7 days in advance.
Price: $9 - $15

Credit Cards:	■	Restaurant:	■
Driving Range:	■	Lounge:	■
Practice Green:	■	Meeting Rooms:	■
Locker Room:	■	Tennis:	
Rental Clubs:	■	Swimming:	
Walkers:	■	Jogging Trails:	
Snack Bar:	■	Boating:	■

COURSE DESCRIPTION

Queensbury Golf Course is an average layout that features scenic mountain views, and despite its rolling terrain, it's quite easy to walk.

The challenge is mostly directed towards high-handicappers who happen to be short on distance and accuracy. The shape of the course is favorable to a fade, but if your natural shot is a draw, you'll still find enough room to move the ball in the desired direction you want — that is, of course, if you hit it right. The friendly atmosphere coupled with its low admission price has worked in the establishment's favor by building a faithful following of amateur golfers.

DIRECTIONS

Take I-87 north to Exit 20 and proceed to Rt. 9N to Rt. 149. The course will be approximately 5-miles further on your left.

42

WARREN / WASHINGTON COUNTIES

SAGAMORE RESORT & GOLF CLUB
Federal Hill Rd., Bolton Landing, NY 12814 / (518) 644-9400

BASIC INFORMATION

Course Type: Public Resort
Year Built: 1928
Architect: Donald Ross
Local Pro: Tom Snack

Course: N/A
Holes: 18 / Par 70

Back : 6,910 yds. Rating: 72.9 Slope: 138
Middle: 6,490 yds. Rating: 71.9 Slope: 132
Ladies: 5,261 yds. Rating: 73.0 Slope: 122

Tee Time: 1 day in advance for resort guests.
Price: $59 - $75

Credit Cards:	■	Restaurant:	■
Driving Range:	■	Lounge:	■
Practice Green:	■	Meeting Rooms:	■
Locker Room:	■	Tennis:	■
Rental Clubs:	■	Swimming:	■
Walkers:	■	Jogging Trails:	■
Snack Bar:	■	Boating:	■

COURSE DESCRIPTION
The *Sagamore Resort & Golf Club* is a quintessential vacation resort with an unbelievable golfing venue. You'll be playing through one of the most scenic settings in New York. The course was expertly designed by the late Donald Ross. His trademark bunkers are evident throughout, his expertly crafted undulating greens sit majestically at the end of each hole, and if that's not enough, you'll also find towering trees upwards of a hundred feet towering around you.

DIRECTIONS
Take the New York State Thruway to Rt. 87N (Adirondacks) and get onto Exit 22. Take Rt. 9. for about 6-miles and look for the course on your right.

SKENE VALLEY COUNTRY CLUB
Rd. 2, Box 2975 Norton Rd., Whitehall, NY 12887 / (518) 499-1685

BASIC INFORMATION

Course Type: Public
Year Built: 1966
Architect: Mark Cassidy
Local Pro: N/A

Course: N/A
Holes: 18 / Par 72

Back : 6,823 yds. Rating: 71.8 Slope: 121
Middle: 6,455 yds. Rating: 70.3 Slope: 116
Ladies: 5,688 yds. Rating: 71.8 Slope: 117

Tee Time: 2 days in advance.
Price: $15 - $17

Credit Cards:		Restaurant:	■
Driving Range:	■	Lounge:	■
Practice Green:	■	Meeting Rooms:	
Locker Room:		Tennis:	
Rental Clubs:	■	Swimming:	
Walkers:		Jogging Trails:	
Snack Bar:	■	Boating:	

COURSE DESCRIPTION
Skene Valley Country Club is usually set up for fast play and low numbers. The fairways are wide and generous, which allows the golfer to shape his/her drives in either direction, the rough is kept low for a minimum of difficulty, and most of the greens are big enough for golfers to choose from two-to-three clubs on their approach shots.

The course is very scenic and fun to play. You'll find the back-nine a little harder than the front and because of the natural shape of the layout, a draw would be the favored shot of a given round.

DIRECTIONS
The course is a 1/2-mile north of Rt. 4 on Rt. 9A on Norton rd. Look for the course on your right.

ALTERNATIVE COURSES - NORTH

Clinton
Military

Plattsburgh AFB Golf Club
380th CSG Plattsburgh AFB
Plattsburgh, NY 12903
(518) 565-5773

Essex
Private

Ausable Club
Adirondack Mountain Reserve
Saint Huberts, NY 12943
(518) 576-4411

Essex
9-hole

Cobble Hill Golf Course
C/O Golf Shop
Elizabeth Town, NY 12932
(518) 873-9974

Saranac Lake Golf Club
Lake Placid Rd.
Saranac Lake, NY 12983
(518) 891-2675

Town Of Schroon Golf
Hoffman Rd.
Schroon Lake, NY 12870
(518) 532-9359

Willsboro Golf Club
Willsboro
Schroon Lake, NY 12996
(518) 963-8989

Franklin
9-hole

Ouleout Creek Golf Course
HC 87, Box 37
Franklin, NY 13775
(607) 829-2100

Franklin
Executive

Loon Lake Golf Course
Rt. 99,
Loon Lake, NY 12968
(518) 891-3249

Fulton
Private

Pine Brook Golf Club
P.O. Box 549
Gloversville, NY 12968
(518) 725-5242

44

Fulton
9-hole

Kingsboro Golf Club
301 N. Kingboro Ave.
Gloversville, NY 12078
(518) 773-4600

Sacandaga Golf Club
Sacandaga Park
Northville, NY 12134
(518) 863-4887

Fulton
Executive

Holland Meadows Golf Course
Rd. 2, Box 1257
Gloversville, NY 12078
(518) 883-3318

Hamilton
9-holes

Cedar River Club
180 W. Main St.
Indian Lake, NY 12842
(518) 648-5906

Lake Pleasant Golf
RR 8 Box 709
Lake Pleasant, NY 12108
(518) 548-7071

Wakely Lodge Golf Course
Cedar River Rd.
Indian Lake, NY 12842
(518) 648-5011

Herkimer
Public

Grygiel's Pine Hills Golf
Jones Rd.
Frankfort, NY 13340
(315) 733-5030

Herkimer
9-hole

Doty's Golf Course
RR1 Box 412
Ilion, NY 13357
(315) 894-2860

Maple Crest Golf Course
Upper Barringer Rd.
Frankfort, NY 13340
(315) 895-7258

Jefferson
Private

Bartlett Country Club
32 Euclid Ave.
Orlean, NY 14760
(716) 372-5176

Ives Hill Country Club
435 Flower Ave. W.
Watertown, NY 13601
(315) 782-1771

Jefferson
9-hole

Bedford Creek Golf Course
Scenic Hwy.
Sackets Harbor, NY 13634
(315) 646-3400

Clayton Country Club
Outer State St., P.O. Box 404
Clayton, NY 13624
(315) 386-4242

Rustic Golf & Country Club
Box 88B Rd. 1
Dexter, NY 13634
(315) 639-6800

Willowbrook Golf Club
RR5 Route 37
Westertown, NY 13601
(315) 782-8192

Lewis
Executive

Cedars Golf Course
Rt. 1, East Rd., Box 246
Lowville, NY 13367
(315) 376-6267

Montgomery
Public

City Golf Course
Van Dyke Ave.
Amerstam, NY 12010
(518) 842-4265

Montgomery
Private

Antlers Country Club
P.O. Box 203
Amerstam, NY 12010
(518) 829-7423

Oneida
Public

Brook Barker Golf Course
Rogers Rd.
Oriskany Falls, NY 13425
(315) 821-9992

Sleepy Hollow Golf Club
5909 Sleepy Hollow Rd.
Rome, NY 13440
(315) 336-4110

Oneida
Private

Oswego Country Club
West River Rd.
Oswego, NY 13126
(315) 343-9881

Sadaquada Golf Club
P.O. Box 556
New Hartford, NY 13413
(315) 736-3231

Teugega Country Club
6801 Golf Course Rd.
Rome, NY 13440
(315) 337-7151

Westmoreland Golf Club
Fairway Dr.
Westmoreland, NY 13490
(315) 853-8914

Yahnundasis Golf Club
Seneca Turnpike
New Hartford, NY 13413
(315) 732-3950

Oneida
9-hole

Alder Creek Golf Club
Rt. 12
Alder Creek, NY 13301
(315) 831-5222

Brandy Brook Golf Course
Foster Rd.
Durhamville, NY 13054
(315) 363-9879

Golf Knolls
P.O. Box 848
Rome, NY 13440
(315) 337-0920

Oriskany Hill Golf Club
Rt. 69
Oriskany, NY 13424
(315) 736-4540

Sauquoit Knolls Golf Club
Knolls Dr.
Sauquoit, NY 13456
(315) 737-8959

Woodgate Pines Golf Club
Woodgate Dr.
Booneville, NY 13309
(315) 942-5442

Oswego
Public

Riverside Country Club
River Rd.
Central Square, NY 13036
(315) 676-7714

Oswego
9-hole

Pines Golf Club, The
6919 Scenic Hwy.
Pulaski, NY 13142
(315) 298-9970

Oswego
Execitive

Sadaquada Golf Club
P.O. Box 556
New Hartford, NY 13413
(315) 736-3231

Saratoga
Public

Ballston Spa Country Club
P.O. Box 117
Ballston Spa, NY 12020
(518) 885-7935

River View Country Club
847 River View Rd.
Rexford, NY 12148
(518) 399-1920

Robert Van Patten Golf Course
Main St.
Clifton Park, NY 12065
(518) 877-5400

Saratoga
Private

Edison Club, The
P.O. Box 214, Riverview Rd.
Rexford, NY 12148
(518) 399-2992

McGregor Links Country Club
Box 344
Saratoga, NY 12866
(518) 584-6664

Saratoga
Private

Saratoga Golf & Polo Club
301 Church St.
Saratoga Springs, NY 12866
(518) 584-8122

Saratoga
9-hole

Bend of the River Golf Club
Park Ave.
Hadley, NY 12835
(518) 696-3415

Mechanicville Golf Club
Box 462
Mechanicville, NY 12118
(518) 664-3866

Schenectady
Private

Mohawk Golf Club
1849 Union St.
Schenectady, NY 12309
(518) 374-9121

Schenectady
9-hole

Galway Golf Club
P.O. Box 2762
Glenville, NY 12325
(518) 582-6395

St. Lawrence
Public

Clifton-Fine Golf Course
Main St. Rt. 3
Star Lake, NY 13690
(315) 848-3570

Raymondville Golf & Country Club
Rt. 56
Massena, NY 13662
(315) 697-9324

St. Lawrence State Park Golf
Riverside Dr.,
Ogdensburg, NY 13669
(315) 393-9850

Twin Brook 18-Hole Course
Franklin Rd.
Waddington, NY 13694
(315) 388-4480

St. Lawrence
9-hole

Fore X Four Golf Club
Rt. 11 N.
Gouverneur, NY 13642
(315) 287-3711

Governeur Golf Club
P.O. Box 273, Country Club Rd.
Governeur, NY 13642
(315) 287-2130

Meadowbrook Golf Course
Rt. 1
Winthrop, NY 13697
(315) 389-4562

Potsdam Town & Country Club
Box 5107
Potsdam, NY 13676
(315) 265-2141

St. Lawrence
Executive

FCedar View Golf Course
Rt. 37 C
Massena, NY 13662
(315) 764-9104

Warren
Public

Cronins Golf Resort
Golf Course Rd.
Warrensburg, NY 12885
(518) 623-9336

Thousand Acres Golf Club
Rt. 418
Stonycreek, NY 12878
(518) 696-5246

Warren
Private

Glens Falls Country Club
Round Pond Rd.
Glen Falls, NY 12804
(518) 793-0021

Warren
9-hole

Bay Meadows Golf Club
Cronin Rd.
Glen Falls, NY 12804
(518) 792-1650

Green Meadows Golf Club
Box 463
Chestertown, NY 12817
(518) 494-7222

Top of the World Golf Course
P.O. Box 1390
Lock Heart Mountain Rd.
Lake George, NY 12845
(518) 668-2062

Washington
Public

Tee Bird Country Club
Reservoir Rd., Box 33A Rd. 2
Ford Edward, NY 12828
(518) 792-7727

Washington
Executive

Battenkill Country Club
Box 127, Rt. 29 & 40
Greenwich, NY 12834
(518) 692-9179

4. N.Y. CENTRAL/COUNTIES AND CITIES

Albany
B2 / Albany ... 1
B2 / Cohoes ... 2
B2 / Ravena ... 3

Broome
B2 / Chenango ... 4
B2 / Conklin ... 5
B2 / Endwell ... 6

Delaware
B2 / Margaretville ...17
B2 / Stamford ...18

Greene
B2 / Windom ... 19

Madison
B1 / Canastota ... 20
B1 / Hamilton ... 21

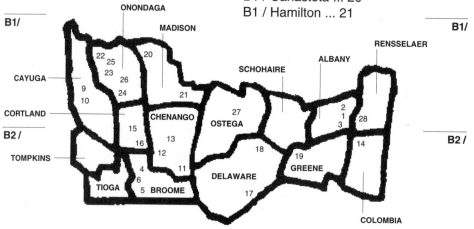

Cayuga
B2 / Auburn ... 9
B2 / Owasco ... 10XX

Chenango
B2 / Afton Lake ... 11
B2 / Greene ... 12
B2 / Norwich ... 13

Colombia
B2 / Valatie ... 14

Cortland
B1 / Cortland ... 15
B2 / Marathon ... 16

Onondaga
B2 / Baldwinsville ... 22
B2 / Camillus ... 23
B2 / Fayetteville ... 24
B2 / Liverpool ... 25
B2 / Syracuse ... 26

Ostega
B2 / Cooperstown ... 27

Rensselaer
B3 / Castleton-On-The-Hudson ... 28

NEW COURSE AT ALBANY, THE
65 O'Neill Rd., Albany, NY 12208 / (518) 438-2208

BASIC INFORMATION

Course Type: Municipal
Year Built: 1930's / 1991
Architect: Bob Smith & Ed Bosse ('91)
Local Pro: Tom Vidulich

Course: N/A
Holes: 18 / Par 71

Back: 6,179 yds. Rating: 69.4   Slope: 117
Middle: 5,726 yds. Rating: 68.7   Slope: 116
Ladies: 4,990 yds. Rating: 72.0   Slope: 113

Tee Time: 2 days in advance.
Price: $10 - $18

Credit Cards:		Restaurant:	■
Driving Range:	■	Lounge:	■
Practice Green:	■	Meeting Rooms:	■
Locker Room:	■	Tennis:	■
Rental Clubs:	■	Swimming:	
Walkers:	■	Jogging Trails:	
Snack Bar:	■	Boating:	■

COURSE DESCRIPTION

The New Course At Albany plays a little harder than the numbers represented in the Basic Information box for its Rating and Slope.

You'll find many mature trees spread along the circumference of the course and along the fairways. To play well here you'll need to hit your drives accurately to strategic points that will allow you to play your approach shots from a short distance to the hole. You'll need to finesse these shots to get the ball close to the pin. Most of the greens are small and feature undulating surfaces that are difficult to putt on.

DIRECTIONS

Take Exit 4 off I-90 (Rt. 85) to the Krumkill Rd. Exit. Make a right at New Scotland Ave. and a left onto O'neill Rd. Look for the course on your left.

SYCAMORE COUNTRY CLUB
Rt. 143, Ravena, NY 12143 / (518) 756-6635

BASIC INFORMATION

Course Type: Semi-private
Year Built: 1972
Architect: Francis Duane
Local Pro: Bary Vaurinek

Course: N/A
Holes: 18 / Par 71

Back: 6,528 yds. Rating: 70.1   Slope: 115
Middle: 6,045 yds. Rating: 68.8   Slope: 113
Ladies: 5,607 yds. Rating: 70.7   Slope: 114

Tee Time: Every Tues. for the weekend.
Price: $15 - $18

Credit Cards:		Restaurant:	■
Driving Range:	■	Lounge:	■
Practice Green:	■	Meeting Rooms:	
Locker Room:	■	Tennis:	
Rental Clubs:	■	Swimming:	
Walkers:	■	Jogging Trails:	
Snack Bar:	■	Boating:	■

COURSE DESCRIPTION

Sycamore Country Club allows a player a good margin of error from the teeing ground, which should help the good majority of players who tend to play many slices and hooks. The front-nine runs along a fairly level terrain while the back-nine, the more difficult half, runs along a rolling surface.

Many golfers consider the 18th hole tho hardest test on the course. It's a 445 yard, par-4 hole that starts off having a golfer play a blind drive to a very narrow, hour-glass shape landing area. Your approach shot needs to be played over water to the right-middle portion of the demanding small green that slopes from right-to-left.

DIRECTIONS

Take the New York Thruway to Exit 21B and take 9W north to Ravena. Go west on Rt. 143 and look for the course on your right.

TOWN OF COLONY GOLF COURSE

Rd. #1, Box 422, Cohoes, NY 12047 / (518) 375-4181

BASIC INFORMATION

Course Type: Public
Year Built: 1969
Architect: John Mitchell
Local Pro: Tom Gunning

Course: White & Blue (18 / Par 72)
Holes: 27

Back: 6,685 yds. Rating: 72.5 Slope: 129
Middle: 6,370 yds. Rating: 70.1 Slope: 120
Ladies: 5,810 yds. Rating: 72.3 Slope: 113

Tee Time: 2 days in advance.
Price: $18 - $19

Credit Cards:		Restaurant:	■
Driving Range:	■	Lounge:	■
Practice Green:	■	Meeting Rooms:	■
Locker Room:	■	Tennis:	■
Rental Clubs:	■	Swimming:	
Walkers:	■	Jogging Trails:	
Snack Bar:	■	Boating:	■

COURSE DESCRIPTION

The **Town Of Colony Golf Course** presents a beautiful challenge for golfers of different abilities. It's a flat course that many people consider easy to walk; from the back-tees at 6,845 yards, you may want to reconsider.

The finishing hole is the hardest rated hole on the course. You'll need to hit your drive over a fairway bunker that sits in the middle of the fairway about 200 yards out on this provocative par-4. If you're going to layup, your second shot will be a difficult long-iron approach to a small green that features bunkers both left and right.

DIRECTIONS

Take I-87 north to Exit 24 and proceed for about 4-miles to Lishakilo Rd. Make a right and follow the signs to the course.

CHENANGO VALLEY STATE GOLF COURSE

153 State Park Rd., Chenango Forks, NY 13746 / (607) 648-9804

BASIC INFORMATION

Course Type: Public
Year Built: 1967
Architect: Hal Purdy
Local Pro: Mark Lange

Course: N/A
Holes: 18 / Par 72

Back: 6,271 yds. Rating: 70.0 Slope: N/A
Middle: 5,878 yds. Rating: 68.9 Slope: N/A
Ladies: 5,254 yds. Rating: 69.5 Slope: N/A

Tee Time: 2 days in advance on weekends.
Price: $12 - $16

Credit Cards:	■	Restaurant:	■
Driving Range:	■	Lounge:	■
Practice Green:	■	Meeting Rooms:	
Locker Room:	■	Tennis:	
Rental Clubs:	■	Swimming:	■
Walkers:	■	Jogging Trails:	■
Snack Bar:	■	Boating:	■

COURSE DESCRIPTION

The original golf course was designed as a 9-hole layout by a New York State Parks landscape architect and built during the era of the Civilian Conservation Corps by crews who had lived on-site during construction. In 1967, the second 9 holes were added to complete the course as it is today.

On rare occasions, you may be privy to some of the fascinating wildlife that includes deer, fox, beaver, coyote, ducks, turkeys, blue-birds, hawks, and many other species.

From start to finish, this course plays straightforward and simple.

DIRECTIONS

Take I-88 to Exit 3 and turn left onto Rt. 369. Follow this road for 4-miles to Chenango Valley State Park.

CONKLIN PLAYERS CLUB
1520 Conklin Rd., Conklin, NY 13748 / (607) 755-3042

BASIC INFORMATION
Course Type: Public (Some members)
Year Built: 1988-1991
Architect: Rickard, Brown, & Brown
Local Pro: N/A

Course: N/A
Holes: 18 / Par 72

Back : 6,772 yds. Rating: 72.5 Slope: 127
Middle: 6,128 yds. Rating: 69.5 Slope: 121
Ladies: 4,699 yds. Rating: 67.8 Slope: 116

Tee Time: 7 days in advance.
Price: $15 - $30

Credit Cards:	■	Restaurant:	■
Driving Range:	■	Lounge:	■
Practice Green:	■	Meeting Rooms:	
Locker Room:		Tennis:	
Rental Clubs:		Swimming:	
Walkers:	■	Jogging Trails:	
Snack Bar:	■	Boating:	

COURSE DESCRIPTION
Conklin Players Club was designed by the owners of the course during a span of three years. It's a comfortable course for most golfers to play on and features lush fairways throughout its interesting variety of championship holes.

The playing field rolls along a hilly terrain that is often demanding if a ball ends up on an uneven lie. You'll need to play an accurate game of golf to score well here. Low-to-mid-handicappers will appreciate the many challenging holes that this course has to offer.

DIRECTIONS
From I-81 north take Exit 1 (Kirkwood/Conklin) and turn left at the end of the exit ramp to the upcoming set of lights. Turn left onto Rt. 7, and look for the course on your right.

ENDWELL GREENS GOLF CLUB
3675 Sally Piper Rd., Endwell, NY 13760 / (607) 785-4653

BASIC INFORMATION
Course Type: Public
Year Built: 1968
Architect: Geoffery Cornish
Local Pro: Stan Lisk

Course: N/A
Holes: 18 / Par 70

Back: 7,010 yds. Rating: N/A Slope: N/A
Middle: 6,258 yds. Rating: N/A Slope: N/A
Ladies: 5,382 yds. Rating: N/A Slope: N/A

Tee Time: 3 day in advance.
Price: $16 - $18

Credit Cards:	■	Restaurant:	■
Driving Range:	■	Lounge:	■
Practice Green:	■	Meeting Rooms:	■
Locker Room:	■	Tennis:	
Rental Clubs:	■	Swimming:	
Walkers:	■	Jogging Trails:	
Snack Bar:	■	Boating:	

COURSE DESCRIPTION
Endwell Greens Golf Club is a monster of a course to tackle from the back-tees at 7,010 yards. If you don't have the ability to hit long drives, do yourself a favor and play from the middle tees instead.

You need to have a good all around game to play well here. You'll find water on ten holes, but only a handful actually come into play between the 4 dogleg lefts, 6 dogleg rights, and the remaining 8 straight holes of golf. An ability to play a draw or a fade will help you out tremendously on your approach shots.

DIRECTIONS
Take Rt.17 west out of Binhamton Exit 69 Endwell to Rt. 17C. Make a right at Hooper Rd., another right at Market Rd., and yet another right on Sally Piper Rd. to the course.

DUTCH HOLLOW COUNTRY CLUB

Benson Rd., Owasco, NY 13130 / (315) 784-5052

BASIC INFORMATION

Course Type: Semi-private
Year Built: 1967
Architect: Wilford S. Hall
Local Pro: Michael Cotela

Course: N/A
Holes: 18 / Par 71

Back : 6,460 yds. Rating: 70.3 Slope: 120
Middle: 6,023 yds. Rating: 78.5 Slope: 116
Ladies: 5,045 yds. Rating: N/A Slope: N/A

Tee Time: 8-13 days in advance.
Price: $15 - $17

Credit Cards:	■	Restaurant:	■
Driving Range:	■	Lounge:	■
Practice Green:	■	Meeting Rooms:	■
Locker Room:	■	Tennis:	
Rental Clubs:	■	Swimming:	
Walkers:	■	Jogging Trails:	
Snack Bar:	■	Boating:	■

COURSE DESCRIPTION

Dutch Hollow Country Club offers a well-balanced mixture of holes that low-to-high-handicappers should comfortably play through. Uneven lies are not uncommon. The course features many undulations along its playing surface.

The front-nine, although shorter, plays harder because of the demanding design of its tight fairways. The sloppy greens tend to play medium-fast and are often difficult to putt on. You'll need to play your approach shots close to the pin for pars and birdies.

DIRECTIONS

Take the New York State Thruway (from the Weeds Port Exit) to Rt. 34 south to Auburn. At Rt. 38 A, you'll need to go through the village of Owasco towards Benson Rd. Make a left and look for the course about a 1/4-mile further on your left.

HIGHLAND PARK GOLF CLUB

Franklin Street Rd., Auburn, NY 11321 / (315) 253-3381

BASIC INFORMATION

Course Type: Public
Year Built: 1925 / 1960's
Architect: Connish
Local Pro: Steve Spinney

Course: N/A
Holes: 18 / Par 71

Back: 6,401 yds. Rating: 70.8 Slope: 120
Middle: 6,161 yds. Rating: 69.5 Slope: 117
Ladies: 5,285 yds. Rating: 73.0 Slope: 122

Tee Time: 2 days in advance.
Price: $20

Credit Cards:	■	Restaurant:	■
Driving Range:	■	Lounge:	■
Practice Green:	■	Meeting Rooms:	■
Locker Room:	■	Tennis:	
Rental Clubs:	■	Swimming:	
Walkers:	■	Jogging Trails:	
Snack Bar:	■	Boating:	■

COURSE DESCRIPTION

Highland Park Golf Club is noted for its fast, undulating greens. The course is also noted for its dual character. Like establishments that have been built between decades (3 1/2 to be exact), you're bound to find some fundamental differences. The old nine, in its traditional form, features smaller greens and a shorter playing field. The front-nine, conforming to the advancement of modern equipment, features better teeing platforms, a larger playing field, more bunkers and hazards, and larger greens.

Water comes into play on four holes.

DIRECTIONS

Go west bound form Sycamore & Rt. 5 and make a left at Prospect St. Make another left on Franklin St. and look for the course on your right.

AFTON GOLF CLUB

Afton Lake Rd., Afton Lake, NY 13730 / (607) 639-2454

BASIC INFORMATION

Course Type: Semi-private
Year Built: N/A
Architect: N/A
Local Pro: Bob Dawson

Course: N/A
Holes: 18 / Par 72

Back: 6,450 yds. Rating: N/A Slope: 113
Middle: 5,807 yds. Rating: N/A Slope: 112
Ladies: 4,580 yds. Rating: N/A Slope: N/A

Tee Time: First come, first serve.
Price: $10 - $24

Credit Cards:		Restaurant:	■
Driving Range:		Lounge:	■
Practice Green:	■	Meeting Rooms:	■
Locker Room:		Tennis:	
Rental Clubs:	■	Swimming:	
Walkers:	■	Jogging Trails:	
Snack Bar:	■	Boating:	■

COURSE DESCRIPTION

You won't have to worry about performing your very best at the *Afton Golf Club*. This course is a simple layout that seems, because of its effortless design, to have been built specifically for quick play.

Hazards are used sparingly and most of the holes can easily be reached in two strokes. If you're a mid-to-high handicapper, you shouldn't find much trouble in picking up a number of pars and birdies by the end of any given round. If that's what you're looking for in a golf course, this is certainly the place to go.

DIRECTIONS

1-mile off Exit 7 on I-88.

CANASAWACTA COUNTRY CLUB

79 South Broad Street Country Club Rd., Norwich, NY 13815 / (607) 336-2685

BASIC INFORMATION

Course Type: Semi-private
Year Built: 1920 / 1969
Architect: Russell Bailey
Local Pro: Fred Zahner

Course: N/A
Holes: 18 / Par 70

Back : 6,271 yds. Rating: 69.9 Slope: 120
Middle: 6,044 yds. Rating: 69.5 Slope: 118
Ladies: 5,166 yds. Rating: 68.8 Slope: 114

Tee Time: 3 days in advance.
Price: $15 - $22

Credit Cards:		Restaurant:	■
Driving Range:		Lounge:	■
Practice Green:	■	Meeting Rooms:	■
Locker Room:	■	Tennis:	
Rental Clubs:	■	Swimming:	
Walkers:	■	Jogging Trails:	
Snack Bar:	■	Boating:	

COURSE DESCRIPTION

Canasawacta Country Club covers a wonderful piece of real estate that features many beautiful trees along its hilly terrain. Each hole has a distinct character that sets it apart from each other, ten of which feature water coming into the play of action. Scoring well on this platform means having the ability to play shots from various lies – it's not often that you'll find your ball rolling on an even one. Besides the fact that the course is made up of many undulations, the fairways are wide, allowing aggressive play from each teeing area.

The course is an exceptional challenge for mid-to-high handicappers.

DIRECTIONS

Take Rt. 12 north of Norwich one mile to Rt. 44 (Country Club Rd.) Look for the course on your left about one mile further.

GENEGANTSLET GOLF CLUB

Rd. 12, Box 444, Greene, NY 13778 / (607) 656-8191

BASIC INFORMATION

Course Type: Semi-private
Year Built: 1953
Architect: Pete McClain
Local Pro: Karen Taylor

Course: N/A
Holes: 36

Back : 6,306 yds. Rating: N/A Slope: N/A
Middle: N/A   Rating: N/A Slope: N/A
Ladies: 5,811 yds. Rating: N/A Slope: N/A

Tee Time: 2 days in advance.
Price: $15 - $22.50

Credit Cards:	■	Restaurant:	■
Driving Range:	■	Lounge:	■
Practice Green:	■	Meeting Rooms:	■
Locker Room:		Tennis:	
Rental Clubs:	■	Swimming:	
Walkers:	■	Jogging Trails:	
Snack Bar:	■	Boating:	■

COURSE DESCRIPTION

Genegantslet Golf Club attracts golfers who enjoy walking while playing the game. At 6,306 yards from the back-tees, and with a playing field that is mostly level, most players shouldn't have a problem scoring low numbers. The course will test your ability to hit accurate drives right from the start. The long and narrow fairways of the front-nine make it important to control your shots to strategic landing areas. If you hit an errant shot, you'll most likely end up losing your ball between one of the maturely grown trees. If you can make it through the first-nine, you'll end up playing a much better game on the easier back-nine.

DIRECTIONS

Take Hwy. 81 N to Exit 6. Make a right and follow the road for about twenty minutes to the course. It will be on your right.

WINDING BROOK COUNTRY CLUB

RFDI Rt. 203, Valatie, NY 12184 / (518) 758-9117

BASIC INFORMATION

Course Type: Semi-private
Year Built: 1960's
Architect: Paul Roth
Local Pro: James Rothenburg

Course: N/A
Holes: 18 / Par 72

Back: 6,614 yds. Rating: 68.2 Slope: 110
Middle: 6,314 yds. Rating: 66.9 Slope: 107
Ladies: 5,865 yds. Rating: 70.2 Slope: 121

Tee Time: 1 day in advance.
Price: $16 - $18

Credit Cards:		Restaurant:	■
Driving Range:		Lounge:	■
Practice Green:	■	Meeting Rooms:	■
Locker Room:	■	Tennis:	■
Rental Clubs:	■	Swimming:	■
Walkers:	■	Jogging Trails:	
Snack Bar:	■	Boating:	

COURSE DESCRIPTION

Winding Brook Country Club is a sporty layout that features a good combination of holes and tree-lined narrow fairways.

Needless to say, you'll need to drive the ball well to steer your ball away from trouble. The majority of the course plays on an even plane of difficulty. Try to feel out the first couple of holes and plan your strategy around them. If they seem simple, choose to play aggressively. If you find them difficult, you can play the course conservatively and still come out shooting a low number.

DIRECTIONS

Take Rt. 9 twenty-miles southeast of Albany to Rt. 203. The course will be one mile off Rt. 9 on Rt. 209.

ELM TREE GOLF COURSE

Rt. 13, Cortland, NY 13045 / (607) 753-1341

BASIC INFORMATION

Course Type: Semi-private
Year Built: 1950's
Architect: N/A
Local Pro: Bruce Martins

Course: N/A
Holes: 18 / Par 70

Back: 6,251 yds. Rating: 66.4 Slope: 100
Middle: 6,103 yds. Rating: 64.8 Slope: 97
Ladies: 5,475 yds. Rating: 66.3 Slope: 99

Tee Time: First come, first serve.
Price: $11 - $13

Credit Cards:	■	Restaurant:	■
Driving Range:	■	Lounge:	■
Practice Green:	■	Meeting Rooms:	
Locker Room:	■	Tennis:	
Rental Clubs:		Swimming:	
Walkers:	■	Jogging Trails:	
Snack Bar:	■	Boating:	■

COURSE DESCRIPTION

The **Elm Tree Golf Course** is the perfect place for a first-time golfer to step off the practice range and give a round of golf a full force effort. This course is extremely easy to play, straightforward in its design, void of surprises, and absolutely unintimidating.

If you're a high-handicapper, the simplicity of this course will surely offer you many chances to score par or better. When you experience the thrill of playing a low numbered round for the first time, you'll remember it for the rest of your life, and somehow, as irrational as it may seem, you'll instinctively force yourself to play better golf on harder courses — ultimately making you a better player in the long run.

DIRECTIONS

Take Rt. 81 to Rt. 13 and head south for about 8-miles.

MAPLE HILL GOLF CLUB

Conrad Rd., Marathon, NY 13803 / (607) 849-3285

BASIC INFORMATION

Course Type: Public
Year Built: 1968
Architect: N/A
Local Pro: N/A

Course: N/A
Holes: 18 / Par 70

Back : 6,440 yds. Rating: 70.5 Slope: 112
Middle: 5,900 yds. Rating: 69.0 Slope: N/A
Ladies: 4,650 yds. Rating: N/A Slope: N/A

Tee Time: 7 days in advance.
Price: $10 - $18

Credit Cards:		Restaurant:	■
Driving Range:		Lounge:	■
Practice Green:	■	Meeting Rooms:	■
Locker Room:	■	Tennis:	
Rental Clubs:	■	Swimming:	
Walkers:	■	Jogging Trails:	
Snack Bar:	■	Boating:	■

COURSE DESCRIPTION

Maple Hill Golf Club rolls through a hilly playing surface that features tight fairways and fast greens. Yet it is simple enough for the newest of novices to play well on.

The toughest hole on the course is the 15th, which is a par-5 that measures 580 yards from the back-tees. You'll need to hit your drive about 230 yards to the left-center portion of the fairway to cut off the right dogleg design of the hole. Your approach shot will have to be played over trees and a lurking pond that sits about 230 yards away from an elevated green that slopes from back-to-front.

DIRECTIONS

The course is 3-miles off the Martin Exit on Rt. 81 on Exit 9.

DELAWARE COUNTY

HANAH COUNTRY CLUB
Rt. 30, Margaretville, NY 12455 / (914) 587-2100

BASIC INFORMATION

Course Type: Public
Year Built: 1992
Architect: N/A
Local Pro: N/A

Course: N/A
Holes: 18 / Par 72

Back : 7,033 yds. Rating: 70.0 Slope: 133
Middle: 6,313 yds. Rating: N/A Slope: 126
Ladies: 5,294 yds. Rating: 72.4 Slope: 123

Tee Time: First come, first serve.
Price: $37- $55

Credit Cards: ■	Restaurant: ■
Driving Range: ■	Lounge: ■
Practice Green: ■	Meeting Rooms: ■
Locker Room: ■	Tennis: ■
Rental Clubs: ■	Swimming: ■
Walkers: ■	Jogging Trails: ■
Snack Bar: ■	Boating:

COURSE DESCRIPTION

This exceptional course will thrill you from the moment you step up to the first tee. The landscaping combined with its natural surroundings of mature trees and beautiful wild mountain flowers makes this an attraction you'll want to come back to more than just once.

The multiple tees on the course are a great challenge for all types of players.

DIRECTIONS

Take the New York Thruway, get off at Exit 19 and enter Rt. 28 west (Pine Hill). Drive 45 miles. When you reach Arkville and see Delaware and Ulster railroad station on your left, go approximately 200 yards and you will see a sign for the Hanah Inn & Resort. Make a right turn at this corner. Go to end of road and make a right onto Rt. 30. The course will be on your left.

STAMFORD GOLF CLUB
Taylor Rd., Stamford, NY 12167 / (607) 652-7398

BASIC INFORMATION

Course Type: Semi-private
Year Built: 1897
Architect: N/A
Local Pro: Jim Schouller

Course: N/A
Holes: 18 / Par 70

Back : 6,585 yds. Rating: 69.7 Slope: 113
Middle: 6,125 yds. Rating: 69.1 Slope: 112
Ladies: 5,249 yds. Rating: 79.9 Slope: 108

Tee Time: 1 day in advance.
Price: $42 - $71

Credit Cards:	Restaurant: ■
Driving Range: ■	Lounge: ■
Practice Green: ■	Meeting Rooms: ■
Locker Room: ■	Tennis:
Rental Clubs: ■	Swimming:
Walkers: ■	Jogging Trails:
Snack Bar: ■	Boating: ■

COURSE DESCRIPTION

Stamford Golf Club, built in the late 1800's, is one of America's long lost golfing jewels. And thank the Lord that it's a semi-private course that allows the general public a chance to experience what it was like to play golf when it was first introduced to our country.

If you're searching for nostalgia, this course is for you.

DIRECTIONS

Take Rt. 88 to Exit 20 and follow that until you get to Rt. 10. The course will be on your right.

WINDHAM COUNTRY CLUB

P.O. Box 53 South St., Windham, NY 12496 / (518) 734-9910

BASIC INFORMATION

Course Type: Public
Year Built: 1927
Architect: N/A
Local Pro: Dave Rarich

Course: N/A
Holes: 18 / Par 71

Back : 6,088 yds. Rating: 69.9 Slope: 127
Middle: 5,755 yds. Rating: 68.1 Slope: 123
Ladies: 4,879 yds. Rating: 68.4 Slope: 114

Tee Time: 2 days in advance.
Price: $32 - $38

Credit Cards:	■	Restaurant:	■
Driving Range:	■	Lounge:	■
Practice Green:	■	Meeting Rooms:	■
Locker Room:	■	Tennis:	
Rental Clubs:	■	Swimming:	
Walkers:	■	Jogging Trails:	
Snack Bar:	■	Boating:	■

COURSE DESCRIPTION

Windham Country Club flows around an attractive country setting with offerings of beautiful mountain views throughout its playing field. You'll need to hit your drives accurately to well-defined landing areas for proper pin position on your approach shots. Most golfers find the back-nine a little more difficult to play because of its open architecture. It isn't unusual to be playing through windy conditions that make it hard to choose the right club according to distance.

The preferred shot on this course is a draw.

DIRECTIONS

Take the New York State Thruway to Exit 21 and follow that to Rt. 23 W for about 1/2 an hour. Make a left at Rt. 29 and a right when you get to South St. The course will be on your left.

CASELWOOD GOLF COURSE

RR 5 New Boston Rd., Canastota, NY 13032 / (315) 697-9164

BASIC INFORMATION

Course Type: Public
Year Built: 1962 / 1989
Architect: Richard Quick ('89)
Local Pro: N/A

Course: N/A
Holes: 18 / Par 71

Back : 6,144 yds. Rating: N/A Slope: N/A
Middle: 6,093 yds. Rating: N/A Slope: N/A
Ladies: 5,700 yds. Rating: N/A Slope: N/A

Tee Time: First come, first serve.
Price: $12 - $14.50

Credit Cards:	■	Restaurant:	■
Driving Range:		Lounge:	■
Practice Green:	■	Meeting Rooms:	■
Locker Room:		Tennis:	
Rental Clubs:	■	Swimming:	
Walkers:	■	Jogging Trails:	
Snack Bar:	■	Boating:	■

COURSE DESCRIPTION

Caselwood Golf Course was built for the masses. It's a place where an average golfer can have a go at par without having to perform like a professional. The course features many willow trees that often come into play along side the fairways.

The 9th-hole, which measures 595 yards from the championship tees, is the hardest hole on the course. A long drive is required to hit the ball over a fairway pond, followed by two well-placed approach shots, en route to a demanding, elevated green that slopes from front-to-back.

DIRECTIONS

Take the New York State Thruway to Exit 34 and make a left at New Boston Rd. The course will be 2 miles further up the road. You'll see it on your right.

60

COLGATE UNIVERSITY SEVEN OAKS GOLF CLUB
Huntington Gymnasium, Hamilton, NY 13346 / (315) 824-1432

BASIC INFORMATION

Course Type: Semi-private
Year Built: N/A
Architect: Robert Trent Jones
Local Pro: Mary Ann Burke

Course: N/A
Holes: 18 / Par 72

Back : 6,915 yds. Rating: 73.4 Slope: 128
Middle: 6,423 yds. Rating: 71.4 Slope: 124
Ladies: 5,849 yds. Rating: 75.0 Slope: 125

Tee Time: 14 days in advance.
Price: $35

Credit Cards: ■   Restaurant: ■
Driving Range: ■   Lounge: ■
Practice Green: ■   Meeting Rooms: ■
Locker Room: ■   Tennis:
Rental Clubs: ■   Swimming:
Walkers: ■   Jogging Trails:
Snack Bar: ■   Boating: ■

COURSE DESCRIPTION

This club offers an excellent opportunity for all types of players to enjoy a fine challenge of golf.

You'll find the course opening up immediately on most of the holes, allowing you to work the ball in several directions towards generously wide fairways. It makes for a very exciting, purposely aggressive type of golf — the type that has become a favorite to watch on the PGA Tour. Due to its fine implementation of hole designs, this course has hosted a Nike Tour event and a New York State Mens Amateur competition.

You're going to love playing here!

DIRECTIONS
Please call for directions.

ARROWHEAD GOLF COURSE
7185 East Taft Rd., East Syracuse, NY 13057 / (315) 656-7563

BASIC INFORMATION

Course Type: Semi-private
Year Built: 1968 / 1971 / 1989
Architect: N/A
Local Pro: N/A

Course: N/A
Holes: 18 / Par 72

Back : 6,637 yds. Rating: 70.9 Slope: 113
Middle: 6,272 yds. Rating: 69.2 Slope: 109
Ladies: 5,156 yds. Rating: 68.5 Slope: 109

Tee Time: First come, first serve.
Price: $15

Credit Cards: Restaurant:
Driving Range: Lounge: ■
Practice Green: ■   Meeting Rooms:
Locker Room: Tennis:
Rental Clubs: ■   Swimming:
Walkers: ■   Jogging Trails:
Snack Bar: ■   Boating:

COURSE DESCRIPTION

Arrowhead Golf Course emphasizes an ability to conform to a nonconforming design. One interesting distinction that becomes quite evident on this course is that it features not a single sand trap throughout its entire layout. The architect chose to take a different direction by moving a lot of earth, incorporating a good amount of water, placing grass bunkers instead of sand, and building many different types of greens — both in size and shape.

DIRECTIONS
This course is 5 miles from Hwy. 481 (Bridge Port Exit) where you'll need to make a left at the first set of lights (Freemont Rd.) followed by a left towards Taft Rd. and a right to the course. Look for the course about a 1/4-mile further on your right.

CAMILLUS COUNTRY CLUB

5690 Bennetts Cors Rd., Camillus, NY 13031 / (315) 672-3770

BASIC INFORMATION

Course Type: Semi-private
Year Built: 1962
Architect: N/A
Local Pro: Bill Tooley

Course: N/A
Holes: 18 / Par 72

Back : 6,368 yds. Rating: 70.1 Slope: N/A
Middle: N/A Rating: N/A Slope: N/A
Ladies: 5,573 yds. Rating: 71.4 Slope: N/A

Tee Time: 7 days in advance.
Price: $14 - $35

Credit Cards:	■	Restaurant:	■
Driving Range:	■	Lounge:	■
Practice Green:	■	Meeting Rooms:	■
Locker Room:	■	Tennis:	
Rental Clubs:	■	Swimming:	
Walkers:	■	Jogging Trails:	
Snack Bar:	■	Boating:	■

COURSE DESCRIPTION

Camillus Country Club holds its strength on the many blind shots that it will force you to play through. The difficulty doesn't lie so much in the distance of every shot, but rather the direction of a given shot under different circumstances.

The hilly terrain will inevitably navigate your rolling ball onto an uneven lie. If you're not used to playing shots above and below your stance, you'll need to get to the driving range early to get a feel for them.

The course features a good variety of trees with tighter fairways on the back-nine.

DIRECTIONS

This course is off Hwy. 690 (Rt. 81), heading west to Hwy. 695 and onto Rt. 5. When you reach Bennetts Rd., make a right and look for the course about 1/2 further on your right.

FOXFIRE GOLF & TENNIS CLUB

1 Village Blvd., Baldwinsville, NY 13027 / (315) 638-2930

BASIC INFORMATION

Course Type: Public
Year Built: 1978
Architect: Phelps & Benz
Local Pro: Fred Elliott

Course: N/A
Holes: 18 / Par 72

Back : 6,909 yds. Rating: 72.8 Slope: 128
Middle: 6,451 yds. Rating: 70.4 Slope: 123
Ladies: 5,775 yds. Rating: 72.3 Slope: 120

Tee Time: 4 days in advance.
Price: $18 - $20

Credit Cards:	■	Restaurant:	■
Driving Range:	■	Lounge:	■
Practice Green:	■	Meeting Rooms:	■
Locker Room:	■	Tennis:	■
Rental Clubs:	■	Swimming:	
Walkers:	■	Jogging Trails:	
Snack Bar:	■	Boating:	■

COURSE DESCRIPTION

Foxfire Golf & Tennis Club provides a fully irrigated, well-trapped layout with lurking water hazards that test the average as well as the expert golfer. This par-72 beauty stretches to 6,900 yards from the championship tees. The white tees provide an ample test at 6,466 yards. Constructed in the early '70's, Foxfire has hosted the New York State Woman's Amateur in 1980 and the annual Babe Zaharis tournament since 1976.

If you're in Onondaga County, you'll want to take a day off to play this thoughtfully designed golf course.

DIRECTIONS

Take I-690 west (8 miles from downtown Syracuse) and exit at Van Buren Rd. The course will be on your right. You'll need to make three rights to get to the parking lot.

ONONDAGA COUNTY

GREEN LAKES STATE PARK CLUB

7000 Green Lakes Rd., Fayetteville, NY 13066 / (315) 637-5515

BASIC INFORMATION

Course Type: Public
Year Built: 1936
Architect: Robert Trent Jones
Local Pro: Anthony Marino

Course: N/A
Holes: 18 / Par 71

Back   : 6,212 yds. Rating: 68.4 Slope: 113
Middle: 5,920 yds. Rating: 67.0 Slope: 110
Ladies: 5,481 yds. Rating: N/A   Slope: N/A

Tee Time: 2 days in advance.
Price: $7 - $14

Credit Cards:		Restaurant:	■
Driving Range:		Lounge:	■
Practice Green:	■	Meeting Rooms:	■
Locker Room:		Tennis:	
Rental Clubs:	■	Swimming:	
Walkers:	■	Jogging Trails:	
Snack Bar:	■	Boating:	■

COURSE DESCRIPTION

Green Lakes State Park Club plays a little harder than the numbers indicated for the Rating and Slope in the Basic Information box. Robert Trent Jones built an interesting layout with many difficult lies that will subject you to manufacture a swing on the numerous uneven lies your ball is bound to roll onto. Accurate drives are also needed to keep the ball in play between the tight fairways and away from the higher than average rough.

The small greens on this course can be brutal at times with their many built-in mounds. It makes for an interesting round.

DIRECTIONS

Take Rt. 81 north to Rt. 481 and follow that to Rt. 5 where you'll have to go east — into Fayettville, N.Y. —and you'll see signs that will lead you directly to the course, off Rt. 5.

LIVERPOOL GOLF & COUNTRY CLUB

7209 Morgan Rd., Liverpool, NY 13088 / (315) 457-7170

BASIC INFORMATION

Course Type: Public
Year Built: 1949
Architect: Archie S. Ajemian
Local Pro: Jim Doherty

Course: N/A
Holes: 18 / Par 71

Back   : 6,412 yds. Rating: 70.7 Slope: 114
Middle: 6,032 yds. Rating: 68.3 Slope: 111
Ladies: 5,487 yds. Rating: 69.3 Slope: 113

Tee Time: 7 days in advance.
Price: $15 - $17

Credit Cards:		Restaurant:	■
Driving Range:	■	Lounge:	■
Practice Green:	■	Meeting Rooms:	■
Locker Room:	■	Tennis:	
Rental Clubs:	■	Swimming:	
Walkers:		Jogging Trails:	
Snack Bar:	■	Boating:	■

COURSE DESCRIPTION

Liverpool Golf & Country Club allows a mid-to-high handicapper to score well throughout the layout. It's a flat course that prefers a fade over a draw on the majority of the holes. Confidence should easily be built once you take your stance on the first tee and look out towards the generously sized fairways — open and inviting in nature and wide enough for a variety of shaped shots. The rest of the course follows in its footsteps.

Water comes into play on eleven holes.

DIRECTIONS

Take the New York State Thruway to Exit 38 and make a left and make a right at the first set of lights. Make your first left from here, and a right onto Morgan Rd. You'll see the course on your right.

RADISSON GREENS GOLF COURSE

8055 Potter Rd., Baldwinsville, NY 13027 / (315) 638-0092

BASIC INFORMATION

Course Type: Semi-private
Year Built: 1972
Architect: Robert Trent Jones
Local Pro: Jeff Thompson

Course: N/A
Holes: 18 / Par 72

Back : 7,010 yds. Rating: 73.3 Slope: 128
Middle: 6,360 yds. Rating: 71.9 Slope: 124
Ladies: 5,543 yds. Rating: 70.0 Slope: 124

Tee Time: 1 day in advance.
Price: $22

Credit Cards:		Restaurant:	■
Driving Range:	■	Lounge:	■
Practice Green:	■	Meeting Rooms:	■
Locker Room:	■	Tennis:	
Rental Clubs:		Swimming:	
Walkers:	■	Jogging Trails:	
Snack Bar:	■	Boating:	■

COURSE DESCRIPTION

The *Radisson Greens Golf Course* is an outstanding design that is a further example of the incredible mind of architect Robert Trent Jones. The course is just as exciting today as the day that it first opened in 1975.

If you choose to play from the championship tees, you'll need to play both accurately and long to navigate your ball through the elongated fairways that are tree-lined and narrow. A generous amount of bunkering is present, set in strategic areas, to challenge you from each one of its tees.

The course is fundamentally strong in the sense that it offers a level challenge from beginning to end.

DIRECTIONS

Take Hwy. 690 W to Rt. 31 E. The course will be on your left.

LEATHERSTOCKING GOLF COURSE

P.O. Box 510 Nelson Avenue, Cooperstown, NY 13326 / (607) 547-5275

BASIC INFORMATION

Course Type: Public (Resort)
Year Built: 1909
Architect: Devereaux Emmett
Local Pro: Rick Wolcott

Course: N/A
Holes: 18 / Par 72

Back : 6,324 yds. Rating: 71.0 Slope: 124
Middle: 6,053 yds. Rating: 69.3 Slope: 120
Ladies: 5,254 yds. Rating: 69.2 Slope: 116

Tee Time: 6 days in advance.
Price: $45 - $55

Credit Cards:	■	Restaurant:	■
Driving Range:		Lounge:	■
Practice Green:	■	Meeting Rooms:	■
Locker Room:	■	Tennis:	■
Rental Clubs:	■	Swimming:	■
Walkers:	■	Jogging Trails:	
Snack Bar:	■	Boating:	■

COURSE DESCRIPTION

Leatherstocking Golf Course is a rich looking, traditionally-styled layout that provides a wonderful playing field along a colorfully expansive lake.

Both the front- and the back-nines play in similar fashion and are equally challenging with neither favoring a draw nor a fade; a good combination of both is needed to shoot par or better for an average golfer who carries about a 15-handicap.

Aggressive play is recommended along the majority of the open fairways, even though the course features a healthy combination of trees that run along the parallel design of the holes.

DIRECTIONS

Take Rt. 80 south-bound towards Cooperstown. The course will be on your left.

EVERGREEN COUNTRY CLUB

1400 Schuurman Rd., Castleton-On-The-Hudson, NY 12033 / (518) 477-6224

BASIC INFORMATION

Course Type: Public (Private)
Year Built: 1960
Architect: Paul Roth
Local Pro: Barney Bell

Course: Birches (18 / Par 70)
Holes: 36

Back : 6,001 yds. Rating: 68.0 Slope: 111
Middle: N/A   Rating: N/A   Slope: N/A
Ladies: 5,134 yds. Rating: 72.0 Slope: 117

Tee Time: 1 day in advance.
Price: $12 - $20

Credit Cards: ■   Restaurant: ■
Driving Range: ■   Lounge: ■
Practice Green: ■   Meeting Rooms: ■
Locker Room: ■   Tennis: ■
Rental Clubs: ■   Swimming: ■
Walkers: ■   Jogging Trails:
Snack Bar: ■   Boating:

COURSE DESCRIPTION

The non-private course (Birches) is the shorter of the two, yet it does provide a nice playing field for an enjoyable round of golf for mid-to-high handicappers. If you're an above average golfer, you won't find much to challenge here, unless you're specifically working on your short game.

DIRECTIONS

From Albany, take I-90 east to Exit 11W and horseshoe around to the first set of traffic lights. Turn left and proceed straight for about a half-mile to the course which will appear on your left.

ALTERNATIVE COURSES - CENTRAL

Albany
Private

Albany Country Club
Wormer Rd.
Voorheesville, NY 12186
(518) 765-2854

Colonie Country Club
P.O. Box 322, Rt. 85 A
Voorheesville, NY 12186
(518) 765-4103

Normanside Country Club
Box 159, End of Salisbury Rd.
Delmar, NY 12054
(518) 439-6204

Pinehaven Country Club
P.O. Box 567, Silver Rd.
Guilderland, NY 12084
(518) 456-7111

Schuyler Meadows Club
Box 11500 Schuler Meadows Rd.
Laudonville, NY 12211
(518) 785-8558

Shaker Ridge Country Club
802 Albany Shaker Rd.
Laudonville, NY 12211
(518) 869-5101

Wolferts Roost Country Club
Van Roost Country Club
Albany, NY 12204
(518) 462-2115

Albany
9-hole

French's Hollow Fairways
Hurst Rd., P.O. Box 116
Guilderland, NY 12085
(518) 861-8837

Mill Road Acres Golf Course
30 Mill Rd.
Latham, NY 12110
(518) 785-4653

Van Schaick Island Country Club
Continental Ave.
Cohoes, NY 12047
(518) 237-6127

Albany
Executive

Western Turnpike Golf Course
72 Main St.
Bemus Point, NY 14712
(716) 386-2893

Albany
Par-3

Hiawatha Trails
State Farm Rd.
Guilderland, NY 12084
(518) 456-9512

Broome
Public

En Joie Golf Club
722 West Main St.
Endicott, NY 13760
(607) 785-1661

Broome
Private

Binghampton Country Club
Robinson Hill Rd.
Endwell, NY 13760
(607) 797-5828

IBM Country Club
Watson Blvd.
Johnson City, NY 13790
(607) 797-2381

Vestal Hills Country Club
P.O. Box 142, SVS Webb Rd.
Binghampton, NY 13903
(607) 723-7658

Broome
Executive

Golden Oak Golf Club
Rt. 79 South Rd. 2
Windsor, NY 13865
(607) 655-3217

Cayuga
Public

Auburn Country Club
East Lake Rd.
Auburn, NY 13021
(315) 253-0359

Cayuga
Private

Owasco Country Club
Box 2248 East Lake Rd.
Auburn, NY 13021
(315) 253-3971

Cayuga
9-hole

Cato Golf Club
12981 NY Rt. 34
Cato, NY 13033
(315) 626-2291

Cranebrook Golf Club
Conoga Rd.
Auburn, NY 13021
(315) 252-7887

Meadowbrook Golf Club
Ball Rd.
Weedsport, NY 13166
(315) 834-9358

Wells College Golf Course
Box. 58, Corn St.
Aurora, NY 13026
(315) 364-8024

Cayuga
Executive

Fillmore Golf Course
Tolgate Hill Rd.
Locke, NY 13092
(315) 497-3145

Chenango
Public

Riverbend Golf Course
8 New Berlin Rd.
Oxford, NY 13411
(607) 847-8481

Chenango
9-hole

Mountain Top Golf Course
RD 1, Box 26
Sherburne, NY 13460
(607) 674-4005

Sundown Golf & Country Club
RD 3, Box 242D, Hay Half Lane
Bainbridge, NY 13733
(607) 895-6888

Chenango
Executive

Bluestone Golf Course
Corner of Grant St. & Scott St.
Oxford, NY 13830
(607) 843-8352

Columbia
Public

Copake Country Club
44 Golf Course Rd.
Crayville, NY 12521
(518) 325-4338

Columbia
Private

Colombia Golf & Country Club
P.O. Box 646, Rt. 217
Claverack, NY 12513
(518) 851-9894

Cortland
Private

Cortland Country Club
Box 277
Cortland, NY 13045
(607) 753-3336

Cortland
9-hole

Knickerbocker Country Club
Telephone Rd.
Cincinnatus, NY 13040
(607) 863-3800

Delaware
Private

Sidney Golf & Country Club
Box 175 STAR Rt.
Sidney, NY 13838
(607) 563-8381

Delaware
9-hole

College Golf Course
Sunny Delhi
Delhi, NY 13753
(607) 746-4281

Greene
Public

Colonial Country Club
Rt. 23 A, Box 595
Tannersville, NY 12485
(518) 589-9807

Greene
9-hole

Blackhead Mountain Lodge & C.C.
Craws Nest Rd.
Roundtop, NY 12473
(518) 622-3157

Pleasant Valley Golf
Rt. 23
Windham, NY 12496
(518) 734-4230

Pleasant View Lodge
Freehold - Gayhead Rd.
Freehold, NY 12431
(518) 634-2523

Rainbow Country Club
Box 169, Rd. 2
Greenville, NY 12083
(518) 966-5343

Rip Van Winkle
Rt. 23 A, P.O. Box 190
Palenville, NY 12463
(518) 678-9779

Greene
Executive

Onteora Club
P.O. Box 546
Tannersville, NY 12485
(518) 589-5310

Sunnyhill Resort
Sunnyhill Rd.
Greenville, NY 12083
(518) 634-7698

Madison
Private

Kanon Valley Country Club
Rd. 2, Box 215
Oneida, NY 13421
(315) 363-8283

Oneida Community Golf Club
Kenwood Station
Oneida, NY 13421
(315) 361-3241

Madison
9-hole

Oneida Country Club
409 Genese St.
Oneida, NY 13421
(315) 363-8879

Pleasant Knolls Golf Course
Stoney Brook Rd.
Oneida, NY 89502
(315) 829-4653

Skyridge Chalet & Golf
Salt Springs Rd.
Chittenango, NY 13037
(315) 687-6900

Onondago
Public

Lyndon Golf Courses
Fayetteville Rd.
Fayetteville, NY 13066
(315) 446-1885

Skyline Golf & Country Club
9113 Brewerton Rd.
Brewerton, NY 13029
(315) 699-5338

Tanner Valley Golf
4040 Tanner Rd.
Syracuse, NY 13215
(315) 492-9856

Towne Isle Golf Club & Range
6113 Towne Isle Rd.
Kirkville, NY 13082
(315) 656-3522

Wa-Noa Golf Club
Bridgeport Rd.
East Syracuse, NY 13057
(315) 656-8213

Onondago
Private

Beaver Meadows Golf & Recreation
Box 522
Liverpool, NY 13088
(315) 695-5187

Onondago
Private - Continued

Bellevue Country Club
Glenwood Ave.
Syracuse, NY 13207
(315) 475-1984

Cavalry Club
P.O. Box 158, Troop Rd.
Manlius, NY 13104
(315) 682-9510

Drumlins Golf Course
800 Nottingham Rd.
Syracuse, NY 13244
(315) 446-5580

Lafayette Country Club
4480 Lafayette Rd.
Jamesville, NY 13078
(315) 469-3298

Lske Shore Yacht & Country Club
6777 Lake Shore Rd.
Cicero, NY 13039
(315) 699-5118

Onondaga Golf & Country Club
7003 East Genese
Fayetville, NY 13066
(315) 446-3500

Pompey Club
7200 Hamilton Rd.
Pompey, NY 13138
(315) 677-3559

Skaneateles Country Club
Drawer 29, Westlake Rd.
Skaneateles, NY 13152
(315) 685-7131

Tuscarora Golf Club
Howlett Hill Rd.
Marcellus, NY 13108
(315) 673-2679

Onondago
9-hole

Burnett Park Golf Course
412 Spencer
Syracuse, NY 13204
(315) 487-6285

Northern Pines Golf
Rt. 31
Cicero, NY 13039
(315) 699-2939

Northern Pines Range & Golf Course
215 Gerant Drive
Syracuse, NY 13204
(315) 699-2939

Orchard Valley Golf Club
4693 Cherry Valley Turnpike
Lafayette, NY 13084
(315) 677-5180

Point East Golf Course
200 Warring Rd.
Syracuse, NY 13244
(315) 445-0963

Seneca Golf Course
State Fair Blvd.
Baldwinsville, NY 13027
(315) 635-7571

Sunnycrest Golf Course
412 Spencer
Syracuse, NY 13204
(315) 473-2674

Vesperhills Golf Course
Octagon Rd.
Tully, NY 13159
(315) 696-8328

Wildwood Golf Course
7954 Brewerton Rd.
Cicero, NY 13039
(315) 669-5255

Onondago
Executive

Brooklawn Golf Course
Old Thompson Rd.
Syracuse, NY 12180
(315) 463-1831

Delphi Falls Golf Course
2127 Oran Delphi Rd.
Delphi Falls, NY 13051
(315) 662-3611

Pine Grove Country Club
3185 Milton Ave. (Exit)
Camillus, NY 13031
(315) 672-8107

West Hill Golf & Country Club
West Hill
Camillus, NY 13031
(315) 672-8677

Westvale Golf Club
100 Golf View Dr.
Camillus, NY 13031
(315) 487-9815

Otsego
Private

Country Club Of Ithaca
189 Pleasant Grove Rd.
Ithaca, NY 14850
(607) 257-1808

Country Club Of Troy
P.O. Box 125, Brunswick Rd.
Troy, NY 12181
(518) 274-4207

Oneonta Country Club
Country Club Drive
Oneonta, NY 13820
(607) 432-9074

Otsego
9-hole

Edgewood Golf Course
RR1 Box 166,
Laurens, NY 13796
(607) 432-2713

Otsego Golf Club
Box 217, Rt. 80
Springfield Center, NY 13468
(607) 547-9290

Woodhaven Park Golf Course
Woodhaven Park
West Oneonta, NY 13861
(607) 433-2301

Otsego
Executive

Cee Jay Golf Course
Rd 1, Box 127
Laurens, NY 13796
(607) 263-5291

Rensselaer
9-hole

Burden Lake Country Club
Todem Lodge Road, Rt. 3, Box 179 A
Averill Park, NY 12018
(518) 674-8917

Schoharie
9-hole

Cobleskill Golf & Country Club
Rt. 7, Box 367
Cobleskill, NY 12043
(518) 234-4045

Tioga
Public

Catatonk Golf Club
71 Golf Club Rd.
Candor, NY 13743
(607) 659-4600

Tioga Country Club
RO-KI Blvd., P.O. Box 220
Nichols, NY 13812
(607) 699-3881

Tioga
Private

Shepard Hills Country Club
P.O. Box 516, Shemung St. (17 C)
Waverly, NY 14892
(607) 432-9074

Tioga
9-hole

Apalachin Golf Course
South Apalachin Rd.
Apalachin, NY 13732
(607) 625-2682

Grandview Farms
400 Hartwell Rd.
Berkshire, NY 13736

Tioga
Executive

Newark Valley Golf Club
10626 Rt. 38
Newark Valley, NY 13811
(607) 642-3376

Tomkins
Public

Stonehedges Golf Course
P.O. Box 25 Licks & Stevens Rd.
Groton, NY 13073
(607) 898-3754

Tomkins
Private

**Robert Trent Jones Course
at Cornell University**
Warren Rd.
Ithaca, NY 14850
(607) 257-3661

Tomkins
9-hole

Dryden Lake Golf Course
430 Lake Rd.
Dryden, NY 13053
(607) 844-9173

Indian Head Golf Course
Rd. 1, Box 590
Cayuga, NY 13034
(315) 253-6812

Ithaca City Golf Course
10 Pier Rd.
Ithica, NY 14850
(607) 273-6262

Trumansburg Golf Club
23 Halsey St.
Trumansburg, NY 14886
(607) 387-8844

Tomkins
Executive

Hillendale Golf Course
218 Applegate Rd.
Ithaca, NY 14850
(607) 273-2363

Washoe
Private

Hidden Valley Country Club
3575 East Hidden Valley Dr.
Reno, NY 89502
(702) 857-4735

5. N.Y. SOUTH /COUNTIES AND CITIES

Bronx
B2 / Bronx ... 1

Dutchess
B1 / Hopewell Junc. ... 2
B1 / Pine Plains ... 3
B1 / Poughkeepsie ... 4

Rockland
B2 / Pearl River ... 10
B2 / Thiells ... 11

Suffolk
B2 / Babylon ...12
B2 / Brentwood ...13

B1 / Liberty ... 20
B1 / Loch Sheldrake
... 21
B1 / Roscoe... 22

Ulster
B1 / Ellenville ... 23
B1 / Kerhonkson ... 24

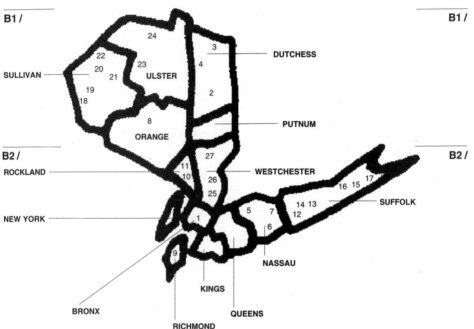

Nassau
B2 / Glenwood ... 5
B2 / Lido Beach ... 6
B2 / Woodbury ... 7

Orange
B1 / Montgomery ... 8

Richmond
B2 / Statan Island ... 9

B2 / Hauppuge ...14
B2 / Manorville ...15
B2 / Middle island ...16
B2 / Montauk ...17

Sullivan
B1 / Callicoon ... 18
B1 / Kiamesha Lake
... 19

Westchester
B2 / Scarsdale ... 25
B2 / White Plains ... 26
B1 / Yorktown Heights
... 27

PELHAM SPLIT ROCK AMERICAN GOLF CLUB

870 Shore Rd., Bronx, NY 10464 / (718) 885-1258

BASIC INFORMATION

Course Type: Public
Year Built: 1898
Architect: T.J. Tillinghast
Local Pro: Charles Kilkenny

Course: Split Rock (18 / Par 71)
Holes: 36

Back : 6,585 yds. Rating: 71.9 Slope: 125
Middle: 6,239 yds. Rating: 70.1 Slope: 122
Ladies: 5,509 yds. Rating: 71.7 Slope: 122

Tee Time: 10 days in advance.
Price: $8.50 - $23

Credit Cards:	■	Restaurant:	
Driving Range:		Lounge:	
Practice Green:	■	Meeting Rooms:	
Locker Room:	■	Tennis:	
Rental Clubs:	■	Swimming:	
Walkers:	■	Jogging Trails:	■
Snack Bar:	■	Boating:	■

COURSE DESCRIPTION

Pelham Split Rock American Golf Club
is an understated attraction that offers a playing field that most golfers will feel comfortable playing. The terrain is surprisingly hilly with extensions of long narrow fairways. The 16th hole, a par-4 measuring 440 yards is the hardest test on the course. You'll be hitting your drive off an elevated tee towards a tight fairway featuring a swamp on the left and mature oak trees on the right. You'll need to follow that with a blind uphill approach to a two-tiered hour-glass shape green surrounded by bunkers.

DIRECTIONS

Take I-95 to Exit 8B and go over the bridge. Make a left at the first traffic light and follow the circle half-way around. From that point on, you'll see signs that will lead you to the course.

VAN CORTLAND PARK GOLF COURSE

Van Cortland & Bailey Avenues, Bronx, NY 10471 / (212) 543-4595

BASIC INFORMATION

Course Type: Public
Year Built: 1895
Architect: Tom Bendlon
Local Pro: Tom Terlease

Course: N/A
Holes: 18 / Par 70

Back: 6,122 yds. Rating: N/A Slope: N/A
Middle: 5,913 yds. Rating: 67.7 Slope: 110
Ladies: 5,421 yds. Rating: 73.0 Slope: 120

Tee Time: 9 -10 days in advance.
Price: $8.50 - $19

Credit Cards:	■	Restaurant:	■
Driving Range:		Lounge:	■
Practice Green:		Meeting Rooms:	
Locker Room:	■	Tennis:	
Rental Clubs:	■	Swimming:	
Walkers:	■	Jogging Trails:	
Snack Bar:	■	Boating:	

COURSE DESCRIPTION

Van Cortland Park Golf Course was built in 1895 and is still inviting enough to excite some of the local gentry, mostly made up of golf-hungry New Yorkers, who had to fight a bitter cold winter to get a chance to play their favorite game.

This is not a difficult course to play, and as such will most likely appeal to high handicappers and short hitters alike. Most players usually opt to play the first fourteen holes because the remaining four are a good distance away.

DIRECTIONS

From downtown Manhattan: Take Hwy. 87N and make a left at 230th St. and another left onto Barly Ave. Go north for about a half-a-mile and stay on the right side of the road as it starts to fork out.

DUTCHESS COUNTY

BEEKMAN GOLF COURSE
11 Country Club Rd., Hopewell Junction, NY 12533 / (914) 226-7700

BASIC INFORMATION
Course Type: Public
Year Built: 1965
Architect: N/A
Local Pro: Todd Barker

Course: Highland & Valley (18 / Par 72)
Holes: 27

Back: 6,300 yds. Rating: 71.6 Slope: 123
Middle: 6,000 yds. Rating: 69.5 Slope: 118
Ladies: 5,300 yds. Rating: 72.1 Slope: 122

Tee Time: 7 days in advance.
Price: $29.50 - $37

Credit Cards:	■	Restaurant:	■
Driving Range:	■	Lounge:	■
Practice Green:	■	Meeting Rooms:	■
Locker Room:	■	Tennis:	
Rental Clubs:	■	Swimming:	
Walkers:	■	Jogging Trails:	
Snack Bar:	■	Boating:	■

COURSE DESCRIPTION
Beekman Golf Course is a good test of golf for mid-to-high handicappers.

It's a simple playing field that will entice you to play as aggressively as possible. Don't get carried away though, because you may want to consider clubbing down to a 3-wood or even a 4-wood on some of the holes, for hitting your drives too long will usually result in your ball being driven into unwanted trouble.

The course features hilly terrain that runs through open holes, with other holes surrounded by trees. You'll find playing a draw to your advantage on both the Highland-nine and the Valley-nine.

DIRECTIONS
Take the Taconic Pkwy. to Beekman Rd. and make a left. Look for the course about a half-mile further on your right.

McCANN MEMORIAL GOLF COURSE
155 Wilbur Blvd., Poughkeepsie, NY 12603 / (914) 454-1968

BASIC INFORMATION
Course Type: Municipal
Year Built: 1972
Architect: W.M. Mitchell
Local Pro: Bob Paquet

Course: N/A
Holes: 18 / Par 72

Back: 6,524 yds. Rating: 72.0 Slope: 128
Middle: 6,090 yds. Rating: 70.0 Slope: 124
Ladies: 5,354 yds. Rating: 71.4 Slope: 123

Tee Time: 1 day in advance.
Price: $10 - $48

Credit Cards:		Restaurant:	■
Driving Range:	■	Lounge:	■
Practice Green:	■	Meeting Rooms:	
Locker Room:	■	Tennis:	
Rental Clubs:	■	Swimming:	
Walkers:	■	Jogging Trails:	
Snack Bar:	■	Boating:	

COURSE DESCRIPTION
McCann Memorial Golf Course is within reach for many golfers to feel comfortable with. It's not a terribly hard course to maneuver around, so if you have the ability, play it aggressively from first tee to the 18th green.

The course places a good amount of emphasis on your putting skills. Many of the greens feature subtle undulations that can make reading them a bit tricky at times.

A low numbered round usually consists of accurate approach shots that land close to the pins.

DIRECTIONS
From New York City, follow Rt. 684 north to Rt. 84 west. Follow Rt. 84 west to Exit 13. Follow Rt. 9 north (9 miles) and turn left at the second set of lights. Look for the course about 1 mile further on your left.

DUTCHESS / NASSAU COUNTIES

THOMAS CARVEL COUNTRY CLUB

Taconic State Pkwy. & Ferris Rd., Pine Plains, NY 12567 / (518) 398-7101

BASIC INFORMATION

Course Type: Municipal
Year Built: 1967
Architect: N/A
Local Pro: Ed Gentile

Course:N/A
Holes: 18 / Par 73

Back : 7,025 yds. Rating: 73.5 Slope: 127
Middle: 6,600 yds. Rating: 71.6 Slope: 123
Ladies: 5,066 yds. Rating: 79.0 Slope: 115

Tee Time: 7 days in advance.
Price: $30 - $35

Credit Cards:	■	Restaurant:	■
Driving Range:	■	Lounge:	■
Practice Green:	■	Meeting Rooms:	■
Locker Room:	■	Tennis:	
Rental Clubs:	■	Swimming:	
Walkers:		Jogging Trails:	
Snack Bar:	■	Boating:	■

COURSE DESCRIPTION

Thomas Carvel Country Club is a great place to experience if you're serious about your game. It's a tremendous challenge that offers a chance to play professional caliber golf at an affordable price.

The course flows beautifully through its hilly terrain and offers incredible mountain views that you'll enjoy looking at as you drive your cart between holes. The first hole, a par-4 measuring 422 yards from the championship tees, can be deceiving for a first-time player. Just remember to approach it with at least two clubs more than you normally would; it always seems to play against strong prevailing winds.

DIRECTIONS

Take the Taconic State Pkwy. to the Ferris Rd. Exit. The course will be on its east side.

BETHPAGE STATE PARK

Bethpage State Park, Farmingdale, NY 11735 / (516) 249-0700

BASIC INFORMATION

Course Type: Public
Year Built: 1940
Architect: John Tillinghurst
Local Pro: Chuck Workman

Course: Black (18 / Par 71)
Holes: 90 holes

Back : 7,065 yds. Rating: 75.4 Slope: 144
Middle: 6,556 yds. Rating: 73.1 Slope: 140
Ladies: N/A Rating: N/A Slope: N/A

Tee Time: 7 days in advance.
Price: $14 - $16

Credit Cards:	■	Restaurant:	■
Driving Range:	■	Lounge:	■
Practice Green:	■	Meeting Rooms:	■
Locker Room:	■	Tennis:	■
Rental Clubs:	■	Swimming:	
Walkers:	■	Jogging Trails:	
Snack Bar:	■	Boating:	■

COURSE DESCRIPTION

It is difficult to choose one of these five courses as the best, but most locals and better players agree that the Black course is the one to beat.

Pars don't come easy on this layout. With a course rating of 75.4 and a slope rating of 144, it is undoubtedly one of the hardest tests of golf in the entire state of New York. You'll find many demanding hole designs that will force you to think about strategy above all else. It's a terrific course you'll want to play more than just once.

DIRECTIONS

Take the Long Island Expressway to Exit 44 and go south to Exit 8 where you'll need to make a left. Follow the signs to the course.

HOLLAND HILLS GOLF COURSE

10438 Holland-Glenwood Rd., Glenwood, NY 14069 / (716) 537-2345

BASIC INFORMATION

Course Type: Semi-private
Year Built: 1959 / 1976
Architect: N/A
Local Pro: N/A

Course: N/A
Holes: 18 / Par 72

Back : 6,355 yds. Rating: 71.3 Slope: 115
Middle: N/A   yds. Rating: N/A   Slope: N/A
Ladies: 6,140 yds. Rating: 72.0 Slope: 108

Tee Time: 2 days in advance.
Price: $14 - $16

Credit Cards:		Restaurant:	■
Driving Range:	■	Lounge:	■
Practice Green:	■	Meeting Rooms:	
Locker Room:	■	Tennis:	
Rental Clubs:	■	Swimming:	
Walkers:	■	Jogging Trails:	
Snack Bar:	■	Boating:	

COURSE DESCRIPTION

Holland Hills Golf Course is a fun-filled layout that offers many opportunities to score low numbers. It's a high-handicappers' layout that features wide landing areas and very few hazards to slow down play. It's not a terribly long course, and if you play golf in the mid-80's, you'll find yourself shooting for birdies quite often.

Play the course as you see it, for it doesn't hold anything back from the tees.

DIRECTIONS

Take Hwy. 400 to its end and continue southbound on Rt. 16 into Holland. Turn right at the first set of lights (Holland Glenwood Rd.). The course will be approximately 4-miles further up the road on the right.

LIDO GOLF COURSE

Lido Blvd., Lido Beach, NY 11561 / (516) 431-8778

BASIC INFORMATION

Course Type: Public
Year Built: 1920's
Architect: Robert Trent Jones
Local Pro: Shane Higuera

Course: N/A
Holes: 18 / Par 72

Back: 6,868 yds. Rating: N/A   Slope: N/A
Middle: 6,387 yds. Rating: 71.8 Slope: 128
Ladies: 5,603 yds. Rating: N/A   Slope: N/A

Tee Time: 1 day in advance.
Price: $13.50 - $40

Credit Cards:		Restaurant:	■
Driving Range:	■	Lounge:	■
Practice Green:	■	Meeting Rooms:	
Locker Room:		Tennis:	
Rental Clubs:	■	Swimming:	
Walkers:	■	Jogging Trails:	
Snack Bar:	■	Boating:	

COURSE DESCRIPTION

Lido Golf Course is a formidable challenge for players that carry about a 15+ handicap. The 16th hole, a par-5 that measures 487 yards from the championship tees, is the hardest test on the course. From the tee, you'll be facing a "horseshoe" shaped fairway that features water in the middle of it. Choose to play your drive to the left fairway of the horseshoe for both position and safety. If you land on a good lie, you may want to crush a 3-wood for an eagle opportunity. The green slopes severely from back-to-front, so play your ball back-center.

DIRECTIONS

Take the Middlebrook Pkwy. south to Loop Pkwy. and follow that to its end. At Toledo Blvd, you'll need to make a right. Follow this road to the course which will be about 2 miles further down on your right.

OYSTER BAY GOLF COURSE
Duane Stage Rd., Box 26, Woodbury, NY 12953 / (516) 364-3977

BASIC INFORMATION

Course Type: Public
Year Built: 1989
Architect: Tom Fazio
Local Pro: Gene Miller

Course:N/A
Holes: 18 / Par 70

Back : 6,351 yds. Rating: 71.5 Slope: 133
Middle: 5,795 yds. Rating: N/A Slope: N/A
Ladies: 5,109 yds. Rating: N/A Slope: N/A

Tee Time: 1 day in advance.
Price: $14 - $16

Credit Cards: Restaurant: ■
Driving Range: ■   Lounge: ■
Practice Green: ■   Meeting Rooms: ■
Locker Room: ■   Tennis:
Rental Clubs: ■   Swimming:
Walkers: ■   Jogging Trails:
Snack Bar: ■   Boating: ■

COURSE DESCRIPTION

You couldn't find a more inventive architect, with a keen imagination for building unique golf courses that are equally challenging for both the amateur and professional golfer, in respect to their various styles and abilities. Tom Fazio has been recognized by national golfing publications and a host of his peers for his incredible work in the field of golf architecture.

You'll need to manage your game well to score low numbers. Most people tend to play the course several times to get a feel for where they should place their drives. It's a wonderful course with many beautiful sights.

DIRECTIONS

Take the Long Island Expressway to Exit 44 N and follow that to Exit 14 E. At the third set of lights, make a left and look for the course on your left, too.

STONY FORD GOLF COURSE
550 Rt. 416, Montgomery, NY 12549 / (914) 457-3000

BASIC INFORMATION

Course Type: Public
Year Built: 1965
Architect: Hal Purdy
Local Pro: John Healy

Course:N/A
Holes: 18 / Par 72

Back : 6,651 yds. Rating: 72.4 Slope: 128
Middle: 6,182 yds. Rating: 70.3 Slope: 124
Ladies: 5,856 yds. Rating: 74.0 Slope: 128

Tee Time: 7 days in advance.
Price: $9 - $28

Credit Cards: Restaurant: ■
Driving Range: ■   Lounge:
Practice Green: ■   Meeting Rooms: ■
Locker Room: ■   Tennis: ■
Rental Clubs: ■   Swimming:
Walkers: ■   Jogging Trails: ■
Snack Bar: ■   Boating: ■

COURSE DESCRIPTION

Stony Ford Golf Course features rolling fairways and scenic mountain views. Favoring neither a draw nor a fade, the course has ample room for novices, yet will reward strategically placed shots by better golfers.

You'll find four reachable par-5's, and four difficult par-3's. Well-placed bunkers guard most of the greens left and right, yet allow many opportunities to pitch and run the ball as an alternative to sending the ball high in the air without any roll.

DIRECTIONS

Take Rt. 80 between the cities of Middletown and Newburgh to Exit 5. Follow that to Rt. 208 and head south to Rt. 99. Make a right and follow Rt. 99 to its end. You'll see a stop-sign. Go left onto Rt 416 and look for the course about 1 mile further on your right.

AMERICAN GOLF CORP.

1001 Richmond & Hill Rd., Staten Island, NY 10306 / (718) 351-1889

BASIC INFORMATION

Course Type: Semi-private
Year Built: 1990
Architect: Arnold Palmer
Local Pro: Tom Duncan

Course: N/A
Holes: 18 / Par 72

Back : 7,218 yds. Rating: 72.9 Slope: 136
Middle: 6,637 yds. Rating: 70.1 Slope: 130
Ladies: 5,897 yds. Rating: 67.2 Slope: 124

Tee Time: 14 days in advance.
Price: $25 - $55

Credit Cards:	■	Restaurant:	■
Driving Range:	■	Lounge:	■
Practice Green:	■	Meeting Rooms:	■
Locker Room:	■	Tennis:	■
Rental Clubs:	■	Swimming:	■
Walkers:	■	Jogging Trails:	■
Snack Bar:	■	Boating:	■

COURSE DESCRIPTION

American Golf Corp. features rolling fairways and undulating greens, adorned with strategically placed bunkers and natural hazards. The course plays at a distance of 6,732 yards from the back-tees and features a plethora of tree-lined fairways you'll need to guide your ball between to set yourself up successfully for your following approach shots.

You may find it interesting to note that the tenth tee is the highest point on Staten Island.

DIRECTIONS

From the Verranzo Bridge, go north to Bradley Ave. and follow that to Service Rd. Make your second left to Wooley Ave and follow that with a left at Richmond Hill Rd. You'll see the course on both sides of the road.

BLUE HILL GOLF CLUB

285 Blue Hill Rd., Pearl River, NY 10965 / (914) 735-2094

BASIC INFORMATION

Course Type: Semi-private
Year Built: 1920's
Architect: N/A
Local Pro: Jimmy Stewart

Course: N/A
Holes: 18 / Par 72

Back : 6,431 yds. Rating: 70.0 Slope: 116
Middle: 6,132 yds. Rating: 68.6 Slope: 114
Ladies: 5,601 yds. Rating: 70.6 Slope: 117

Tee Time: First come, first serve.
Price: $15 - $32

Credit Cards:		Restaurant:	■
Driving Range:		Lounge:	■
Practice Green:	■	Meeting Rooms:	■
Locker Room:	■	Tennis:	
Rental Clubs:		Swimming:	
Walkers:	■	Jogging Trails:	
Snack Bar:	■	Boating:	

COURSE DESCRIPTION

Blue Hill Golf Club is a pretty simple course that will appeal mostly to high-handicappers in general. The course features wide fairways that will allow you to play a variety of shots from all three teeing grounds. You can play both aggressively or conservatively, depending on your style, and still come out shooting a good number.

The course features five holes along its rolling terrain. Players who naturally draw the ball will find the course a little easier than players who prefer to play a fade.

DIRECTIONS

Take the Palisades Pkwy. to Exit 6W and go to the third set of traffic lights. Make a right, and look for the course about another 1/2-mile further on your right.

PHILLIP J. ROTELLA MUNICIPAL

Thiells Mt. Izy Rd., Thiells, NY 10984 / (914) 354-1616

BASIC INFORMATION

Course Type: Public
Year Built: 1983
Architect: N/A
Local Pro: Howard Pearson

Course: N/A
Holes: 18 / Par 72

Back: 6,502 yds. Rating: 70.7 Slope: 122
Middle: 6,068 yds. Rating: 68.6 Slope: N/A
Ladies: 4,856 yds. Rating: 70.7 Slope: N/A

Tee Time: 2 days in advance.
Price: Please call to confirm.

Credit Cards:
Driving Range: ■
Practice Green: ■
Locker Room:
Rental Clubs: ■
Walkers: ■
Snack Bar: ■
Restaurant: ■
Lounge: ■
Meeting Rooms:
Tennis:
Swimming:
Jogging Trails:
Boating:

COURSE DESCRIPTION

Phillip J. Rotella Municipal is an easy course to master by better players. If you're a mid-to-low handicapper, you'll find the course to be a good challenge.

It features a unique combination of six par-3's, six par-4's, and six par-5's. Most players will find the fairways wide enough to move the ball on either side without much trouble, but you do need to know where to drive the ball to set yourself up on your following approach shots.

You won't find surprises on this course, so play it aggressively and reach for as many birdies as you can possibly make. Good luck!

DIRECTIONS

Take the New York State Thruway to Exit 13 N and follow that to Palisades. Follow the signs to the course.

BERGEN POINT GOLF CLUB

Bergen Avenue West, Babylon, NY 11704 / (516) 661-8282

BASIC INFORMATION

Course Type: Public
Year Built: 1969
Architect: N/A
Local Pro: Bill McCumiskey

Course: N/A
Holes: 18 / Par 71

Back : 6,637 yds. Rating: 71.4 Slope: 116
Middle: 6,197 yds. Rating: 69.2 Slope: 112
Ladies: 5,707 yds. Rating: 71.8 Slope: 122

Tee Time: 7 days in advance.
Price: $7 - $30

Credit Cards:
Driving Range: ■
Practice Green: ■
Locker Room: ■
Rental Clubs: ■
Walkers: ■
Snack Bar: ■
Restaurant: ■
Lounge: ■
Meeting Rooms: ■
Tennis:
Swimming:
Jogging Trails:
Boating: ■

COURSE DESCRIPTION

Bergen Point Golf Club offers a linksland style course traditionally designed in an open environment.

When wind conditions start picking up, the course can play a lot harder than the numbers indicated in the Information box. The key to playing well here is to keep the ball on a low trajectory, below the wind, and towards your target. This can be accomplished by playing a knockdown shot. You can do this by playing a longer club and, rather than taking a full swing, keep it back to about three quarters. You'll be surprised at how easy and valuable this shot can be.

DIRECTIONS

Take the New York State Thruway to Exit 33S (Babylon, Rt. 109) to Great Neck Rd. The road will start forking out into two directions. Take the right side to the course.

SUFFOLK COUNTY

BRENTWOOD COUNTRY CLUB

100 Pennsylvania Ave., Brentwood, NY 11717 / (516) 436-6060

BASIC INFORMATION

Course Type: Public
Year Built: 1920's
Architect: N/A
Local Pro: Rich Loughlin

Course: N/A
Holes: 18 / Par 72

Back   : 6,273 yds. Rating: 69.3 Slope: 121
Middle: 5,835 yds. Rating: 67.8 Slope: 118
Ladies: 5,093 yds. Rating: 68.4 Slope: 111

Tee Time: 1 day in advance.
Price: $8.50 - $26

Credit Cards:	■	Restaurant:	■
Driving Range:		Lounge:	■
Practice Green:	■	Meeting Rooms:	■
Locker Room:	■	Tennis:	
Rental Clubs:	■	Swimming:	
Walkers:	■	Jogging Trails:	
Snack Bar:	■	Boating:	■

COURSE DESCRIPTION

Brentwood Country Club, built on flat terrain, is a good choice for mid-to-high handicappers.

Most of the holes are straightforward, and if you play them correctly, you'll often find yourself putting for a birdie or a par. You can pursue making your birds as often as possible on the front-nine by playing an aggressive game, but be forewarned: the tighter back-nine features narrow fairways, making it much harder to place your drives onto the proper landing areas. It's almost like playing two different courses.

DIRECTIONS

Take the Long Island Expressway to Brentwood Rd. and follow the signs to the course.

HAUPPAUGE COUNTRY CLUB

P.O. Box 237, Veterans Memorial Hwy., Hauppuge, NY 11788 / (516) 724-7500

BASIC INFORMATION

Course Type: Semi-private
Year Built: 1960
Architect: N/A
Local Pro: Keven Beatty

Course: N/A
Holes: 18 / Par 72

Back   : 6,525 yds. Rating: 71.0 Slope: 122
Middle: 6,350 yds. Rating: 69.9 Slope: 120
Ladies: 5,970 yds. Rating: 75.5 Slope: 131

Tee Time: 1 day in advance.
Price: $25 - $50

Credit Cards:		Restaurant:	■
Driving Range:	■	Lounge:	■
Practice Green:	■	Meeting Rooms:	■
Locker Room:	■	Tennis:	■
Rental Clubs:	■	Swimming:	
Walkers:	■	Jogging Trails:	
Snack Bar:	■	Boating:	■

COURSE DESCRIPTION

Hauppauge Country Club stretches 6,525 yards from its championship tees on a relatively flat piece of land that features wide fairways, water coming into play on six holes, trees, and much more. The 12th hole is one of the most exciting attractions on the course. It's a slight dogleg-right par-4 that measures 417 yards from the championship back-tees. You'll find water coming into play at a distance of 200 yards, and if you don't hit over it, you'll be faced with a long difficult approach shot that features trees on the left side of the fairway and out-of-bounds coming into play on the right.

DIRECTIONS

Take the Northern St. Pkwy. east to its end and it will turn into Veterans Memorial Hwy. The course is about 2 1/2 miles further from that point on the left.

MARRIOTT'S GOLF CLUB AT WIND WATCH

1717 Vanderbilt Motor Pkwy., Hauppauge, NY 11788 / (516) 232-9850

BASIC INFORMATION

Course Type: Public
Year Built: 1990
Architect: Joe Lee
Local Pro: Robert Bartley

Course: N/A
Holes: 18 / Par 71

Back : 6,425 yds. Rating: 72.2 Slope: 133
Middle: 6,138 yds. Rating: 69.5 Slope: 129
Ladies: 5,135 yds. Rating: 68.6 Slope: 118

Tee Time: 3-7 days in advance.
Price: $40 - $70

Credit Cards: ■	Restaurant: ■
Driving Range: ■	Lounge: ■
Practice Green: ■	Meeting Rooms: ■
Locker Room: ■	Tennis: ■
Rental Clubs: ■	Swimming: ■
Walkers: ■	Jogging Trails:
Snack Bar: ■	Boating: ■

COURSE DESCRIPTION

This course is a beautiful tribute to the art of golf architecture. Joe Lee did a fantastic job of building a course that will appeal to all types of players by offering them a playing field open to their particular type of play.

If you enjoy playing a shot-makers course, the type that will force you to play a variety of shots both left and right, you'll find all of that here and more! Many of the holes feature mature oak trees that come into play, and bent grass is featured on the tees, along the fairways, and throughout the many undulating greens. You'll be playing on Long Islands's second highest point.

DIRECTIONS

Take the Long Island Expy. east to Exit 57. Turn left at the light and proceed on Motor Pkwy. Look for both the course and the hotel on your left.

MIDDLE ISLAND COUNTRY CLUB

P.O. Box 205, Yaphank Rd., Middle Island, NY 11953 / (516) 924-5100

BASIC INFORMATION

Course Type: Public
Year Built: 1964
Architect: N/A
Local Pro: Michael A. Wands

Course: Oaktree & Spruce (18-Par 72)
Holes: 27

Back : 7,027 yds. Rating: N/A Slope: N/A
Middle: 6,681 yds. Rating: N/A Slope: N/A
Ladies: 5,906 yds. Rating: N/A Slope: N/A

Tee Time: 1-7 days in advance.
Price: $22 - $25

Credit Cards:	Restaurant: ■
Driving Range:	Lounge: ■
Practice Green: ■	Meeting Rooms:
Locker Room: ■	Tennis:
Rental Clubs: ■	Swimming:
Walkers: ■	Jogging Trails:
Snack Bar: ■	Boating:

COURSE DESCRIPTION

Middle Island Country Club has three nine-hole championship golf courses. The Dogwood and Oaktree courses are hilly with tree-lined fairways. Spruce is more open, flatter, and a little bit longer. All three will challenge you to manufacture a wide assortment of shots.

All three courses demand a subtle touch around the many undulating greens that each features.

DIRECTIONS

Heading east-bound on the Long Island Expy. (495), get off at Exit 66. Turn left off ramp and go north to the second set of lights, make a right onto Mill Rd. and proceed a quarter-mile to the stop sign. At the red blinking light, turn left onto Yaphank Rd. The course on your right.

84

MONTAUK DOWNS STATE PARK

South Fairview Avenue, Montauk, NY 11954 / (516) 668-1100

BASIC INFORMATION

Course Type: Public
Year Built: 1920 / 1968
Architect: Robert Trent Jones (1968)
Local Pro: Keven Smith

Course: N/A
Holes: 18 / Par 72

Back   : 6,762 yds. Rating: 75.9 Slope: 135
Middle: 6,289 yds. Rating: 70.5 Slope: 128
Ladies: 5,689 yds. Rating: 73.3 Slope: 133

Tee Time: Call: (316) 668-5000
Price: $16 - $18

Credit Cards:		Restaurant:	■
Driving Range:	■	Lounge:	■
Practice Green:	■	Meeting Rooms:	■
Locker Room:	■	Tennis:	■
Rental Clubs:	■	Swimming:	■
Walkers:	■	Jogging Trails:	
Snack Bar:	■	Boating:	■

COURSE DESCRIPTION

Montauk Downs State Park is the kind of course that will make you earn your pars on every hole.

There are no gimmies on this course; you'll need to hit the ball both long and accurately on every drive and approach to make your pars. Many of the greens are elevated and are well-protected by strategically placed sand bunkers. The middle-tees are a great alternative for those who find the back-tees too difficult to play.

DIRECTIONS

Take the Long Island Expy. to Exit 70 (Rt. 11) to the end. At Rt. 27 you'll need to make a right. Follow that road to the Town of Montauk and make a left at Hwy. 27 towards Westlake Dr. Make another left at South Fairway Ave. and the course will be on your right.

ROCKHILL GOLF & COUNTRY CLUB

105 Clancy Rd., Manorville, NY 11949 / (516) 878-2250

BASIC INFORMATION

Course Type: Public
Year Built: N/A
Architect: Frank Duane
Local Pro: Barney Bell

Course: N/A
Holes: 18 / Par 71

Back   : 7,050 yds. Rating: 73.7 Slope: 128
Middle: 6,464 yds. Rating: 71.3 Slope: 124
Ladies: 5,390 yds. Rating: 71.4 Slope: 121

Tee Time: 7 days in advance.
Price: $12 - $26

Credit Cards:	■	Restaurant:	■
Driving Range:	■	Lounge:	
Practice Green:	■	Meeting Rooms:	
Locker Room:		Tennis:	
Rental Clubs:	■	Swimming:	
Walkers:	■	Jogging Trails:	
Snack Bar:	■	Boating:	

COURSE DESCRIPTION

Rockhill Golf & Country Club sits on top the third highest point on Long Island. You'll be playing golf along a demanding playing field that features hilly fairways throughout its scenic outlines.

The back-nine is a bit longer and tougher than the front-nine. So try to get your birdies early. The 18th-hole has been rated as one of the hardest finishing holes in Long Island.

DIRECTIONS

Take the Long Island Expy. to Exit 70 south to the first set of lights and make a right, which will be just under 2-miles from Clancy Rd. Make a left and follow the road to the course.

CONCORD RESORT HOTEL & GOLF COURSE

Concord Rd., Kiamesha Lake, NY 12751 / (914) 794-4000

BASIC INFORMATION

Course Type: Public
Year Built: 1962
Architect: Joe Finger
Local Pro: Bill Burke

Course: Monster (18 / Par 72)
Holes: 54

Back : 7,471 yds. Rating: 76.4 Slope: 142
Middle: 6,989 yds. Rating: 74.1 Slope: 137
Ladies: 6,548 yds. Rating: 78.5 Slope: 144

Tee Time: 1 day in advance.
Price: $80 - $90

Credit Cards:	■	Restaurant:	■
Driving Range:	■	Lounge:	■
Practice Green:	■	Meeting Rooms:	■
Locker Room:	■	Tennis:	■
Rental Clubs:	■	Swimming:	■
Walkers:		Jogging Trails:	■
Snack Bar:	■	Boating:	■

COURSE DESCRIPTION

Golf and **Golf Digest** magazines both placed this course as one of their top 100 courses to play in the United States.

The monster course, the longest of the three, is an incredible creation that attracts golfers from all parts of the globe. A fourth set of tees measures the layout at an astonishing 7,966 yards, quite possibly the longest course in the world!

Every element is grandiose here: long tee boxes, wide fairways, and large undulating greens. It's a tremendous challenge you won't want to miss.

DIRECTIONS

From Buffalo: Take the New York State Thruway Rt. 90 E. to Exit 36. Follow that to Rt. 81 S and that to Rt. 17 E. At Exit 105 B (Kiamesha Lakes) turn onto Rt. 42 N and follow the signs to the course.

GROSSINGER GOLF COURSE

State Hwy. 52, Liberty, NY 12734 / (914) 292-9000

BASIC INFORMATION

Course Type: Public
Year Built: 1915 / 1960
Architect: Joe Finger
Local Pro: Jeff Marks

Course: Valley & Lake (18 / Par 72)
Holes: 27

Back : 6,839 yds. Rating: 72.9 Slope: 133
Middle: 6,450 yds. Rating: 71.0 Slope: 129
Ladies: 5,875 yds. Rating: 73.2 Slope: 129

Tee Time: 14 days in advance.
Price: $39 - $69

Credit Cards:	■	Restaurant:	■
Driving Range:	■	Lounge:	■
Practice Green:	■	Meeting Rooms:	■
Locker Room:	■	Tennis:	■
Rental Clubs:	■	Swimming:	■
Walkers:	■	Jogging Trails:	■
Snack Bar:	■	Boating:	■

COURSE DESCRIPTION

Grossinger Golf Course is a Joe Finger-designed 6,839 yard layout that presents many attractive hole designs both challenging and unique in their style.

The course evenly spaces the severity of each hole on both sets of nine, making it easily understood from the first hole to the last. You'll find a good mixture of fairway widths, multiple size greens, many sand bunkers, grass mounds, and five holes bringing the element of water into play.

This is a terrific and memorable challenge for all who choose to play it.

DIRECTIONS

Take the New York State Thruway north to Exit 16 and follow that to Rt. 17 W. Get off at the Liberty Exit and make a left. The course will appear directly in front of you.

SULLIVAN COUNTIES

LOCHMOR GOLF COURSE

P.O. Box 830, County Rt. 104, Loch Sheldrake, NY 12759 / (914) 434-9079

BASIC INFORMATION

Course Type: Municipal
Year Built: 1958
Architect: N/A
Local Pro: Glenn Sonnenschein

Course: N/A
Holes: 18 / Par 72

Back   : 6,402 yds. Rating: 70.2 Slope: 121
Middle: 6,248 yds. Rating: 69.9 Slope: 119
Ladies: 5,210 yds. Rating: 69.6 Slope: 116

Tee Time: 3 days in advance.
Price: $18 - $24

Credit Cards:		Restaurant:	
Driving Range:	■	Lounge:	
Practice Green:	■	Meeting Rooms:	
Locker Room:		Tennis:	
Rental Clubs:	■	Swimming:	
Walkers:	■	Jogging Trails:	
Snack Bar:	■	Boating:	■

COURSE DESCRIPTION

The *Lochmor Golf Course* offers many spectacular views of Morningside Lake.

The front-nine is fairly open with demanding small-sized greens, usually elevated, and at times appearing on top of a long horizon, making it difficult to judge distance. The back-nine is more wooded and features water coming into play on 3-holes.

The course is mostly hilly and thus plays a lot harder and longer than the numbers indicated on the score-card.

DIRECTIONS

From New York City, take Rt. 17 west to Exit 105B. Make a left at the first set of lights and stay on Anawana Lake Rd. Follow signs to Loch Sheldrake and look for the course on your right about 8-miles from Rt. 17.

TENNANAH LAKE GOLF & TENNIS CLUB, INC.

Roscoe Ave. & Hakins Rd., Roscoe, NY 12776 / (607) 498-5502

BASIC INFORMATION

Course Type: Semi-private
Year Built: 1952
Architect: Sam Snead
Local Pro: Gregory Scott Smith

Course: N/A
Holes: 18 / Par 72

Back   : 6,850 yds. Rating: 71.2 Slope: 121
Middle: 6,510 yds. Rating: 69.3 Slope: 119
Ladies: 6,300 yds. Rating: 72.5 Slope: 115

Tee Time: First come, first serve.
Price: $20 - $26

Credit Cards:	■	Restaurant:	■
Driving Range:		Lounge:	
Practice Green:	■	Meeting Rooms:	■
Locker Room:		Tennis:	■
Rental Clubs:	■	Swimming:	■
Walkers:	■	Jogging Trails:	■
Snack Bar:	■	Boating:	

COURSE DESCRIPTION

Tennanah Lake Golf & Tennis Club is located on 1,000 sq. acres in the beautiful Catskill Mountains of Roscoe, N.Y.

Sam Snead, one of the true legends of American golf, designed this course in a user-friendly manner for more than just the above-average golfer. With three teeing areas to choose from on each hole, golfers shouldn't have a problem feeling confident while standing over their ball.

The course will mostly appeal to mid-to-high handicappers yet is long enough for the enjoyment of a scratch golfer.

DIRECTIONS

Take Rt. 17 to Exit 94 to Roscoe, N.Y. Follow the signs that will lead you directly to the course.

VILLA ROMA RESORT HOTEL

Rd. 1, Villa Roma Rd., Callicoon, NY 12723 / (914) 887-4880

BASIC INFORMATION

Course Type: Public Resort
Year Built: 1986
Architect: David Postlenatt
Local Pro: Matt Kleiner

Course: N/A
Holes: 18 / Par 71

Back : 6,350 yds. Rating: 70.6 Slope: 125
Middle: 6,050 yds. Rating: 66.9 Slope: 118
Ladies: 4,800 yds. Rating: 68.3 Slope: 117

Tee Time: 1-30 days in advance.
Price: $38 - $48

Credit Cards:	■	Restaurant:	■
Driving Range:	■	Lounge:	■
Practice Green:	■	Meeting Rooms:	■
Locker Room:	■	Tennis:	■
Rental Clubs:	■	Swimming:	■
Walkers:		Jogging Trails:	
Snack Bar:	■	Boating:	■

COURSE DESCRIPTION

You'll find a pleasant challenge as you play through the rolling terrain that makes up the distance of the *Villa Roma Resort Hotel*. It's a scenic course that's equally challenging for different types of playing styles.

A player that can work the ball both left and right will be at an advantage to take control of the many holes that offer multiple angles towards the pin. Good course management plays an important part in setting yourself up for a clear approach shot from the proper side of the fairway.

DIRECTIONS

Coming from New York City you can take the New York Thruway north to Rt. 17 (Harriman) Exit 16. Take Rt. 17 to Exit 104 and get onto Rt. 17B heading west for at least 16-miles. Follow the signs to the course.

GRANIT HOTEL & COUNTRY CLUB

Granit Rd., Kerhonkson, NY 12446 / (914) 626-3141

BASIC INFORMATION

Course Type: Public Resort
Year Built: 1962
Architect: Robert Trent Jones, Sr.
Local Pro: John Magaletta

Course: N/A
Holes: 18 / Par 70

Back : 6,310 yds. Rating: 69.1 Slope: 115
Middle: 5,888 yds. Rating: 67.2 Slope: 111
Ladies: 5,180 yds. Rating: 69.3 Slope: 110

Tee Time: First come, first serve.
Price: $18

Credit Cards:		Restaurant:	■
Driving Range:	■	Lounge:	■
Practice Green:	■	Meeting Rooms:	■
Locker Room:		Tennis:	■
Rental Clubs:	■	Swimming:	■
Walkers:	■	Jogging Trails:	
Snack Bar:	■	Boating:	■

COURSE DESCRIPTION

This may not be the longest course in New York, but you should keep in mind that its course designer was none other than the legendary architect himself, Robert Trent Jones, Sr.

The course is a diversified challenge from the moment you step onto the first tee and the moment you hole your last putt on the 18th green. Most players won't find the challenge too difficult, but should have fun using their short-irons nonetheless.

It's a great course for players who can't hit their drives a long distance.

DIRECTIONS

Take the New York State Thruway south to Exit 18. Get onto Rt. 299 and go west to Rt. 44-55. From this point, follow the signs to the course.

88

NEVELE HOTEL & COUNTRY CLUB
P.O. Box 344, Rt. 209, Ellenville, NY 12428 / (914) 647-6000

BASIC INFORMATION

Course Type: Public Resort
Year Built: 1975 (Redesigned)
Architect: Tom Fazio
Local Pro: Jack Breno

Course: N/A
Holes: 18 / Par 72

Back : 6,500 yds. Rating: 71.9 Slope: 128
Middle: 5,853 yds. Rating: 69.4 Slope: 123
Ladies: 4,570 yds. Rating: 71.1 Slope: 126

Tee Time: 14 days in advance.
Price: $22 - $35+

Credit Cards: ■   Restaurant: ■
Driving Range: ■   Lounge: ■
Practice Green: ■   Meeting Rooms: ■
Locker Room: ■   Tennis: ■
Rental Clubs: ■   Swimming: ■
Walkers: ■   Jogging Trails: ■
Snack Bar: ■   Boating: ■

COURSE DESCRIPTION

The **Nevele Hotel & Country Club** offers a uniquely exciting golfing venue for a course that only measures 6,500 yards from the back-tees. The quality of the course coupled with its picturesque setting make this an exciting and comforting place to relax and play golf.

Tom Fazio expertly mixed a nice combination of hole designs to make this a very interesting and challenging course. Gentle slopes roll along the well manicured fairways of the longer front-nine and the shorter but more demanding back-nine.

DIRECTIONS

Take the New York City Thruway north to Exit 16, Rt. 17 west to Exit 113, and Rt. 209 north for approximately 12 miles to the Resort. The course will be on your right.

LOCH LEDGE GOLF COURSE
Rt. 118, Yorktown Heights, NY 10598 / (914) 962-8050

BASIC INFORMATION

Course Type: Public
Year Built: 1964
Architect: N/A
Local Pro: Gary Goodwin

Course: N/A
Holes: 18 / Par 72

Back : 5,810 yds. Rating: N/A Slope: N/A
Middle: 5,503 yds. Rating: 66.0 Slope: 114
Ladies: 5,125 yds. Rating: N/A Slope: N/A

Tee Time: 1 day in advance.
Price: $15 - $20

Credit Cards: ■   Restaurant:
Driving Range: Lounge:
Practice Green: ■   Meeting Rooms:
Locker Room: Tennis:
Rental Clubs: ■   Swimming:
Walkers: ■   Jogging Trails:
Snack Bar: ■   Boating:

COURSE DESCRIPTION

If you don't have the distance that it takes to play longer courses, you'll enjoy playing the **Loch Ledge Golf Course**. The course plays at a distance of just under 6,000 yards and features a good array of holes that allow a wide margin of error. It's the perfect course for a beginner who isn't quite ready for a championship length course.

You'll find plenty of room to work the ball in both directions, off the tees, towards the generously sized fairways. It makes for an aggressive game of golf.

DIRECTIONS

Take the Taconic Pkwy. east on Underhill Ave. to Rt. 118. Make a right and look for the course approximately 2 1/2 miles on your right.

MAPLE MOOR GOLF COURSE

1128 North St., White Plains, NY 10605 / (914) 946-1830

BASIC INFORMATION

Course Type: Public
Year Built: 1920's
Architect: N/A
Local Pro: Ricky Paonessa

Course: N/A
Holes: 18 / Par 71

Back : 6,226 yds.	Rating: 72.1	Slope: 118
Middle: N/A	Rating: N/A	Slope: N/A
Ladies: 5,812 yds.	Rating: N/A	Slope: N/A

Tee Time: 7 days in advance.
Price: $35 - $40

Credit Cards:	■	Restaurant:	■
Driving Range:		Lounge:	
Practice Green:	■	Meeting Rooms:	■
Locker Room:	■	Tennis:	
Rental Clubs:	■	Swimming:	
Walkers:	■	Jogging Trails:	
Snack Bar:	■	Boating:	■

COURSE DESCRIPTION

Maple Moor Golf Course has been attracting beginners who feel intimidated by the longer and more difficult championship length courses that are common everywhere for quite some time.

The flat terrain of this 6,226 yard layout makes it a pleasure to walk, if you choose to do so. It's an open design that's sometimes susceptible to strong winds, making it play a little harder than the numbers indicated in the Basic Information box – but not to the point where a beginner will feel totally out of place.

DIRECTIONS

Take the Hutchinson River Pkwy. to Exit 25 westbound. Look for the signs that will lead you to the course.

MOHANSIC GOLF COURSE

Balwin Rd., Yorktown Heights, NY 10598 / (914) 962-4049

BASIC INFORMATION

Course Type: Public
Year Built: 1923
Architect: Tom Winton
Local Pro: John Panessa

Course: N/A
Holes: 18 / Par 70

Back : 6,029 yds.	Rating: 69.8	Slope: 120
Middle: N/A	Rating: N/A	Slope: N/A
Ladies: 5,594 yds.	Rating: 75.2	Slope: 127

Tee Time: 1 day in advance.
Price: $35 - $45

Credit Cards:	■	Restaurant:	■
Driving Range:	■	Lounge:	■
Practice Green:	■	Meeting Rooms:	■
Locker Room:		Tennis:	
Rental Clubs:	■	Swimming:	
Walkers:	■	Jogging Trails:	
Snack Bar:	■	Boating:	■

COURSE DESCRIPTION

Mohansic Golf Course offers a strong venue that plays a bit harder than its indicated Rating & Slope. It's the type of course that makes you think you've got it figured out from the first tee — but somehow, later on in the game, it starts to seriously challenge your ability to make par, and you'll be wondering why you didn't take the course more seriously when you first started playing!

DIRECTIONS

Take the Taconic Pkwy. north to Baldwin Rd. and make a left towards the course. It will be straight in front of you.

SAXON WOODS GOLF CLUB

Mamaroneck Ave., Scarsdale, NY 10583 / (914) 725-3814

BASIC INFORMATION

Course Type: Public
Year Built: 1931
Architect: WDA Construction
Local Pro: Anthony Masciola

Course: N/A
Holes: 18 / Par 71

Back   : 6,397 yds. Rating: 70.2 Slope: 119
Middle: N/A   Rating: N/A   Slope: N/A
Ladies: 5,617 yds. Rating: 71.2 Slope: 120

Tee Time: 1 day in advance.
Price: Please call to confirm.

Credit Cards:		Restaurant:	■
Driving Range:		Lounge:	■
Practice Green:	■	Meeting Rooms:	■
Locker Room:	■	Tennis:	■
Rental Clubs:	■	Swimming:	■
Walkers:	■	Jogging Trails:	■
Snack Bar:	■	Boating:	■

COURSE DESCRIPTION

Saxon Woods Golf Club provides an easily understood playing field that is open to many pars and birdies if you're willing to take the time to manage your game to its strategic design. You don't have to be pin-point accurate on every shot; but do consider your options. You'll find many situations that will favor a 3-wood instead of a driver for both accuracy and distance. And that's the key: having the ability to determine the right amount of club that will set you up for your next shot.

Mid-to-high handicappers will gain the most amount of enjoyment on this playing field.

DIRECTIONS

Go south on Hutchinson Pkwy. to Exit 22 and follow the signs that will lead you to the course.

ALTERNATIVE COURSES - SOUTH

Dutchess
Public

James Baird State Park Course
Baird State Park Grounds
Pleasant Valley, NY 12569
(914) 473-1052

Dutchess
Private

Dutchess Golf & Country Club
South Rd. P.O., Box 1670
Poughkeepsie, NY 12603
(914) 452-5403

IBM Country Club
P.O., Box 1913
Poughkeepsie, NY 12601
(914) 433-2222

Millbrook Golf & Tennis Club
Rt. 343
Millbrook, NY 12545
(914) 677-3810

Queens Hill Country Club
Rural Rt. I
Pawling, NY 12564
(914) 855-1040

Skenandoa Club Of Clinton
Norton Ave. Box 284
Clinton, NY 13323
(315) 853-6612

Southern Duchess Country Club
53 North Ave., Beacon, NY 12508
(914) 831-0762

Dutchess
9-holes

College Hill Golf Course
North Clinton St., P.O., Box 587
Poughkeepsie, NY 12601
(914) 486-9112

Dutchess Golf Course
East Main St.
Pawling, NY 12564
(914) 855-9845

Fishkill Golf Course
P.O. Box 594
Fishkill, NY 12524
(914) 896-5220

Rea Hook Golf Club
Rd. 2, Box 131
Red Hook, NY 12571
(914) 758-8652

Vassar Golf Course
Raymond Ave.
Poughkeepsie, NY 12601
(914) 473-1550

Dutchess
Executive

Beekman Golf Course
11 Country Club Rd.
Hopewell Junction, NY 12533
(914) 226-7700

Kings
Public

Dyker Beach American Golf Club
7th Avenue & 86th St.
Brooklyn, NY 11228
(718) 836-9722

Nassau
Private

Brookville Country Club
Chicken Valley Rd.
Glen Head, NY 11545
(516) 671-8466

Cedarbrook Club
Oak Lane
Old Brookville, NY 11545
(516) 759-1600

Cherry Valley Club
Rockaway Ave. & Third St.
Garden City, NY 11530
(516) 741-1980

Creek Club, The
Horse Hollow Rd.
Locust Valley, NY 11560
(516) 671-1001

Deepdale Golf Club
North Service Rd.
Manhasett, NY 11030
(516) 365-91111

Engineers Country Club
Glenwood Rd.
Roslyn Harbor, NY 11576
(516) 621-5350

Garden City Country Club
206 Stewart Ave.
Garden City, NY 11530
(516) 747-2929

Glen Head Country Club
Cedar Swamp Rd.
Glen Head, NY 11545
(516) 676-4057

Glen Oaks Club
Box 249, 175 Post Rd.
Old Westbury, NY 11568
(516) 626-0161

IBM Country Club
10 Astor Lane
Port Washington, NY 11050
(516) 944-7840

Lawrence Golf Club
Causeway & Rock Hill Rd.
Lawrence, NY 11559
(516) 239-8263

Meadows Brook Club
Cedar Swamp Rd.
Jericho, NY 11753
(516) 822-3354

Merrick Rd. Park Golf Club
2550 Clubhouse Rd.
Merrick, NY 11566
(516) 868-4650

Middle Bay Country Club
3600 Skillman Ave.
Oceanside, NY 11572
(516) 763-1658

Mill River Club
P.O. Box 90
Oyster Bay, NY 11771
(516) 922-0463

North Hempstead Country Club
Port Washington Blvd.
Port Washington, NY 11050
(516) 365-2321

North Hills Country Club
North Service Rd. L1 Expressway
Manhasset, NY 11030
(516) 627-9139

North Shore Country Club
P.O. Box 101
Glen Head, NY 11545
(516) 676-4225

Old Westbury Golf & Country Club
270 Wheatley Rd.
Old Westbury, NY 11568
(516) 626-1810

Pine Hollow Country Club
Rt. 25 A
East Norwich, NY 11732
(516) 922-0300

Piping Rock Club
Piping Rock Rd.
Locust Valley, NY 11560
(516) 676-0460

Plandome Country Club
145 Stoneytown Rd.
Plandome, NY 11030
(516) 627-1200

Rockville Links Course
Long Beach Rd.
Rockville Centre, NY 11570
(516) 766-7446

Sands Point Golf Club
Middle Neck Rd.
Sands Point, NY 11050
(516) 883-3130

Sewane Club, The
1 Club Dr.
Hewlett Harbor, NY 11557
(516) 374-1110

Tam O'Shanter Club
Fruitledge Rd.
Brookville, NY 11545
(516) 626-7579

Towers Country Club
27286 Grand Central Pkwy.
Floral Park, NY 11005
(718) 279-1848

Wheatley Hill Golf Course
East Williston Ave.
East Williston, NY 11596
(516) 747-7358

Woodcrest Club, The
225 East Woods Rd.
Syosset, NY 11791
(516) 496-8673

Woodmere Club, The
Meadow Drive
Woodmere, NY 11598
(516) 374-1110

Nassau
Executive

Glen Core Golf Club
Lattingtown Rd.
Glen Cove, NY 11542
(516) 671-0033

Nassau
9-holes

Bay Park Golf Course
East Rockaway
Long Island, NY 11518
(516) 571-7242

Cantiague Park Golf Course
West John St.
Hicksville, NY 11801
(516) 932-1600

Christopher Morley Park
Searingtown Rd.
North Hills, NY 11040
(516) 621-9107

North Woodmere Golf Course
Hungry Harbor
North Woodmere, NY 11598
(516) 791-7705

Peninsula Golf Club
50 Nassau Rd.
Massapegua, NY 11758
(516) 798-9776

Nassau
Executive

Glen Core Golf Club
Lattingtown Rd.
Glen Cove, NY 11542
(516) 671-0033

Orange
Public

Central Valley Golf Course
Smith Clove Rd., P.O. Box 116
Cenrtral Valley, NY 10917
(914) 928-6924

Orange
Private

Orange County Golf Club
Golf Links Rd., P.O. Box 3117
Middletown, NY 10940
(914) 343-1284

Osiris Country Club
Osiris Rd.
Walden, NY 12586
(914) 778-5795

Port Jervis Country Club
Neversink Dr.
Port Jervis, NY 12771
(914) 856-5391

Powelton Club, The
29-63 Balmville Rd.
Newburgh, NY 12550
(914) 561-7409

Storm King Golf Club
Ridge Rd.
Cornwall, NY 12518
(914) 534-8834

Tuxedo Club, The
West Lake Rd.
Tuxedo Park, NY 10987
(914) 351-4543

Warwick Valley Country Club
P.O. Box 321
Warwick, NY 10990
(914) 986-9609

Orange
9-holes

Eddy Farm Resort Hotel
Eddy Farm Rd.
Sparrowbush, NY 12780
(914) 856-4333

Green Ridge Golf Course
Gregory Rd.
Johnson, NY 10933
(914) 355-1317

Monroe Country Club
P.O. Box 472, Still Rd.
Monroe, NY 10950
(914) 3783-9045

Scott's Corners Golf Course
1207 Rt. 17 K
Montgomery, NY 12549
(914) 457-9141

Orange
Military

West Point Golf Course
Building 622 USMA
West Point, NY 10996
(914) 938-2435

Putnum
Private

Mahopac Golf Club
North Lake Blvd.
Mahopac, NY 10996
(914) 628-8090

Putnum
9-holes

Vails Grove Golf Course
Rt. 121 - Peach Lake Rd.
Brewster, NY 10509
(914) 669-5721

Queens
Public

Silver Lake Golf Course
915 Victoria Blvd.
Statan Island, NY 10301

(718) 447-5686

Queens
Executive

Douglaston Golf Club
6320 Marathon Pkwy.
Douglaston Queens, NY 11363
(718) 224-6566

Forest Park Golf Course
P.O. Box K
Jamaica, NY 11411
(718) 296-0999

Kissena Park Golf Course
16415 Booth Memorial Ave.
Flushing, NY 11365
(718) 939-4594

Richmond
Private

Richmond County Country Club
1122 Todt Hill Rd.
Staton Island, NY 10304
(718) 351-0600

Rockland
Public

Rockland Lake Championship G.C.
P.O. Box 217, Rt. 9W & Lake Rd.
Congress NY 10920
(914) 268-7275

Rockland
Private

Broadacres Golf Club
Rockland Psychiatric Center
Orangesburg, NY 10962
(914) 359-8218

Dellwood Country Club
Zucker Rd.
New City, NY 10962
(914) 634-4626

Rockland Country Club
Rt. 9 W
Sparkill, NY 10976
(914) 359-3072

Rockland
9-hole

Spook Rock Golf Course
199 Spook Rock Rd.
Suffern, NY 10901
(914) 357-6466

Suffolk
Public

Cold Spring Country Club
East Gate Dr.
Cold Spring Harbor, NY 11724
(516) 367-3513

Indian Island Golf Course
Riverside Dr.
Riverhead, NY 11901
(516) 727-7776

Island's End Golf & Country Club
Rt. 25
Greeport, NY 11944
(516) 477-9457

Pine Hills Country Club
162 Wading River Rd.
Manorville, NY 11949
(516) 878-4343

Smithtown Landing Golf Club
495 Landing Ave.
Smithtown, NY 11787
(516) 360-7618

Spring Lake Golf Course
950 Barlett Rd., Rt. 25
Middle Island, NY 11953
(516) 924-5115

Swan Lake Golf Club
388 River Rd.
Manorville, NY 11949
(516) 369-1818

Timber Point Country Club
Great River Rd.
Great River, NY 11739
(516) 581-2401

West Sayville Golf Course
Montauk Hwy.
West Sayville, NY 11796
(516) 567-1704

Suffolk
Private

Atlantic Golf Club
Scuttle Hide Rd.
Bridgehampton, NY 11932
(516) 537-5450

Bellport Country Club
South Country Rd.
Bellport, NY 11713
(516) 286-7206

Fisher Island Club
Fisher's Island
Fisher's Island, NY 16390
(516) 788-7223

Fox Hill Golf & Country Club
100 Fox Hill Dr.
Baiting Hollow, NY 11933
(516) 727-6363

Gardiner's Bay Country Club
12 Dinah Rock Rd.
Shelter Island, NY 11964
(516) 549-1033

Hampton Hills Golf & Country Club
P.O. Box 1087
Country Rd. 51 & Riverside
Westhampton, NY 11978
(516) 727-6862

Huntington Cresent Club
Washington Dr. & Rt. 25 A
Huntington, NY 11743
(516) 421-5180

Suffolk
Private - Continued

Indian Hills Country Club
21 Breeze Hills Rd.
Northport, NY 11768
(516) 757-7718

Island Hills Golf Club
Lakeland Ave.
Sayville, NY 11782
(516) 563-1492

Maidstone Golf Club
Old Beach Land
East Hampton, NY 11937
(516) 324-5530

National Golf Links of America
Sabonac Inlet Rd.
Southhampton, NY 11968
(516) 283-0559

Nissequgue Golf Course
Moriches Rd.
St. James, NY 11780
(516) 584-7989

North Fork Country Club
Main Rd.
Cutchogue, NY 11935
(516) 734-7758

Noyac Golf & Country Club
Wildwood Rd.
Sag Harbour, NY 11963
(516) 725-1889

Port Jefferson Country Club
44 Fairway Drive
Port Jefferson, NY 11777
(516) 473-1464

Quogue Field Club
P.O. Box 700
Quogue, NY 11959
(516) 653-9885

St. George's Golf & Country Club
Sheep Pasture Rd.
Stony Brook, NY 11790
(516) 751-0585

Shinnecock Hills Golf Course
North Hwy.
South Hampton, NY 11968
(516) 283-3525

South Fork Country Club
Abraham Landing Rd.
Amagansett, NY 11930
(516) 267-6827

South Hampton Golf Club
671 North Highway
South Hampton, NY 11968
(516) 283-4975

Southward Ho Country Club
Montauk Hwy.
Bayshore, NY 11706
(516) 665-1753

Westhampton Country Club
35 Potunk Lane
Westhampton, NY 11978
(516) 288-1110

Suffolk
9-hole

Cedars Golf Club
Cases Lane
Cutchogue, NY 11935
(516) 734-6363

Dix Hills Golf Course
527 Half Hollow Rd.
Dix Hills, NY 11746
(516) 271-4788

Dix Hills Park Golf Course
575 Vanderbilt Pkwy.
Dix Hills, NY 11746
(516) 499-8005

Hollow Hills Golf Course
49 Ryder Ave.
Dix Hills, NY 11746
(516) 242-0010

Poxabogue Golf Course
Montauk Hwy.
Bridge Hampton, NY 11963
(516) 537-0025

Sag Harbor Golf Course
Box 463, Northwest Rd.
Sag Harbor, NY 11963
(516) 725-9739

**Sunken Meadow State
Park Golf Course**
Sunken Meadow State Park
Kings Park, NY 11754
(516) 669-4333

Suffolk
Executive

Tall Tree Golf Course
Rt. 25 A
Rocky Point, NY 11778
(516) 744-3200

Sullivan
Public

Swan Lake Golf & Country Club
Mount Hoke Rd.
Swan Lake, NY 12783
(914) 292-0323

Tarry Brae Golf Course
Pleasant Valley Rd.
South Fallsburg, NY 12779
(914) 434-2622

Sullivan
Private

Kutsher's Country Club
Kutsher Rd.
Monticello, NY 12701
(914) 794-6000

**Sullivan County
Golf & Country Club**
P.O. 468
Liberty, NY 12754
(914) 292-9584

Sullivan
9-hole

Homowack Hotel Golf Course
C/O Golf Shop
Spring Glen, NY 12483
(914) 647-6800

Island Glenn Country Club
Rt. 17 B
Bethel, NY 12720
(914) 583-9898

Pines Hotel & Golf Club, The
Laural Ave.
South Fallsburg, NY 12779
(914) 434-6000

Ulster
Public

Roundout Country Club
P.O. Box 194 Whitfield Rd.
Accord, NY 12404
(914) 626-2513

Ulster
Private

Country Club Of Rochester
2935 East Ave.
Rochester, NY 14610
(716) 385-1600

Irondequoit Country Club
P.O. Box 10149
Rochester, NY 14610
(716) 586-0156

Ridgemont Country Club
3717 Ridge Road West
Rochester, NY 14626
(716) 225-7650

Twaalfskill Club
282 W. O'Reilly St.
Kingston, NY 12401
(914) 331-6266

Wiltwyck Golf Club
Lucas Ave. Extension
Kingston, NY 12401
(914) 331-5178

Woodstock Golf Club
Box 303, Routes 212 & 375
Woodstock, NY 12498
(914) 679-2914

Ulster
9-hole

Katsbaan Golf Club
1754 Old Kings Hwy.
Saugerties, NY 12477
(914) 246-8182

Mohonk Mountain Golf Course
Route 299
New Paltz, NY 12561
(914) 255-1000

New Paltz Golf Club
215 Huguenot St.
New Paltz, NY 12561
(914) 255-8282

Shawangunk Country Club
Nevel Rd., P.O. Box 367
Ellenville, NY 12428
(914) 647-6090

Woodcliff Golf Course
P.O. Box 22850, 199 Woodcliff Dr.
Rochester, NY 14692
(716) 248-4845

Westchester
Private

Apawamis Club, The
Club Rd.
Rye, NY 10580
(914) 967-2100

Ardsley Country Club
North Mountain Dr.
Ardsley-On-Hudson, NY 10503
(914) 591-8403

Arrowwood Golf Course
Anderson Hill Rd.
Rye Brook, NY 10573
(914) 939-5500

Bedford Golf And Tennis Club
Rt. 22
Bedford, NY 10506
(914) 234-3325

Blind Brook Country Club
P.O. Box 229
Purchase, NY 10577
(914) 939-1450

Bonnie Brian Country Club
808 Weaver St.
Larchmont, NY 10538
(914) 834-1627

Brae Burn Country Club
Brae Burn Dr., Box 214
Purchase, NY 10577
(914) 328-8478

Briar Hall Country Club
Pine Rd.
Briarcliff, NY 10510
(914) 941-4300

Century Country Club
P.O. Box 248
Purchase, NY 10577
(914) 761-0400

Doral Arrowwood Resort
Anderson Hill Rd.
Rye Brook, NY 10573
(914) 939-5500

Elmwood Country Club
Dobbs Ferry Rd.
White Plains, NY 10607
(914) 592-6600

Fenway Golf Club
Old Mamaroneck Rd.
Scarsdale, NY 10583
(914) 723-1095

Heritage Hills Country Club
Rt. 202, P.O. Box 167
Somers, NY 10589
(914) 276-2169

Highlands Country Club
Rt. 9 D, Bear Mountain Bridges Rd.
Garrison, NY 10524
(914) 424-3727

Knollwood Country Club
Knollwood Rd.
Elmsford, NY 10523
(914) 592-6182

Leewood Golf Club
1 Leewood Dr.
Eastchester, NY 10707
(914) 793-5821

Metropolis Country Club
Dobbs Ferry Rd.
White Plains, NY 10607
(914) 946-8814

Mount Kisco Country Club
Taylor Rd.
Mount Kisco, NY 10549
(914) 666-7300

Old Oaks Country Club
Purchase St.
Purchase, NY 10577
(914) 949-5100

Pelham Country Club
Wynnewood Rd.
Pelham Manor, NY 10803
(914) 738-5074

Pleasantville Country Club
110 Nannohangan
Pleasantville, NY 10570
(914) 769-8600

Quaker Ridge Golf Club
Griffen Ave.
Scarsdale, NY 10583
(914) 723-3701

Ridgeway Country Club
Ridgeway Ave.
White Plains, NY 10605
(914) 946-0681

Rye Golf Club
330 Boston Post Rd.
Rye, NY 10580
(914) 835-1354

Salem Golf Club
Bloomer Rd.
North Salem, NY 10560
(914) 669-5551

Scarsdale Golf Club
Clubway
Harstale, NY 10530
(914) 723-5202

Siwanoy Country Club
Pondfield Rd.
Bronxville, NY 10708
(914) 337-8858

Sleepy Hollow Country Club
Albany Post Rd., Box 345
Scarborough, NY 10510
(914) 941-3062

St. Andrews Golf Club
Old Jackson Ave.
Hastings-On-The-Hudson, NY 10510
(914) 478-3475

Sunningdale Country Club
P.O. Box 249
Scardale, NY 10583
(914) 472-6972

Waccabuc Country Club
Mead St.
Waccabuc, NY 10597
(914) 763-8410

Westchester Country Club
North St.
Rye, NY 10580
(914) 967-6000

Westchester Hills Golf Club
Ridgeway Ave.
White Plains, NY 10605
(914) 761-7639

Wippoorwill Club
150 Whipporwill Rd.
Armonk, NY 10504
(914) 273-3059

Winged Foot Golf Club
Fenimore Rd.
Mamaroneck, NY 10543
(914) 381-5821

Wykagyl Country Club
1195 North Ave.
New Rochelle, NY 10804
(914) 632-2359

Westchester
9-hole

Pehquenakonck Country Club
Peach Lake
North Salem, NY 10560
(914) 669-9380

Vails Grove Golf Course
Peach Lake
North Salem, NY 10560
(914) 669-5721

Westchester
Executive

Dunwoodie Golf Club
Wasylenko Lane
Yonkers, NY 10701
(914) 969-9217

6. NEW YORK - WEST/COUNTIES & CITIES

Allegany

B2 / Belfast ... 1
B2 / Wellsville ... 2

Cattaraugus

B2 / Randolph ... 3

B2 / Eden ... 16
B1 / Elma ... 17
B1 / Grand Island ... 18
B1 / Tonawanda ... 19

Genesee

B1 / Batavia ... 21

B1 / Webster ... 36

Niagara

B1 / Lockport ... 37
B1 / Middleport ... 38
B1 / Niagara Falls ... 39
B1 / Tonawanda ... 40

B1 /

B1 /

B2 /

B2 /

B2 / Ellicottville ... 4
B2 / Salamanca ... 5

Chautauqua

B2 / Chautauqua ... 6
B2 / Clymer ... 7
B2 / Forestville ... 8
B2 / Fredonia ... 9
B2 / Jamestown ... 10
B2 / Lakewood ... 11

Chemung

B2 / Flats ... 12
B2 / Horsehead ... 13

Erie

B1 / Akron ... 14
B1 / Amhurst ... 15

B1 / Darien ... 22

Livingston

B1 / Conesus ... 23
B2 / Geneseo ... 24
B2 / Lima ... 25
B2 / Livonia ... 26
B1 / Nunda ... 27

Monroe

B1 / Brockport ... 28
B1 / Churchville ... 29
B1 / Fairport ... 30
B1 / Penfield ... 31
B1 / Rochester ... 32
B1 / Rush ... 33
B1 / Scottsville ... 34
B1 / Spencerport ... 35

Ontario

B2 / Campbell Hall ... 41
B1 / Canandaigua ... 42
B1 / Geneva ... 43
B1 / Shortsville ... 44
B1 / Victor ... 45

Steuben

B2 / Hornell ... 46

Wayne

B1 / Lyons ... 47

Wyoming

B2 / Varyburg ... 48

SIX-S COUNTRY CLUB

Transit Bridge, Belfast, NY 14711 / (716) 365-2201

BASIC INFORMATION

Course Type: Public
Year Built: 1964
Architect: Bill & Larry Short
Local Pro: Marcia Short

Course: Championship (18 / Par 72)
Holes: 27

Back : 6,210 yds. Rating: 75.8 Slope: 120
Middle: 5,941 yds. Rating: 69.5 Slope: 115
Ladies: 4,826 yds. Rating: 64.9 Slope: 110

Tee Time: First come, first serve.
Price: $10 - $12

Credit Cards:		Restaurant:	■
Driving Range:	■	Lounge:	■
Practice Green:	■	Meeting Rooms:	■
Locker Room:	■	Tennis:	
Rental Clubs:		Swimming:	
Walkers:	■	Jogging Trails:	
Snack Bar:	■	Boating:	

COURSE DESCRIPTION

Six-S Country Club is a family operation that features one championship course and an additional nine-hole layout. A back-side nine is currently under construction and is due for its debut about May 1995.

The current championship course offers a short layout with a good number of interesting holes to play through. Mid-to-high handicappers will enjoy this layout the most. The course offers a peaceful setting that's far away from noisy traffic, void of having to cross over roads, and is open from March 15th up to late November.

Strict etiquette is enforced.

DIRECTIONS

Exit the Southern Tier Expressway at Rt. 19 and go north to Allegany County Rt. 16. Turn right and go one half mile to the course.

WELLSVILLE COUNTRY CLUB

Riverside Dr., Box 290, Wellsville, NY 14895 / (716) 593-6337

BASIC INFORMATION

Course Type: Semi-private
Year Built: N/A
Architect: N/A
Local Pro: Robert Todd

Course: N/A
Holes: 18 / Par 70

Back: 6,063 yds. Rating: 69.5 Slope: 117
Middle: 5,802 yds. Rating: 69.0 Slope: 115
Ladies: 5,320 yds. Rating: 70.6 Slope: 108

Tee Time: 1 day in advance.
Price: $19.88

Credit Cards:	■	Restaurant:	■
Driving Range:	■	Lounge:	■
Practice Green:	■	Meeting Rooms:	■
Locker Room:	■	Tennis:	
Rental Clubs:	■	Swimming:	
Walkers:		Jogging Trails:	
Snack Bar:	■	Boating:	

COURSE DESCRIPTION

Wellsville Country Club is open to golfers of all abilities. Its relatively short distance makes it quite attractive to play aggressively. If you can keep the ball in play with your drives, you'll often find yourself in good position for an easy approach shot to the green. The layout favors good shot-makers over long-hitters on the majority of holes. A strong architectural design is the foundation that sits below these many thought-provoking, uniquely structured holes.

It's a great competitive venue for mid-to-high handicappers.

DIRECTIONS

Take I-17 to Rt. 19 (Belmont/Wesville Exit). Look for the course approximately 12 miles further on your left.

CATTARAUGUS COUNTY

CONEWANGO FORKS GOLF CLUB INC.

Rt. 241 Conewango Rd., Randolph, NY 14772 / (716) 358-5409

BASIC INFORMATION

Course Type: Public
Year Built: N/A
Architect: N/A
Local Pro: Steve Beattie

Course: N/A
Holes: 18 / Par 72

Back: 6,358 yds. Rating: N/A   Slope: N/A
Middle: 6,058 yds. Rating: N/A   Slope: N/A
Ladies: 5,753 yds. Rating: N/A   Slope: N/A

Tee Time: 7 days in advance.
Price: $12 - $19

Credit Cards:	■	Restaurant:	■
Driving Range:	■	Lounge:	■
Practice Green:	■	Meeting Rooms:	■
Locker Room:	■	Tennis:	
Rental Clubs:	■	Swimming:	
Walkers:	■	Jogging Trails:	
Snack Bar:	■	Boating:	■

COURSE DESCRIPTION

Conewango Forks Golf Club sits atop a unique vantage point that offers beautiful mountain views of an orthodox Anabaptist sect; this area is known as Amish country.

It's not a course that a low handicapper has to fear, but rather it's a nice venue for a double-digit handicapper to experience. You'll often need to hit your ball out of an uneven lie because of the rolling terrain that the course was built on. You can get yourself in good par position with well placed drives. Accuracy is much more important than distance.

DIRECTIONS

Take Rt. 17 north to the Randolph Exit and go north to Rt. 241. Make a left and look for the course about a 1/4-mile further on your right.

ELKDALE COUNTRY CLUB

Rt. 353, P.O. Box 544, Salamanca, NY 14779 / (716) 945-5553

BASIC INFORMATION

Course Type: Semi-private
Year Built: 1946
Architect: N/A
Local Pro: N/A

Course: N/A
Holes: 18 / Par 70

Back: 6,132 yds. Rating: 68.4 Slope: 112
Middle: N/A   Rating: N/A   Slope: N/A
Ladies: 5,221 yds. Rating: 67.4 Slope: N/A

Tee Time: 7 days in advance.
Price: $18 - $24

Credit Cards:	■	Restaurant:	■
Driving Range:		Lounge:	■
Practice Green:	■	Meeting Rooms:	■
Locker Room:		Tennis:	
Rental Clubs:	■	Swimming:	■
Walkers:	■	Jogging Trails:	
Snack Bar:	■	Boating:	■

COURSE DESCRIPTION

Elkdale Country Club is a laid-back place, infamous in this part of the state.

You'll find traces of days gone by when architects chose to design small demanding greens to offset the short distance of the blueprints that had been given to them. At a distance of only 6,132 yards, it was generally accepted that players would be using high-lofted irons on their approach shots. These small greens forced the golfer to play an absolutely accurate shot to get the ball on the green and close to the pin.

If you're a mid-to-high handicapper looking for a course to test your short game — this may be it.

DIRECTIONS

Take Rt. 17 to Hwy. 353 north and look for the course on your right side.

HOLIDAY VALLEY RESORT
Holiday Valley Rd., Ellicottville, NY 14731 / (716) 699-2346

BASIC INFORMATION
Course Type: Public
Year Built: 1957 / 1980's
Architect: N/A
Local Pro: Peter Stransky

Course: N/A
Holes: 18 / Par 72

Back: 6,555 yds. Rating: 71.3 Slope: 125
Middle: 6,167 yds. Rating: 70.0 Slope: 120
Ladies: 5,381 yds. Rating: 74.0 Slope: 115

Tee Time: 3 days in advance.
Price: $15 - $25

Credit Cards: ■	Restaurant: ■
Driving Range: ■	Lounge: ■
Practice Green: ■	Meeting Rooms: ■
Locker Room: ■	Tennis: ■
Rental Clubs: ■	Swimming: ■
Walkers:	Jogging Trails: ■
Snack Bar: ■	Boating: ■

COURSE DESCRIPTION
Holiday Valley Resort is a pleasurable course that caters to every type of golfer, regardless of ability and experience.

You'll need to play a strong game to score low numbers. Tight fairways make it difficult to keep the ball in play when driving the ball from the championship tees. The longer front-nine is more open and can play like a monster if the wind picks up — which it does quite often.

If your natural shot is a draw, you're in luck, because most of the holes seem to cater to that line of play. Don't despair; middle-tees are much friendlier at 6,167 yards. Enjoy!

DIRECTIONS
Take Rt. 219, 1-mile short of Main St. and Ellicottville town. The course will be on your left.

CHAUTAUQUA GOLF COURSE
Rt. 394, Chautaqua, NY 14722 / (716) 357-6211

BASIC INFORMATION
Course Type: Public
Year Built: 1920's
Architect: Donald Ross
Local Pro: Stan Marshalls

Course: Lake (18 / Par 72)
Holes: 36

Back: 6,462 yds. Rating: 71.1 Slope: 115
Middle: 6,148 yds. Rating: 69.6 Slope: 113
Ladies: 5,423 yds. Rating: 71.7 Slope: 108

Tee Time: 7 days in advance.
Price: $12 - $25

Credit Cards: ■	Restaurant:
Driving Range: ■	Lounge:
Practice Green: ■	Meeting Rooms:
Locker Room: ■	Tennis:
Rental Clubs: ■	Swimming:
Walkers: ■	Jogging Trails:
Snack Bar: ■	Boating: ■

COURSE DESCRIPTION
Chautauqua Golf Course is a nice challenge with many interesting holes for an amateur golfer to enjoy. At 6,462 yards from the championship tees, it's neither too short for a better player or too long for a higher handicapper. You'll find reachable par-5's egging you on to go for that dream eagle approach shot — and you will. The rolling terrain of the course features four ponds that come into play, elevated tees, and many subtle undulations.

As always, the brilliance that made the late Donald Ross one of the most respected architects of all time is evident throughout this beautiful design.

DIRECTIONS
Take I-90 to the Westfield Exit (Rt. 394 East). The course will be 14 miles further on your right.

CHAUTAUQUA COUNTY

HILLVIEW GOLF COURSE
4717 Berry Rd., Fredonia, NY 14063 / (716) 679-4571

BASIC INFORMATION
Course Type: Public
Year Built: 1936
Architect: R.R. Shephard & A.W. Porter
Local Pro: Steve Dole

Course: N/A
Holes: 18 / Par 70

Back: 6,149 yds. Rating: 68.3 Slope: 106
Middle: N/A   Rating: N/A Slope: N/A
Ladies: N/A   Rating: N/A Slope: N/A

Tee Time: First come, first serve.
Price: $12 - $15 (for the entire day).

Credit Cards:		Restaurant:	
Driving Range:	■	Lounge:	■
Practice Green:	■	Meeting Rooms:	
Locker Room:	■	Tennis:	
Rental Clubs:	■	Swimming:	
Walkers:	■	Jogging Trails:	
Snack Bar:	■	Boating:	■

COURSE DESCRIPTION
Hillview Golf Course offers a playing field that is best suited for high-handicappers.

The bad news is that the course only offers a single set of tees to accommodate every type of player; the good news is once you've paid for your round, you've earned a VIP pass to play the course as many times as you want for that particular day — sort of like going back for seconds at a food buffet! Think of it as an advanced driving range.

DIRECTIONS
Take Rt. 20 west to Village of Fredonia and make a right at Chesnut, another right at Berry Rd., and yet another right towards the course which will be on your right.

MAPLEHURST COUNTRY CLUB
1508 Big Tree Rd., Lakewood, NY 14750 / (716) 763-1225

BASIC INFORMATION
Course Type: Public
Year Built: 1930's
Architect: N/A
Local Pro: Wallace Holmes

Course: N/A
Holes: 18 / Par 70

Back : 6,250 yds. Rating: 67.0 Slope: 114
Middle: 6,127 yds. Rating: 66.0 Slope: 113
Ladies: 5,376 yds. Rating: 68.0 Slope: 115

Tee Time: 1 day in advance.
Price: $10 - $18

Credit Cards:	■	Restaurant:	■
Driving Range:		Lounge:	■
Practice Green:	■	Meeting Rooms:	■
Locker Room:	■	Tennis:	
Rental Clubs:	■	Swimming:	
Walkers:	■	Jogging Trails:	
Snack Bar:	■	Boating:	■

COURSE DESCRIPTION
You won't find many hazards that will hold you back on this course, and that's just how the local players prefer to play to play here. It isn't unusual to play a round in a matter of four hours.

The course has a dual personality by offering two distinctive nine-holes to play through. The front half is the harder of the two because of its hilly terrain, which often will have your ball roll onto an uneven lie; the back side is much more manageable because of its flatness and shorter distance.

DIRECTIONS
Take Rt. 17 to the Lakewood Exit and make a left. Proceed westbound and make a right at Rt. 394 and follow that to Big Tree Rd. The course will be about 3 miles further on your left.

PEEK 'N' PEEK RECREATION

Rd. 2, Box 135, Clymer, NY 14724 / (716) 355-4141

BASIC INFORMATION

Course Type: Public
Year Built: 1972
Architect: Ferdinand Garbin
Local Pro: N/A

Course: Peek 'N' Peek (18 / Par 72)
Holes: 27

Back: 6,260 yds. Rating: 69.0 Slope: 115
Middle: N/A   Rating: N/A Slope: N/A
Ladies: 5,328 yds. Rating: 69.5 Slope: 112

Tee Time: 1 year in advance.
Price: $29 - $37

Credit Cards: ■	Restaurant: ■
Driving Range: ■	Lounge: ■
Practice Green: ■	Meeting Rooms: ■
Locker Room: ■	Tennis: ■
Rental Clubs: ■	Swimming: ■
Walkers: ■	Jogging Trails: ■
Snack Bar: ■	Boating: ■

COURSE DESCRIPTION

Peek "N' Peek Recreation is a friendly course with well-defined fairways that make it easy to follow the shape of every hole. It's an easy course design that uses very little in the way of hazards to divert a player's thinking. An additional nine-holes is in the works to complement the secondary nine-hole course that already exists (to make up a secondary championship course for visitors to choose from).

The hardest hole on the course is the par-5, number 17. This double-dogleg (left-to-right/right-to-left) stretches 509 yards in length from the championship tees.

DIRECTIONS

Take I-90 to Exit 10 A and onward to the Findley Lake Exit where you'll have to make a right. Follow the signs to the course.

SOUTH HILLS COUNTRY CLUB

3108 Busti-Stillwater Rd., Jamestown, NY 14701 / (716) 487-1471

BASIC INFORMATION

Course Type: Public
Year Built: 1963 / 1974
Architect: N/A
Local Pro: Roger Loop

Course: N/A
Holes: 18 / Par 72

Back : 6,105 yds. Rating: 67.5 Slope: 116
Middle: 5,538 yds. Rating: 65.2 Slope: 114
Ladies: 4,681 yds. Rating: 66.0 Slope: N/A

Tee Time: Fist come, first serve.
Price: $12 - $15

Credit Cards:	Restaurant:
Driving Range:	Lounge: ■
Practice Green: ■	Meeting Rooms: ■
Locker Room: ■	Tennis:
Rental Clubs: ■	Swimming:
Walkers: ■	Jogging Trails:
Snack Bar: ■	Boating:

COURSE DESCRIPTION

This course may not be the toughest course you'll face, but it's an interesting design that will be enjoyed by mid-to-high handicappers. This is a strategic course that integrates features of the surrounding environment: water, creeks, trees, rolling terrain, etc. The result is a colorful blueprint that makes it an enjoyable venue to play and experience. You'll find many doglegs to negotiate through; a peculiar arrangement of three par-5's spread along the front-nine; contoured greens, and more!

The number one handicap hole on the course is number 12. It's a par-4 that extends 370 yards in length from the championship tees.

DIRECTIONS

Please call the course for proper directions.

TRI-COUNTY COUNTRY CLUB
Rt. 39, Forrestville, NY 14062 / (716) 965-2053

BASIC INFORMATION

Course Type: Semi-private
Year Built: 1924
Architect: N/A
Local Pro: Tom Kenyon

Course: N/A
Holes: 18 / Par 71

Back: 6,639 yds. Rating: 70.9 Slope: 120
Middle: 6,434 yds. Rating: 70.5 Slope: 118
Ladies: 5,574 yds. Rating: 70.1 Slope: 113

Tee Time: First come, first serve.
Price: $20 - $22

Credit Cards:	■	Restaurant:	■
Driving Range:	■	Lounge:	■
Practice Green:	■	Meeting Rooms:	■
Locker Room:	■	Tennis:	
Rental Clubs:		Swimming:	■
Walkers:	■	Jogging Trails:	
Snack Bar:	■	Boating:	■

COURSE DESCRIPTION

Tri-County Country Club is a mature course, with many fascinating holes, that blend creatively next to each other, offering a challenging design for all sorts of golfers to enjoy. You'll face rolling fairways that will force you to figure out the best possible landing areas; undulating greens that require a careful read to finesse a putt towards a hole in two; and bunkers along the way to confuse you even more.

The challenge is definitely here for different types of players.

DIRECTIONS

Take the New York State Thruway to the Fredonia Exit and go south to Rt. 60 where you'll need to go east to Rt. 20 and east again on Rt. 39. Look for the course on your left.

SOARING EAGLES GOLF COURSE
4229 Middle Rd., Horseheads, NY 14845 / (607) 739-0551

BASIC INFORMATION

Course Type: Public
Year Built: Archibold "Pete" Craig
Architect: William Grygeil
Local Pro: Steve Bowers

Course: N/A
Holes: 18 / Par 72

Back : 6,625 yds. Rating: 71.6 Slope: 117
Middle: 6,327 yds. Rating: 70.2 Slope: 115
Ladies: 4,930 yds. Rating: 67.5 Slope: 108

Tee Time: 2 days in advance.
Price: $12 - $14

Credit Cards:		Restaurant:	■
Driving Range:	■	Lounge:	■
Practice Green:	■	Meeting Rooms:	■
Locker Room:	■	Tennis:	
Rental Clubs:	■	Swimming:	
Walkers:	■	Jogging Trails:	
Snack Bar:	■	Boating:	

COURSE DESCRIPTION

Soaring Eagles Golf Course features many intriguing holes that force a golfer to play different types of shots en route to a low scoring round.

The course requires a golfer to hit accurate drives to well-defined landing areas for good second shot positions — despite the fact that most of the fairways are generally wide in size. This is not a difficult course by any means, but rather a fun venue for amateur golfers to enjoy. Joey Sindelar and Mike Hulbert considered this their home course while playing high school golf.

DIRECTIONS

Take Rt. 17 to Exit 52 onto Westinghouse Rd. to Rt. 14. Make a left at Rt. 14 to Wygant Rd. and a right at Wygant Rd. to Ridge Rd. Proceed left to Middle Rd. and make another left on Middle Rd. to the course.

WILLOW CREEK GOLF CLUB
Rt. 352, Big Flats, NY 14814 / (607) 562-8898

BASIC INFORMATION

Course Type: Public
Year Built: N/A
Architect: Tallman
Local Pro: N/A

Course: N/A
Holes: 18 / Par 72

Back   : 6,820 yds.   Rating: 71.9   Slope: 131
Middle: 6,424 yds.   Rating: 70.1   Slope: 128
Ladies: 5,400 yds.   Rating: 70.0   Slope: 124

Tee Time: 3 days in advance.
Price: $15

Credit Cards: ■   Restaurant:
Driving Range: ■   Lounge: ■
Practice Green: ■   Meeting Rooms:
Locker Room: ■   Tennis:
Rental Clubs: ■   Swimming:
Walkers: ■   Jogging Trails:
Snack Bar: ■   Boating: ■

COURSE DESCRIPTION

You're bound to find moments of excitement on this thrilling championship-length golf course, which will force you to play long drives with accuracy, onto specific areas on the fairways, for proper position on your following approach shots towards the greens.

All eventful playing fields share a common denominator with each other, as this one does: accuracy above distance is the golden rule. If you haven't mastered the art of playing a draw at will, you'll be much better off playing the course from the middle-tees, for it takes the pressure off on those demanding sharp doglegs.

DIRECTIONS
Please call the course for specific directions.

BEAVER ISLAND STATE PARK GOLF COURSE
Grand Island, NY 14072 / (716) 773-3271

BASIC INFORMATION

Course Type: Public
Year Built: 1960's
Architect: Hal Carlson
Local Pro: N/A

Course: N/A
Holes: 18 / Par 72

Back : 6,595 yds.   Rating: 72.1   Slope: N/A
Middle: N/A   Rating: N/A   Slope: N/A
Ladies: 6,201 yds.   Rating: 70.1   Slope: N/A

Tee Time: 3 days in advance.
Price: $12 - $14

Credit Cards: Restaurant:
Driving Range: Lounge: ■
Practice Green: Meeting Rooms:
Locker Room: ■   Tennis:
Rental Clubs: ■   Swimming:
Walkers: ■   Jogging Trails:
Snack Bar: ■   Boating: ■

COURSE DESCRIPTION

Beaver Island State Park Golf Course gets a lot of play each year by local players. It's not a hard course to master by any means, making it ideal for player's who can hit the ball long, but lack the type of accuracy that is needed to get the ball on the green in regulation par.

The hardest rated hole on the course is the par-5, number 13. The hole stretches out 473 yards in length and features fairway bunkers on both sides of the tight fairway, water left, and trees along the right and around the green. A high-flying fade shot is needed to stop the ball atop the undulating and often demanding green.

DIRECTIONS
Take the New York State Thruway to the Beaver Island State Park Exit. Follow the signs to the course.

ERIE COUNTY

BRIGHTON PARK GOLF COURSE
70 Brompton Rd., Tonawanda, NY 14150 / (716) 695-2580

BASIC INFORMATION

Course Type: Public
Year Built: 1969
Architect: N/A
Local Pro: Dennis Rainey / Manager

Course: N/A
Holes: 18 / Par 72

Back : 6,535 yds. Rating: 70.7 Slope: 108
Middle: N/A   Rating: N/A   Slope: N/A
Ladies: 5,852 yds. Rating: 73.5 Slope: 109

Tee Time: 3 days in advance.
Price: $15 - $18

Credit Cards:		Restaurant:	
Driving Range:	■	Lounge:	■
Practice Green:	■	Meeting Rooms:	
Locker Room:	■	Tennis:	
Rental Clubs:		Swimming:	
Walkers:	■	Jogging Trails:	
Snack Bar:	■	Boating:	

COURSE DESCRIPTION

Brighton Park Golf Course is a wide open layout that's punctuated with fairway traps, lateral hazards, and large greens.

The course will mostly appeal to new players and high-handicappers alike. This is not a very difficult course to take control of. Play it aggressively and you'll soon find yourself shooting for par or better.

Both your short game and your putting game will get a good workout by the end of a given round.

DIRECTIONS
Take I-290 to Exit Colvin Blvd. Go north to Brompton Rd. and make a right. The course will be just less than a mile on your left.

EDEN VALLEY GOLF COURSE
10149 Clarksburg Rd., Eden, NY 14057 / (716) 337-2190

BASIC INFORMATION

Course Type: Public
Year Built: N/A
Architect: N/A
Local Pro: N/A

Course: N/A
Holes: 18 / Par 72

Back: 6,298 yds. Rating: N/A Slope: N/A
Middle: N/A   Rating: N/A Slope: N/A
Ladies: 5,921 yds. Rating: N/A Slope: N/A

Tee Time: 7 days from Sunday.
Price: $10 - $13

Credit Cards:		Restaurant:	■
Driving Range:		Lounge:	■
Practice Green:	■	Meeting Rooms:	■
Locker Room:		Tennis:	
Rental Clubs:	■	Swimming:	
Walkers:		Jogging Trails:	
Snack Bar:	■	Boating:	

COURSE DESCRIPTION

Eden Valley Golf Course is a simple design that tends to draw high-handicappers because of its unpretentious qualities.

Although the front-nine features two water holes and a gorge, it's considered the easier half as opposed to the many doglegs with blind shots featured on the back-nine.

The 481 yard, par-5, 12th hole is the hardest test on the course. Many golfers have second thoughts about going for the green in two because of the pond that is situated close to the green.

DIRECTIONS
Take Rt. 219 to Genese Rd. and make a right towards Rt. 75 where you'll need to make a another right. The course will be about 5 miles further on your right.

ELMA MEADOWS GOLF COURSE
171 Brentwood Dr., Elma, NY 14059 / (716) 652-2022

BASIC INFORMATION

Course Type: Public
Year Built: N/A
Architect: N/A
Local Pro: Peter Cizdziel

Course: N/A
Holes: 18 / Par 70

Back : 6,556 yds. Rating: 70.2 Slope: 108
Middle: 6,316 yds. Rating: 69.8 Slope: 107
Ladies: 6,000 yds. Rating: 73.8 Slope: 108

Tee Time: 1 day in advance.
Price: $11 - $13

Credit Cards:	■	Restaurant:	
Driving Range:	■	Lounge:	
Practice Green:	■	Meeting Rooms:	
Locker Room:	■	Tennis:	
Rental Clubs:	■	Swimming:	
Walkers:	■	Jogging Trails:	
Snack Bar:	■	Boating:	

COURSE DESCRIPTION

If you're looking for an inexpensive place to practice your game, **Elma Meadows Golf Course** is the place you want to be. This unpretentious venue offers many opportunities to make par or better. All you need to do is keep the ball on the fairway and hit your approach shots close. The first should come easy; the second takes skill.

What you will find should keep you enthralled if you're in need of some serious practice. Don't come running too quickly; unless you're a beginner, a senior citizen, or one of many types of players that need to work on their long game.

DIRECTIONS

Go south on Rt. 78 (Transit Rd.) and make a left at Seneca Rd. and another left at Rice Rd. Look for the course at the end of Rice Rd.

GLEN OAK GOLF CLUB
711 Smith Rd., East Amhurst, NY 14051 / (716) 688-5454

BASIC INFORMATION

Course Type: Municipal
Year Built: 1969
Architect: Robert Trent Jones
Local Pro: Mike Clawson

Course: N/A
Holes: 18 / Par 72

Back : 6,730 yds. Rating: 72.4 Slope: 129
Middle: 6,232 yds. Rating: 70.8 Slope: 122
Ladies: 5,561 yds. Rating: 71.9 Slope: 118

Tee Time: 3 days in advance.
Price: $20 - $40

Credit Cards:	■	Restaurant:	■
Driving Range:	■	Lounge:	■
Practice Green:	■	Meeting Rooms:	■
Locker Room:	■	Tennis:	
Rental Clubs:	■	Swimming:	
Walkers:		Jogging Trails:	
Snack Bar:	■	Boating:	

COURSE DESCRIPTION

If you happen to be in Buffalo and you've been searching for an affordable layout that will comfort your thoughts, **Glen Oaks Golf Course** is, without question, one of the best in its class. In 1988, **Golf Digest** magazine placed the course in its prestigious Top 75 Public Courses list for America.

This Robert Trent Jones design beauty will have you playing every shot in your repertoire. You'll find many competitive tournaments held here each year that you may have a chance to play in. Give them a call and ask them about their events.

DIRECTIONS

From Rt. 90 take the Depew Exit (#49) north on Transit Rd. for about 7 miles. Make a left on Smith Rd. and look for the course on your left.

ERIE COUNTY

RIVER OAKS GOLF CLUB
201 Whitehaven Rd., Grand Island, NY 14072 / (716) 773-3336

BASIC INFORMATION

Course Type: Semi-private
Year Built: 1970's
Architect: Desmond Muirhead
Local Pro: Mark Luthringer

Course: N/A
Holes: 18 / Par 72

Back : 7,389 yds. Rating: 75.0 Slope: 129
Middle: 6,588 yds. Rating: 71.0 Slope: 122
Ladies: 5,747 yds. Rating: 70.0 Slope: 118

Tee Time: 2-7 days in advance.
Price: $35 - $42

Credit Cards:	■	Restaurant:	■
Driving Range:	■	Lounge:	■
Practice Green:	■	Meeting Rooms:	■
Locker Room:		Tennis:	
Rental Clubs:	■	Swimming:	
Walkers:	■	Jogging Trails:	
Snack Bar:	■	Boating:	■

COURSE DESCRIPTION
River Oaks Golf Club is one of the most sought after of its kind in the Grand Island, N.Y. area.

At 7,389 yards from the championship tees, this monster is considered to be one of the longest courses in the country. The playing field is mostly open and features a good amount of space to work the ball in several directions among its rolling terrain. Grass moguls are an added hazard that you'll need to negotiate with on most of the holes. Flat lies are a scarcity and you'll be doomed if you don't find a side hill that sends your ball into the rough or worse ... O.B.

DIRECTIONS
Take I-90 south to White Haven Rd. and make a left to the end of the road. Look for the course on your left.

ROTHLAND GOLF COURSE
12089 Clarence Center Rd., Akron, NY 14001 / (716) 542-4325

BASIC INFORMATION

Course Type: Public
Year Built: 1969 / 1973 / 1984
Architect: N/A
Local Pro: Jeff Randall

Course: Red & Gold (18 / Par 72)
Holes: 36

Back : N/A Rating: N/A Slope: N/A
Middle: 6,486 yds. Rating: 69.4 Slope: 115
Ladies: 5,893 yds. Rating: 71.3 Slope: 112

Tee Time: 7 days in advance.
Price: $14 - $17

Credit Cards:		Restaurant:	■
Driving Range:	■	Lounge:	■
Practice Green:	■	Meeting Rooms:	
Locker Room:		Tennis:	
Rental Clubs:	■	Swimming:	
Walkers:	■	Jogging Trails:	
Snack Bar:	■	Boating:	

COURSE DESCRIPTION
All three 9-hole combinations are par-72 layouts. Each of these combinations serve as a good challenge for mid-to-high handicappers and senior citizens alike.

The Red & Gold combination is the preferred layout by better players. It's a strategic design with many generous landing areas for your ball to fall onto following your drives. A casual atmosphere is the rule here, which makes it a fun location to play despite the relative ease of the course.

DIRECTIONS
From Main St. (Rt. 5) turn onto Barnum Rd. This road becomes Clarence Center Rd. approximately 2 1/2 miles further down. Once the name changes, you'll see the course about another 1 1/2 miles further on your right.

SHERIDAN PARK GOLF COURSE
Center Park Dr., Tonawanda, NY 14150 / (716) 875-1811

BASIC INFORMATION

Course Type: Municipal
Year Built: N/A
Architect: N/A
Local Pro: Dennis Rainey

Course: N/A
Holes: 18 / Par 71

Back : N/A	Rating: N/A	Slope: N/A
Middle: 6,534 yds.	Rating: 71.5	Slope: 116
Ladies: 5,656 yds.	Rating: 74.0	Slope: 116

Tee Time: 3 days in advance.
Price: $15 - $18

Credit Cards:	Restaurant:	
Driving Range:	Lounge:	■
Practice Green: ■	Meeting Rooms:	
Locker Room: ■	Tennis:	
Rental Clubs:	Swimming:	
Walkers: ■	Jogging Trails:	
Snack Bar: ■	Boating:	

COURSE DESCRIPTION

The *Sheridan Park Golf Course* is generally recognized as one of the better municipal courses in the area. At Par 71, over 6,534 yards of tight fairways, rolling hills and lots of water, it provides a stiff test to your shot-making ability. You'll need to place your drives onto proper landing areas to get yourself into good position on your following approach shots. These shots are key to playing well here.

The course isn't very long, and if you hit your drives accurately, you'll often have an easy, high-lofted, club in your hands to play your follow-through approach shots.

DIRECTIONS

Take I-290 to the Sheridan Dr. Exit. The course will be on the left side of Sheridan Park Dr.

BATAVIA COUNTRY CLUB
7909 Batavia Byron Rd., Batavia, NY 14020 / (716) 343-7600

BASIC INFORMATION

Course Type: Public
Year Built: 1962
Architect: N/A
Local Pro: N/A

Course: N/A
Holes: 18 / Par 72

Back : 7,134 yds.	Rating: 70.4	Slope: 123
Middle: 6,533 yds.	Rating: 70.2	Slope: 114
Ladies: 5,373 yds.	Rating: 71.1	Slope: 117

Tee Time: 7 days in advance.
Price: $22.00 - $24.00

Credit Cards: ■	Restaurant:	■
Driving Range: ■	Lounge:	■
Practice Green: ■	Meeting Rooms:	■
Locker Room: ■	Tennis:	
Rental Clubs: ■	Swimming:	
Walkers: ■	Jogging Trails:	
Snack Bar: ■	Boating:	■

COURSE DESCRIPTION

Batavia Country Club is a full length championship course that offers a great selection of holes for every type of golfer to enjoy.

Although the wide fairways allow a good amount of space to work your tee-shots, you'll often have to direct them onto specific landing areas for proper position. The 15th hole, a par-4 stretching over 400 yards in length, is the number one handicap hole on the course. It requires a very demanding tee-shot to place the ball on its narrow fairway. Trees come into play on both left and right.

DIRECTIONS

Please call the course for directions.

GENESEE COUNTY

CHESTNUT HILL COUNTRY CLUB
1330 Broadway, Darien, NY 14040 / (716) 547-9699

BASIC INFORMATION

Course Type: Semi-private
Year Built: 1964
Architect: N/A
Local Pro: Billy Kay

Course: N/A
Holes: 18 / Par 72

Back : 6,653 yds. Rating: 72.0 Slope: 119
Middle: 6,437 yds. Rating: 71.0 Slope: 117
Ladies: 5,466 yds. Rating: 70.6 Slope: 115

Tee Time: 10 days in advance.
Price: $15 - $27

Credit Cards:		Restaurant:	■
Driving Range:	■	Lounge:	■
Practice Green:	■	Meeting Rooms:	■
Locker Room:	■	Tennis:	
Rental Clubs:	■	Swimming:	
Walkers:	■	Jogging Trails:	
Snack Bar:	■	Boating:	

COURSE DESCRIPTION
Mid-to-high handicappers will feel right at home on this imaginative layout.

The course is set up to be played aggressively by offering reachable par-5's in two, nice par-4's that require ball placement to get the most out of their doglegs, challenging par-3's, and a host of hazards, strategically placed, to make you step back and think about your following shots.

Don't forget to work on your putting stroke before you play here. Many of the greens feature subtle undulations that make it tough to follow the correct line to the hole.

DIRECTIONS
The course is situated on the corner of Rt. 20 and Rt. 77. Please call for complete directions.

LE ROY COUNTRY CLUB
7759 East Main Rd., Le Roy, NY 14482 / (716) 768-7330

BASIC INFORMATION

Course Type: Semi-private
Year Built: 1920's
Architect: N/A
Local Pro: Ed Mills

Course: N/A
Holes: 18 / Par 72

Back : 6,582 yds. Rating: N/A Slope: N/A
Middle: 6,147 yds. Rating: 67.6 Slope: 107
Ladies: 5,659 yds. Rating: 71.0 Slope: 117

Tee Time: 7 days in advance from Wed.
Price: $13 - $16

Credit Cards:	■	Restaurant:	■
Driving Range:	■	Lounge:	■
Practice Green:	■	Meeting Rooms:	■
Locker Room:	■	Tennis:	
Rental Clubs:	■	Swimming:	■
Walkers:	■	Jogging Trails:	
Snack Bar:	■	Boating:	■

COURSE DESCRIPTION
The old time charisma associated with this course is not easily found anymore. Like many of the courses built during the turn of the century, you'll be playing your drives onto narrow fairways that place an accent on accuracy above distance. If you've positioned your ball properly, you may still have a tough approach towards the many small and elevated greens.

Most compelling of all, is the fact that you'll be playing on a course that has been kept in the same basic order since the day it was built in the '20's.

DIRECTIONS
Take the New York State Thruway to Exit 47 (Le Roy) and follow that to Rt. 19 going south to first set of lights (Rt. 5). Make a left and follow that to the course. It will be on your left.

Page 117

TERRY HILLS GOLF COURSE
5122 Clinton St. Rd., Batavia, NY 14020 / (716) 343-0860

BASIC INFORMATION
Course Type: Public
Year Built: 1936 / 1986
Architect: Ed Ault
Local Pro: Nick Rotundo (Dir. Of Golf)

Course: N/A
Holes: 18 / Par 72

Back : 6,038 yds. Rating: 66.0 Slope: 108
Middle: N/A Rating: N/A Slope: N/A
Ladies: 5,108 yds. Rating: 68.0 Slope: 102

Tee Time: 7 days in advance.
Price: $10 - $18

Credit Cards: ■ Restaurant: ■
Driving Range: ■ Lounge: ■
Practice Green: ■ Meeting Rooms:
Locker Room: Tennis:
Rental Clubs: ■ Swimming:
Walkers: ■ Jogging Trails:
Snack Bar: ■ Boating:

COURSE DESCRIPTION
Terry Hills Golf Course is one of the best kept secrets between Buffalo and Rochester. The beauty of the course lies within the design. Regardless of the fact that the course is only 6,038 yards from the back-tees, you'll be up against a well-planned playing field that has a tendency of creeping up on players who choose to play full bore without thought. It's a strategic design that allows several options on most of the tees.

Better players enjoy the short game that is inherent in its design.

DIRECTIONS
Take the New York State Thruway to Exit 48 and go one mile east of Batavia on Rt. 33 east.

BARBERLEA GOLF COURSE
P.O. Box 878, Nunda, NY 14517 / (716) 468-2116

BASIC INFORMATION
Course Type: Public
Year Built: 1966 / 1985
Architect: Freeman Barber / March Bros.
Local Pro: Scott Brother

Course: N/A
Holes: 18 / Par 69

Back : 5,800 yds. Rating: 69.5 Slope: 110
Middle: N/A Rating: N/A Slope: N/A
Ladies: 4,800 yds. Rating: 70.5 Slope: 110

Tee Time: 7 days in advance.
Price: $12 - $14

Credit Cards: ■ Restaurant: ■
Driving Range: ■ Lounge: ■
Practice Green: ■ Meeting Rooms: ■
Locker Room: ■ Tennis: ■
Rental Clubs: ■ Swimming: ■
Walkers: ■ Jogging Trails: ■
Snack Bar: ■ Boating: ■

COURSE DESCRIPTION
From beginning to end, the driving factor that motivates people to play this course is its relaxed atmosphere. It's an easy course, both on the front-nine and the back-nine, and would most likely appeal to an older crowd; short on distance, but still encouraged to experience a nice sports outing among friends.

If you happen to be new to the game, this course may be the perfect venue to overcome any golfing inhibitons you may have. You'll love the fact that each hole is a short distance, which will ultimately help you get the ball in the cup much quicker.

DIRECTIONS
Take I-390 to the Mount Morris Exit and make a left onto Rt. 408. The course will be 20 miles further on your right.

LIMA GOLF & COUNTRY CLUB

2681 Plank Rd., Rt. 15A, Lima, NY 14485 / (716) 624-1490

BASIC INFORMATION

Course Type: Semi-private
Year Built: 1962
Architect: The Checo Family
Local Pro: N/A

Course: N/A
Holes: 18 / Par 72

Back : 6,768 yds. Rating: 74.2 Slope: N/A
Middle: 6,338 yds. Rating: 72.3 Slope: 115
Ladies: 5,624 yds. Rating: 74.2 Slope: N/A

Tee Time: 7 days in advance.
Price: $12 - $16.50

Credit Cards:		Restaurant:	■
Driving Range:	■	Lounge:	■
Practice Green:	■	Meeting Rooms:	■
Locker Room:	■	Tennis:	
Rental Clubs:	■	Swimming:	
Walkers:	■	Jogging Trails:	
Snack Bar:	■	Boating:	■

COURSE DESCRIPTION

The *Lima Golf & Country Club* posts a commanding fight against par. It's the type of course that will force you to play every club in your bag by the end of a given round. So don't forget to bring your most trusted weapons.

The management assured me that Lima will have an additional nine holes built by the end of 1994 and a complete championship sister course by the end of 1995. This is surely a place to enjoy the game to its fullest. You've got to cheer any establishment that's thinking about their clientele, by progressing right along with the game's popularity.

DIRECTIONS

On Rt. 15 A, you'll need to go 2 1/2 miles south of Rt. 5/20.

LIVINGSTON COUNTRY CLUB

Rt. 20A, Geneseo, NY 14454 / (716) 243-4430

BASIC INFORMATION

Course Type: Semi-private
Year Built: 1928
Architect: Semour Dunn
Local Pro: Jeff Kaye

Course: N/A
Holes: 18 / Par 72

Back : 6,573 yds. Rating: 71.0 Slope: 119
Middle: 6,193 yds. Rating: 69.5 Slope: 116
Ladies: 5,163 yds. Rating: 70.1 Slope: 118

Tee Time: 7 days in advance.
Price: $13 - $18

Credit Cards:	■	Restaurant:	■
Driving Range:	■	Lounge:	■
Practice Green:	■	Meeting Rooms:	
Locker Room:	■	Tennis:	
Rental Clubs:		Swimming:	
Walkers:	■	Jogging Trails:	
Snack Bar:		Boating:	■

COURSE DESCRIPTION

Livingston Country Club is located in the beautiful Finger Lakes region of New York. The course is laid out to challenge golfers of many different abilities. The playing field rolls over gullies and features a good assortment of mature trees that add natural beauty to the spectacular views of Genesee Valley.

You'll be challenged by two 450 yard par-4's, and teased by two well-constructed par-3's. All in all, the course has a good variety of par-5's, too — in its repertoire of fine holes.

DIRECTIONS

Located on Rt. 20A, 2-miles west of the Interstate, Rt. 390 (Exit 8), on the south side of the road. The course is only 30 minutes from Rochester.

OLD HICKORY GOLF CLUB

6653 Bigtree Rd., Livonia, NY 14487 / (716) 346-2450

BASIC INFORMATION

Course Type: Semi-private
Year Built: 1990
Architect: Pete Craig
Local Pro: Bob King

Course: N/A
Holes: 18 / Par 72

Back : 6,700 yds. Rating: 70.5 Slope: 116
Middle: 6,300 yds. Rating: 69.0 Slope: 112
Ladies: 5,400 yds. Rating: 70.7 Slope: 111

Tee Time: 2 days in advance.
Price: $13 - $14

Credit Cards:		Restaurant:	
Driving Range:	■	Lounge:	
Practice Green:	■	Meeting Rooms:	
Locker Room:	■	Tennis:	
Rental Clubs:	■	Swimming:	
Walkers:	■	Jogging Trails:	
Snack Bar:	■	Boating:	■

COURSE DESCRIPTION

Old Hickory Golf Club captures the essence of golf by allowing a wide margin of players a chance to score par. If you're a mid-to-high handicapper, one of the tees will surely accommodate your type of play, in a challenging manner.

What you'll be up against is a sweeping charge of rolling terrain with water coming into play on six holes. It makes for a very interesting day at the links. Many of the trees featured on the course are still a little immature and have lot of growth still left for them in their future, but you'll be surprised at how many will actually come into play on errant shots. Good luck!

DIRECTIONS

Take Hwy. 390 south to Rt. 15 and continue south to Livonia. Make a right at Big Tree Rd. and look for the course on your right.

WHISPERING HILLS GOLF CLUB

1 Pine Alley, Conesus, NY 14435 / (716) 346-2100

BASIC INFORMATION

Course Type: Semi-private
Year Built: 1985
Architect: Joe Checho
Local Pro: Joe Checho

Course: N/A
Holes: 18 / Par 71

Back : 6,503 yds. Rating: N/A Slope: N/A
Middle: 6,058 yds. Rating: N/A Slope: N/A
Ladies: N/A Rating: N/A Slope: N/A

Tee Time: 4 days in advance.
Price: $24 - $25

Credit Cards:		Restaurant:	
Driving Range:	■	Lounge:	■
Practice Green:	■	Meeting Rooms:	■
Locker Room:		Tennis:	
Rental Clubs:	■	Swimming:	
Walkers:	■	Jogging Trails:	
Snack Bar:	■	Boating:	■

COURSE DESCRIPTION

If you enjoy playing courses with an understated feel to them – the type that actually look a lot easier than they actually play; the type that won't demolish you if you haven't developed the skill to hit a golf ball a long way; the type that make you want to take up a new challenge ... then *Whispering Hills Golf Club* awaits you with open arms.

It's a great challenge for mid-to-high handicappers, but if you hold a single digit, the course may not be enough of a challenge for you. Nevertheless, it does offer a good balance of hole designs to get a good short game workout.

DIRECTIONS

Coming west on "80", go north on US-395 and go right off the W. McCarren exit. Make a left on Sullivan Lane to the course.

BRAEMAR COUNTRY CLUB
4704 Ridge Rd. West, Spencerport, NY 14559 / (716) 544-3090

BASIC INFORMATION

Course Type: Semi-private
Year Built: 1928-1967
Architect: N/A
Local Pro: Jon Buttaro Jr

Course: N/A
Holes: 18 / Par 72

Back : 6,767 yds. Rating: 71.4 Slope: 121
Middle: 6,409 yds. Rating: 69.7 Slope: 117
Ladies: 5,428 yds. Rating: 70.2 Slope: 113

Tee Time: 4 days from Tuesday.
Price: $15 - $18

Credit Cards:		Restaurant:	■
Driving Range:	■	Lounge:	■
Practice Green:	■	Meeting Rooms:	■
Locker Room:	■	Tennis:	
Rental Clubs:	■	Swimming:	
Walkers:	■	Jogging Trails:	
Snack Bar:	■	Boating:	■

COURSE DESCRIPTION

Braemar Country Club has two distinctive halves that are well worth the adventure. The first nine will take you on a ride back to the late 1920's, when architects felt compelled to build courses with narrow fairways and demandingly small greens. The second, built in the late 1960's, will take you on a *groovy* ride you'll want to experience more than just once.

In unison, you'll find both sides of the course equally compelling and fun to play.

DIRECTIONS

Take the New York State Thruway to Exit 546 north to Hwy 490, west to Spencer Port Lane and make a right to Manite Rd. Make another right to Ridge Rd. and a left towards the course. It will be on your right.

BROCKPORT COUNTRY CLUB
3739 Monroe Orleans, Brockport, NY 14420 / (716) 638-5334

BASIC INFORMATION

Course Type: Semi-private
Year Built: 1970's
Architect: Joe Bosso
Local Pro: Bill Hoock

Course: N/A
Holes: 18 / Par 72

Back : 6,382 yds. Rating: 70.4 Slope: 115
Middle: 5,932 yds. Rating: 68.6 Slope: 113
Ladies: 5,045 yds. Rating: 72.0 Slope: 112

Tee Time: 7 days in advance.
Price: $15 - $18

Credit Cards:		Restaurant:	■
Driving Range:		Lounge:	■
Practice Green:	■	Meeting Rooms:	■
Locker Room:	■	Tennis:	
Rental Clubs:	■	Swimming:	
Walkers:	■	Jogging Trails:	
Snack Bar:	■	Boating:	

COURSE DESCRIPTION

Brockport Country Club presents a nice outline for a comfortable day of golf. The course isn't particularly hard to play, but it is a nice place to experience the joys of sportsmanship.

The front-nine plays a little more difficult than the back-nine because of its length, and often because of severe winds. Unlike the front-nine, the back-nine features a nice rolling terrain, some water, sand, and more!

If you're a mid-to-low handicapper, give this course a chance. You'll enjoy your birds and pars after the game.

DIRECTIONS

From Rochester, take Rt. 104 to Rt. 272 and make a left towards the course. You'll see it on both sides of the road.

CHILI COUNTRY CLUB
760 Scottsville Chili Rd., Scottsville, NY 14546 / (716) 889-9325

BASIC INFORMATION

Course Type: Semi-private
Year Built: 1919
Architect: N/A
Local Pro: Vince Pompa

Course: N/A
Holes: 18 / Par 72

Back   : 6,628 yds. Rating: 71.7 Slope: 117
Middle: 6,253 yds. Rating: 69.6 Slope: 113
Ladies: 5,498 yds. Rating: 70.4 Slope: 110

Tee Time: 7 days in advance.
Price: $10 - $15

Credit Cards: ■   Restaurant: ■
Driving Range: ■   Lounge: ■
Practice Green: ■   Meeting Rooms:
Locker Room: ■   Tennis:
Rental Clubs: ■   Swimming:
Walkers: ■   Jogging Trails:
Snack Bar: ■   Boating:

COURSE DESCRIPTION

The *Chili Country Club* is a beautiful test of golf with many difficult par-3's. Local folks enjoy playing this course for its well-kept greens.

The playing field features a good mixture of hills and flat areas to work your ball around. Both nines offer a level challenge that's evenly distributed throughout the course. You'll find yourself having to play both a draw and a fade en route to a low score. The playing field is neatly tucked in a secluded area adorned with many beautiful trees that you'll often have to play around.

DIRECTIONS

From Rochester, take 490 west to Exit 5 (Chili Center), go right off the Exit to Rt. 386 south. Follow the signs to the course. It will be about 7 miles further.

CHURCHVILLE GOLF CLUB
Kendall Rd., Churchville, NY 14428 / (716) 293-9906

BASIC INFORMATION

Course Type: Public
Year Built: 1920's
Architect: N/A
Local Pro: Paul Schojan

Course: Old Course (18 / Par 72)
Holes: 27

Back   : 6,671 yds. Rating: 69.8 Slope: 105
Middle: N/A   Rating: N/A   Slope: N/A
Ladies: 6,092 yds. Rating: 72.0 Slope: N/A

Tee Time: 1 day in advance.
Price: $12 - $13

Credit Cards: ■   Restaurant: ■
Driving Range: Lounge:
Practice Green: ■   Meeting Rooms: ■
Locker Room: ■   Tennis:
Rental Clubs: ■   Swimming:
Walkers: ■   Jogging Trails:
Snack Bar: ■   Boating: ■

COURSE DESCRIPTION

You shouldn't be looking for Augusta National at the *Churchville Golf Club*. This is not the type of challenge that's featured each week on the PGA Tour.

If you're going to play this course, be prepared for a simple, straightforward layout, one that doesn't have too many hazards to baffle you or stifle your progress. High-handicappers will find it most appealing because of the many wide fairways that the course features. It's also built on a relatively flat surface, which shouldn't affect the lie of your ball if you hit your drives onto the generously wide fairways.

DIRECTIONS

Drive in an easterly direction to Hwy. 490 and get off at the Churchville Exit heading north. Make your second left to Kendall Rd. and look for the course on your left.

MONROE COUNTY

CRAGIE BRAE GOLF CLUB
4391 Union St., Scottsville, NY 14546 / (716) 889-1440

BASIC INFORMATION

Course Type: Public
Year Built: 1963
Architect: Harrison
Local Pro: N/A

Course: N/A
Holes: 18 / Par 72

Back : 6,468 yds. Rating: N/A   Slope: N/A
Middle: 6,230 yds. Rating: 68.3 Slope: 103
Ladies: 5,930 yds. Rating: 69.0 Slope: 105

Tee Time: 1 day in advance.
Price: $9 - $12

Credit Cards:	Restaurant:	■
Driving Range:	Lounge:	
Practice Green: ■	Meeting Rooms:	
Locker Room:	Tennis:	
Rental Clubs: ■	Swimming:	
Walkers: ■	Jogging Trails:	
Snack Bar: ■	Boating:	■

COURSE DESCRIPTION
Cragie Brae Golf Club owes its character to the many grass bunkers featured throughout its layout. If you've never experienced hitting a ball out of a grass bunker, you'll be surprised at how difficult it can really be to get out of. It's almost like playing your ball out of a terribly bad lie.

You won't find any water lurking in the horizon or any sand along the fairways and greens. The course is just a simple challenge that is pure and simple from beginning to end. Bring along your favorite fade shot!

DIRECTIONS
Take the New York State Thruway to LeRoy (Exit 46) and follow that to the 490 Expressway east to Exit 5 and make a right towards the course. Look for it on your right.

DEERFIELD COUNTRY CLUB
100 Craig Hill Dr., Brockport, NY 14420 / (716) 392-8080

BASIC INFORMATION

Course Type: Semi-private
Year Built: 1963
Architect: Peter Craig
Local Pro: Michael S. McGillicuddy (Director)

Course: North & South (18 / Par 72)
Holes: 27

Back : 7,083 yds. Rating: 73.9 Slope: 138
Middle: 6,704 yds. Rating: 71.9 Slope: 134
Ladies: 5,623 yds. Rating: 72.4 Slope: 124

Tee Time: 5 days in advance.
Price: $18 - $21

Credit Cards: ■	Restaurant:	■
Driving Range: ■	Lounge:	■
Practice Green: ■	Meeting Rooms:	■
Locker Room: ■	Tennis:	
Rental Clubs: ■	Swimming:	
Walkers: ■	Jogging Trails:	
Snack Bar: ■	Boating:	

COURSE DESCRIPTION
The North & South combination is a monster of a course just waiting for someone to tame her. It's also one of the few courses in Brockport that could easily host a PGA event — if it was asked to.

At a length of 7,083 yards from the championship tees, with a slope rating of 138, this course will undoubtedly be too much of a challenge for double-digit handicappers, and should be played from the middle-tees, which incidentally are quite difficult too. Bring your best draw and fade, get to the course early to practice your swing, and make sure your putting game is line for its large greens.

DIRECTIONS
Follow 104 west off of Hwy. 390. Look for the sign that will lead you to the club. Take a right on Clarkson-Parma Town Rd. and look for the course 2 miles further on your left.

DURAND EASTMAN GOLF CLUB

1200 Kings Hwy. North, Rochester, NY 14617 / (716) 266-8364

BASIC INFORMATION

Course Type: Public
Year Built: 1933
Architect: Robert Trent Jones
Local Pro: Terry Decker

Course: N/A
Holes: 18 / Par 70

Back : 6,089 yds. Rating: 68.8 Slope: 112
Middle: N/A   Rating: N/A   Slope: N/A
Ladies: 5,717 yds. Rating: 71.7 Slope: 113

Tee Time: 1 day in advance.
Price: $8 - $13

Credit Cards:		Restaurant:	
Driving Range:		Lounge:	
Practice Green:	■	Meeting Rooms:	
Locker Room:		Tennis:	
Rental Clubs:	■	Swimming:	
Walkers:	■	Jogging Trails:	
Snack Bar:	■	Boating:	■

COURSE DESCRIPTION

The *Durand Eastman Golf Club* is a pleasant course that owes its overall challenge to the many creeks that run along its terrain. The venue features a wide variety of hole designs that will challenge high-handicappers in their best form.

You won't find a single bunker on this playing field to alter your position towards the green. It makes for an interesting environment to practice your ability to hit bump-and-run shots to the hole. The front-nine seems as though it was cut right out of a forest. Most of the holes favor a draw.

DIRECTIONS

Take Rt. 590 north and follow it towards Lake Ontario to Lake Shore Blvd. Make a left and that will take you directly to the course.

EAGLE VALE GOLF COURSE

4400 Nine Mile Point Rd., Fairport, NY 14450 / (716) 377-5200

BASIC INFORMATION

Course Type: Public
Year Built: 1987
Architect: N/A
Local Pro: John Quinzi Jr.

Course: N/A
Holes: 18 / Par 71

Back : 6,932 yds. Rating: 70.9 Slope: 123
Middle: 6,244 yds. Rating: 69.0 Slope: 117
Ladies: 5,415 yds. Rating: 72.8 Slope: 120

Tee Time: 1-30 days in advance.
Price: $20 - $30

Credit Cards:	■	Restaurant:	■
Driving Range:	■	Lounge:	■
Practice Green:	■	Meeting Rooms:	■
Locker Room:	■	Tennis:	
Rental Clubs:	■	Swimming:	
Walkers:		Jogging Trails:	
Snack Bar:	■	Boating:	■

COURSE DESCRIPTION

Eagle Vale Golf Course meanders through natural wetlands and wooded areas, yet it also features a number of linksland type holes too.

Most players will feel comfortable playing from the middle-tees, but if you happen to be a low-handicapper, you'll enjoy the boxing for par from the championship tees. The course also features an excellent drainage system that helps the staff keep it in excellent shape. You'll find the front nine playing about a stroke more difficult than the rest of the playing field, leaving you with a pretty level challenge of golf throughout an array of interesting holes.

DIRECTIONS

Take Rt. 441 east to Rt. 250 south and look for the course on your left.

GENESEE VALLEY GOLF CLUB

100 East River Rd., Rochester, NY 14623 / (716) 424-2920

BASIC INFORMATION

Course Type: Public
Year Built: 1900's
Architect: N/A
Local Pro: Jack Tindale

Course: Old Course (18 / Par 72)
Holes: 36

Back : 6,374 yds. Rating:69.3 Slope: 104
Middle: N/A   Rating: N/A Slope: N/A
Ladies: 5,961 yds. Rating: 73.2 Slope: 112

Tee Time: 1 day in advance.
Price: $12 - $13

Credit Cards:	Restaurant:
Driving Range:	Lounge:
Practice Green: ■	Meeting Rooms:
Locker Room: ■	Tennis:
Rental Clubs: ■	Swimming:
Walkers: ■	Jogging Trails:
Snack Bar: ■	Boating: ■

COURSE DESCRIPTION

There isn't much to worry about on this course. It's a straight challenge that's easily understood, even for a first-time player. It's a great course for beginners to learn the game. You won't find a tree or sand bunker blocking your way to a par.

You also won't have to worry about uneven lies on this course. It features a steadily flat terrain, which makes it easy to keep the ball in play off your drives.

DIRECTIONS

Take the 390 Expressway south to Exit 16 (E. River Rd.) and make a right. The course will be about another mile on your right.

LAKE SHORE COUNTRY CLUB

1165 Greenleaf Rd., Rochester, NY 14212 / (716) 663-0300

BASIC INFORMATION

Course Type: Semi-private
Year Built: 1932
Architect: Calvin Black
Local Pro: Lynn Weilacher

Course: Lake Shore (18 / Par 70)
Holes: 36

Back : 6,343 yds. Rating: 69.0 Slope: 121
Middle: 5,767 yds. Rating: 67.2 Slope: 116
Ladies: 5,561 yds. Rating: 72.0 Slope: 117

Tee Time: First come, first serve.
Price: $10 - $20

Credit Cards: ■	Restaurant: ■
Driving Range: ■	Lounge: ■
Practice Green: ■	Meeting Rooms: ■
Locker Room: ■	Tennis:
Rental Clubs:	Swimming:
Walkers: ■	Jogging Trails:
Snack Bar: ■	Boating: ■

COURSE DESCRIPTION

Lake Shore Country Club offers a relatively easy layout that most golfers will feel comfortable playing. The fairways offer plenty of room to work the ball in several directions from the majority of the tees.

At only 6,343 yards from the championship tees, you don't have to be a power hitter to play well. This is much more of a finesse type of course that you'll want attack with a 3-wood off the tees, which will give you added accuracy, and, on most occasions, will leave you with an easy short-iron approach.

DIRECTIONS

Take 390 to its' end. Take Parkway east to Greenleaf Rd. Turn left on Greenleaf Rd. and go one mile further to the course, which will be on your right.

SALMON CREEK COUNTRY CLUB

355 Washington St., Spencerport, NY 14559 / (716) 352-4300

BASIC INFORMATION

Course Type: Semi-private
Year Built: 1960's
Architect: N/A
Local Pro: Jack Schuth

Course: N/A
Holes: 18 / Par 72

Back : 6,200 yds. Rating: 68.8 Slope: 118
Middle: N/A Rating: N/A Slope: N/A
Ladies: 5,500 yds. Rating: 70.9 Slope: 114

Tee Time: 7 days in advance.
Price: $17 - $20

Credit Cards:	■	Restaurant:	■
Driving Range:	■	Lounge:	■
Practice Green:	■	Meeting Rooms:	■
Locker Room:	■	Tennis:	■
Rental Clubs:	■	Swimming:	■
Walkers:	■	Jogging Trails:	■
Snack Bar:	■	Boating:	■

COURSE DESCRIPTION

Salmon Creek Country Club has fooled many golfers into thinking that it's a much easier layout than it actually is.

The subtle contours of the hilly terrain can be quite demanding at times, often requiring a shot from an uneven lie. Most of the holes tend to favor a draw over a fade. But don't despair if you're a fader: despite the shape of these holes and the many trees that surround the course, the fairways do allow a good amount of room to work the ball in both directions. Many people feel compelled to come back for another try; many feel they should have played better!

DIRECTIONS

The course is situated between Rt. 31 & Rt. 104. Please call for exact directions.

SHADOW LAKE GOLF CLUB

1850 Five Mile Line Rd., Penfield, NY 14526 / (716) 385-2010

BASIC INFORMATION

Course Type: Public
Year Built: 1978
Architect: Pete Craig
Local Pro: Don Richards

Course: N/A
Holes: 18 / Par 71

Back : 6,164 yds. Rating: 68.5 Slope: 111
Middle: N/A Rating: N/A Slope: N/A
Ladies: 5,498 yds. Rating: 70.5 Slope: 112

Tee Time: 1-5 days in advance.
Price: $11.50 - $32

Credit Cards:	■	Restaurant:	■
Driving Range:		Lounge:	■
Practice Green:	■	Meeting Rooms:	
Locker Room:	■	Tennis:	■
Rental Clubs:	■	Swimming:	
Walkers:	■	Jogging Trails:	
Snack Bar:	■	Boating:	■

COURSE DESCRIPTION

Shadow Lake Golf Club offers a respectable playing field that is well attuned to the needs of a mid-to-high handicapper. It's an open course with water coming into play on the following holes: 5,6,7, and 9.

The number one handicap hole on the course happens to be the first, and when you're looking out towards the fairway, you'll see its flag sitting 539 yards to the green. You'll be forced to hit a good drive to stay clear of the two opposing fairway bunkers that hole features.

DIRECTIONS

From New York, take the New York State Thruway (Hwy. 90) west to Exit 45 (Rochester) and go north on Hwy. 390 to the Browncroft Exit, where you'll need to make a right. The course is approximately 5 miles further on the right.

SHADOW PINES GOLF CLUB

600 Whalen Rd., Penfield, NY 14526 / (716) 385-8550

BASIC INFORMATION

Course Type: Public
Year Built: 1983
Architect: N/A
Local Pro: Mark Regan & Don Richards

Course: N/A
Holes: 18 / Par 72

Back : 6,741 yds. Rating: 72.1 Slope: 119
Middle: 6,400 yds. Rating: 70.1 Slope: 121
Ladies: 5,437 yds. Rating: 73.1 Slope: 124

Tee Time: Anytime between Tues. and Sun.
Price: $22.50 - $32

Credit Cards:	■	Restaurant:	■
Driving Range:	■	Lounge:	■
Practice Green:	■	Meeting Rooms:	■
Locker Room:	■	Tennis:	
Rental Clubs:	■	Swimming:	
Walkers:	■	Jogging Trails:	
Snack Bar:	■	Boating:	

COURSE DESCRIPTION

Shadow Pines Golf Club is flexible enough to challenge low- and high-handicappers alike. It's a scenic venue that plays 6,741 yards from the championship tees and features many exciting holes.

Once you take the turn onto the back-nine, you'll need to sharpen game skills considerably; that is, if you haven't been playing a good game up to that point. It's unquestionably the toughest combination of holes. Tight fairways and dense foliage make it tough to play aggressively. In addition, four holes feature water coming into the play of action.

DIRECTIONS

Take Hwy. 590 north. When you get to Browncroft Rd., make a right and follow that to Whalen Rd. where you'll need to make another right to the course. Look for the course on your right.

TWIN HILLS GOLF COURSE

5719 Ridge Rd. West, Spencerport, NY 14559 / (716) 352-4800

BASIC INFORMATION

Course Type: Public
Year Built: 1970
Architect: Pete Craig
Local Pro: N/A

Course: N/A
Holes: 18 / Par 71

Back : 6,300 yds. Rating: 69.1 Slope: 110
Middle: 6,000 yds. Rating: 67.8 Slope: 108
Ladies: 5,200 yds. Rating: 70.4 Slope: N/A

Tee Time: 1 day in advance.
Price: $15 - $20

Credit Cards:		Restaurant:	
Driving Range:	■	Lounge:	■
Practice Green:	■	Meeting Rooms:	
Locker Room:	■	Tennis:	
Rental Clubs:	■	Swimming:	
Walkers:	■	Jogging Trails:	
Snack Bar:	■	Boating:	

COURSE DESCRIPTION

Twin Hills Golf Course is a good platform for mid-to-high handicappers to enjoy. At only 6,300 yards from the back-tees, most golfers rarely feel intimidated by the course and find the distance of each hole a comfort to play through.

The course requires accuracy above distance. It's often a difficult task to get your ball rolling on the tight fairways from the tees. You should consider playing a 3-wood for increased spin and added control. The course also features a good amount of water, sand, and plenty of trees.

DIRECTIONS

From Rochester, take Hwy. 490 west to Exit 8 and make a right onto Manator Rd. followed by a left onto Rt. 104. Look for the course about 5 1/2 miles further on your left.

WEBSTER GOLF COURSE
440 Salt Rd., Webster, NY 14580 / (716) 265-1920

BASIC INFORMATION
Course Type: Semi-private
Year Built: 1956
Architect: N/A
Local Pro: Bob Mackowsky

Course: East (18 / Par 71)
Holes: 36

Back : 6,900 yds. Rating: N/A Slope: N/A
Middle: 6,466 yds. Rating: 71.4 Slope: 115
Ladies: 5,800 yds. Rating: 73.0 Slope: 121

Tee Time: 1 day in advance.
Price: $17 - $19

Credit Cards: Restaurant: ■
Driving Range: ■   Lounge: ■
Practice Green: ■   Meeting Rooms: ■
Locker Room: ■   Tennis:
Rental Clubs: ■   Swimming:
Walkers: ■   Jogging Trails:
Snack Bar: ■   Boating: ■

COURSE DESCRIPTION
This course is really quite unusual in its design and use of materials. A common characteristic that it shares with many other courses built during our country's first six decades is its use of small greens, the type that will force you to hit pinpoint accurate approach shots to get close the pin. You'll also find a wide variety of grass bunkers. If you've never experienced playing out of one, don't be judgmental until you do. An unusual lie and stance is not uncommon, and you'll often need to manufacture a swing you've never used before. They can be drastically unforgiving.

DIRECTIONS
Take Hwy.104 east to Rochester to the Salt Exit and go north to the course. It will be on your right.

WILDWOOD COUNTRY CLUB
1201 West Rush, NY 14543 / (716) 344-5860

BASIC INFORMATION
Course Type: Semi-private
Year Built: N/A
Architect: N/A
Local Pro: Mike Judy

Course: N/A
Holes: 18 / Par 71

Back : 6,431 yds. Rating: 70.2 Slope: 120
Middle: 6,140 yds. Rating: 68.8 Slope: 118
Ladies: 5,368 yds. Rating: 70.1 Slope: 116

Tee Time: 1 day in advance.
Price: $18 - $40

Credit Cards: ■   Restaurant: ■
Driving Range: ■   Lounge:
Practice Green: ■   Meeting Rooms: ■
Locker Room: ■   Tennis:
Rental Clubs: ■   Swimming:
Walkers: ■   Jogging Trails:
Snack Bar: ■   Boating:

COURSE DESCRIPTION
Wildwood Country Club is a course with many fine qualities to enjoy. It's not a long course, and so will appeal mostly to mid-to-high handicappers.

The terrain is hilly in its nature and with the front-nine being the more open side of the course. Once you cross over to the 10th tee, you'll quickly notice the fairways tightening up, adding pressure to your drives and forcing you to be a little more accurate.

Many of the greens are of different shapes and sizes. It's imperative that you stroke the ball well with your putter, for the subtle undulations along their surfaces make two putting difficult at times.

DIRECTIONS
Please call for directions.

DEERWOOD GOLF COURSE

1818 Sweeny St., N. Tonawanda, NY 14120 / (716)

BASIC INFORMATION

Course Type: Public
Year Built: 1975
Architect: Russell Tyron
Local Pro: Barney Bell

Course: N/A
Holes: 18 / Par 72

Back : 6,948 yds. Rating: 73.0 Slope: 117
Middle: 6,752 yds. Rating: 72.0 Slope: 115
Ladies: 6,150 yds. Rating: 75.0 Slope: 123

Tee Time: 1 day in advance.
Price: $10.25 - $18.75

Credit Cards:		Restaurant:	■
Driving Range:	■	Lounge:	■
Practice Green:	■	Meeting Rooms:	■
Locker Room:		Tennis:	
Rental Clubs:		Swimming:	
Walkers:	■	Jogging Trails:	
Snack Bar:	■	Boating:	■

COURSE DESCRIPTION

Deerwood Golf Course is terrific for long-hitters who are short on accuracy but enjoy hitting the ball with all that they have for the sheer joy of it. It's also a good challenge for other types of players from the middle-tees.

The fairways are wide and generous, always allowing a fair margin of error without punishing a player too severely on their following shots. You can choose to work the ball as a draw or a fade on the majority of the holes.

DIRECTIONS

Take Exit. 290 west at Niagara Falls Blvd. and get on Rt. 62. Go north to Robinson St. and make a left until you get to Sweeney St. Make a left and look for the course on your right.

HYDE PARK GOLF COURSE

4343 Porter Rd., Niagara Falls, NY 14305 / (716) 297-2067

BASIC INFORMATION

Course Type: Public
Year Built: 1910
Architect: N/A
Local Pro: Kenneth J. Ruggiero

Course: North (18 / Par 70)
Holes: 36

Back : 6,400 yds. Rating: 69.0 Slope: 110
Middle: N/A Rating: N/A Slope: N/A
Ladies: N/A Rating: N/A Slope: N/A

Tee Time: First come, first serve.
Price: Please call to confirm.

Credit Cards:		Restaurant:	■
Driving Range:	■	Lounge:	■
Practice Green:	■	Meeting Rooms:	
Locker Room:	■	Tennis:	■
Rental Clubs:	■	Swimming:	
Walkers:	■	Jogging Trails:	
Snack Bar:	■	Boating:	■

COURSE DESCRIPTION

Hyde Park Golf Course is a simple design with very little trouble between its tees and greens. Once played, you'll come to the conclusion that it neither favors a draw nor a fade. Each hole seems to continue on a relatively even level of difficulty without much change to the individuality and character between each of them.

High handicappers should find this level of golf a good exercise to strengthen their psychological ability, for its relative ease of play lends itself to many low scoring rounds of golf.

DIRECTIONS

Take I-90 (New York Interstate) off at Packard Rd. one block to Porter Rd. Make a left on Porter and the course will be about a mile further. You'll see it on both sides of the road.

NIAGARA COUNTRY GOLF COURSE
314 Davison Rd., Lockport, NY 14094 / (716) 434-6669

BASIC INFORMATION
Course Type: Public
Year Built: N/A
Architect: N/A
Local Pro: Dave Jason

Course: N/A
Holes: 18 / Par 72

Back : 6,464 yds. Rating: 69.3 Slope: 108
Middle: N/A   Rating: N/A   Slope: N/A
Ladies: 5,182 yds. Rating: 68.5 Slope: 108

Tee Time: First come, first serve.
Price: $11 - $12

Credit Cards:		Restaurant:	■
Driving Range:	■	Lounge:	■
Practice Green:	■	Meeting Rooms:	■
Locker Room:	■	Tennis:	
Rental Clubs:	■	Swimming:	
Walkers:	■	Jogging Trails:	
Snack Bar:	■	Boating:	■

COURSE DESCRIPTION
Niagara Country Golf Course offers amateur-level golf that should inspire mid-to-high handicappers to play their best.

You won't have to worry about having to hit from uneven lies on your approach shots, because the majority of the course is built on a level and flat terrain that makes it easy to hit the ball with confidence – the type of confidence you'll need to get the ball close to the pin on many of the large greens.

A well structured short-game is needed to score a low numbered round.

DIRECTIONS
Take Rt. 78 to Transit Rd. and make a right to Lincolin Ave. Follow that to the third set of lights where you'll need to make a left onto Davidson Rd. Look for the course on your right.

NIAGARA ORLEANS COUNTRY CLUB
Telegraph Rd., Middleport, NY 14105/ (716) 735-9000

BASIC INFORMATION
Course Type: Public
Year Built: 1931
Architect: N/A
Local Pro: Dan Graney

Course: N/A
Holes: 18 / Par 71

Back : 6,013 yds. Rating: 65.0 Slope: 106
Middlo: N/A   Rating: N/A   Slope: N/A
Ladies: 5,097 yds. Rating: 70.0 Slope: 105

Tee Time: 1 day in advance.
Price: $18 - $23

Credit Cards:		Restaurant:	■
Driving Range:		Lounge:	■
Practice Green:	■	Meeting Rooms:	■
Locker Room:	■	Tennis:	
Rental Clubs:	■	Swimming:	
Walkers:	■	Jogging Trails:	
Snack Bar:	■	Boating:	

COURSE DESCRIPTION
If you happen to be a mid-to-high handi-capper and you're in the mood to play a course that isn't too difficult, the **Niagara Orleans Country Club** is just that.

You'll be playing along a rolling surface that propels you towards small traditionally-designed greens. Playing well here usually consists of hitting the ball with a certain amount of finesse to get it rolling close to the pin. The hardest challenge on the course is hole number 2. This par-4 measures 400 yards in length and requires a 240 yard uphill drive for position. Your second shot will be anywhere from a 5-iron to a 7-iron, downhill to the green.

DIRECTIONS
Please call the course for directions.

OAK RUN GOLF CLUB
4185 Lake Avenue, Lockport, NY 14094 / (716) 434-8851

BASIC INFORMATION

Course Type: Public
Year Built: 1989
Architect: Joe O'Shoaughnessy
Local Pro: Tom Yeager

Course: N/A
Holes: 18 / Par 70

Back : 6,400 yds. Rating: 70.5 Slope: 115
Middle: 6,100 yds. Rating: 68.0 Slope: 108
Ladies: 5,100 yds. Rating: 68.0 Slope: 109

Tee Time: 1-4 days in advance.
Price: $8 - $16

Credit Cards:	■	Restaurant:	■
Driving Range:		Lounge:	■
Practice Green:	■	Meeting Rooms:	
Locker Room:		Tennis:	
Rental Clubs:	■	Swimming:	
Walkers:	■	Jogging Trails:	
Snack Bar:	■	Boating:	■

COURSE DESCRIPTION

Oak Run Golf Club is a fine establishment that best serves mid-to-high handicappers. It's not a difficult course, and, because of the relative short distance of each hole, you'll often find yourself in an opportunity to make par or better. It's a great course to build self-confidence.

The 16th hole is the hardest test on the course. This interesting par-4 features 360 yards of real-estate towards the pin. It's a straight hole that demands a nicely placed drive to the middle portion of the fairway. The longer the better, for a creek wraps around the green at a distance of only ten yards.

DIRECTIONS

Take the New York State Thruway to Buffalo and get onto Hwy. 290 & 990 to Lockport. Take that to Rt. 78 going north to the course. It will be on your right.

BRISTOL HARBOR GOLF COURSE
Seneca Point Rd., Canandaigua, NY 14424 / (716) 396-2460

BASIC INFORMATION

Course Type: Semi-private
Year Built: 1972
Architect: Robert T. Jones
Local Pro: Sue Ellen Northrop

Course: N/A
Holes: 18 / Par 72

Back : 6,692 yds. Rating: 72.6 Slope: 126
Middle: 6,095 yds. Rating: 69.6 Slope: 121
Ladies: 5,482 yds. Rating: 73.0 Slope: 126

Tee Time: 7 days in advance.
Price: $22 - $40

Credit Cards:	■	Restaurant:	■
Driving Range:	■	Lounge:	■
Practice Green:	■	Meeting Rooms:	■
Locker Room:	■	Tennis:	
Rental Clubs:	■	Swimming:	
Walkers:		Jogging Trails:	
Snack Bar:	■	Boating:	■

COURSE DESCRIPTION

Bristol Harbor Golf Course is a traditional style course that offers a great combination of holes to play through. It's a scenic course that features a lake and rolling terrain. The first nine holes are open in their design and offer plenty of room to work the ball in both left and right. But once you step onto the tenth-tee, the course takes a turn that you'll need to be prepared for. The fairways are much tighter and you'll find many trees that come into play.

It's a fun challenge of golf for many different types of players.

DIRECTIONS

Take the New York State Thruway to Exit 44 and make a right towards Rt. 5 & 20. Make another right going to Rt. 21 heading southbound to Seneca Port Rd. Look for the course on your right.

CANAJOHARIE COUNTRY CLUB

Seneca Point Rd., Canandaigua, NY 14424 / (518) 673-8183

BASIC INFORMATION

Course Type: Public
Year Built: 1946 / 1991
Architect: Scott Norris / Horace Smith
Local Pro: Mark Lane

Course: N/A
Holes: 18 / Par 70

Back : 5,744 yds. Rating: 66.4 Slope: 109
Middle: N/A Rating: N/A Slope: N/A
Ladies: 4,833 yds. Rating: 65.7 Slope: 105

Tee Time: 1 day in advance.
Price: $10 - $15

Credit Cards:	■	Restaurant:	■
Driving Range:	■	Lounge:	■
Practice Green:	■	Meeting Rooms:	
Locker Room:		Tennis:	
Rental Clubs:	■	Swimming:	
Walkers:	■	Jogging Trails:	
Snack Bar:	■	Boating:	■

COURSE DESCRIPTION

Canajoharie Country Club has all the charm and appeal normally associated with a much longer course. It's a unique layout that features water coming into play on half of its holes.

Keep your tee-shots on target and try to stay away from the many undulations that the fairways feature. If you're not careful, your ball will most likely end up leaving you with a very difficult and demanding side hill lie making it difficult to hit a good approach shot to the various small greens throughout the course.

DIRECTIONS

Take the New York State Thruway to Exit 29 and follow that to Rt. 10 heading south for about 4 miles where you'll make a right at Rt. 163. Look for the course on the right.

CENTER POINT COUNTRY CLUB

1940 Brickyard Rd., Canandaigua, NY 14425 / (716) 924-5346

BASIC INFORMATION

Course Type: Semi-private
Year Built: 1963
Architect: Elmer Michaels
Local Pro: Jim Buchanan

Course: N/A
Holes: 18 / Par 71

Back : 6,717 yds. Rating: 70.7 Slope: 116
Middle: 6,478 yds. Rating: 69.6 Slope: 114
Ladies: 5,213 yds. Rating: 68.3 Slope: 107

Tee Time: N/A
Price: Please call to confirm.

Credit Cards:	■	Restaurant:	■
Driving Range:	■	Lounge:	■
Practice Green:	■	Meeting Rooms:	■
Locker Room:	■	Tennis:	
Rental Clubs:	■	Swimming:	
Walkers:	■	Jogging Trails:	
Snack Bar:	■	Boating:	■

COURSE DESCRIPTION

Center Point Country Club is set on a nice piece of real estate that's both beautiful and enjoyable to play in its peaceful environment. It's truly a great course for many different types of players — because of the placement of each one of its tees and the amount of expertise each one commands.

The 7th hole is the longest on the course, reaching 547 yards from the back-tees. You'll need to hit your tee-shot to left-center of the fairway to set yourself up for the first of two approach shots on this slight double-dogleg design.

Most of the greens are big enough for a two-to-three club length variance.

DIRECTIONS

Take Rt. 90 to 332 and make a right at Thomas and then another right onto Brickyard Rd. You'll see the course on the right.

132

SENECA LAKE COUNTRY CLUB

P.O. Box 909, Geneva, NY 14456/ (315) 789-4681

BASIC INFORMATION

Course Type: Semi-private
Year Built: 1930's
Architect: N/A
Local Pro: Doug Bartlett

Course: N/A
Holes: 18 / Par 72

Back : 6,259 yds. Rating: N/A Slope: 113
Middle: 6,044 yds. Rating: N/A Slope: 111
Ladies: 5,341 yds. Rating: N/A Slope: 114

Tee Time: 7 days in advance.
Price: $25

Credit Cards: ■		Restaurant: ■
Driving Range:		Lounge: ■
Practice Green: ■		Meeting Rooms: ■
Locker Room: ■		Tennis:
Rental Clubs: ■		Swimming: ■
Walkers: ■		Jogging Trails:
Snack Bar: ■		Boating: ■

COURSE DESCRIPTION

Seneca Lake Country Club is a shot-makers course above all else.

The fairways are average in size and most of the holes feature a healthy combination of bunkers. You'll also find seven of the holes playing into water. The hilly terrain, on this traditionally designed layout, can be difficult to play from at times, especially when you're stuck with a difficult approach shot from an uneven lie to one of many small greens.

This is not a difficult course by any means, so don't worry about playing it if you're prone to make mistakes.

DIRECTIONS

Take the New York State Thruway to Exit 42 (Geneva) and follow that to Rt. 14. The course will be on your right.

VICTOR HILLS GOLF CLUB

1460 Brace Rd., Victor, NY 14564 / (716) 924-3480

BASIC INFORMATION

Course Type: Semi-private
Year Built: 1973
Architect: Jack Dianetti
Local Pro: Tony Durante

Course: South (18 / Par 72)
Holes: 45

Back : 6,663 yds. Rating: 71.5 Slope: 121
Middle: 6,259 yds. Rating: 69.9 Slope: 117
Ladies: 5,670 yds. Rating: 72.9 Slope: 119

Tee Time: 7 days in advance.
Price: $16 - $17

Credit Cards: ■		Restaurant: ■
Driving Range:		Lounge: ■
Practice Green:		Meeting Rooms:
Locker Room: ■		Tennis:
Rental Clubs: ■		Swimming:
Walkers: ■		Jogging Trails:
Snack Bar: ■		Boating: ■

COURSE DESCRIPTION

Victor Hills Golf Club is a shot-makers course that offers a wonderful playing field for different types of players to enjoy.

From the tee, the hilly terrain is quite evident. You'll often need to read this terrain to place your ball correctly for position. Some of the hills slope sideways; others tend to play above and below the pin. You can use these hills to your advantage by hitting onto them and watching your ball roll towards the destination you had envisioned. It just takes a little practice.

Both a draw or a fade can be used liberally on each of the holes.

DIRECTIONS

Take the New York State Thruway to Exit 45 (Rt. 96 S.) through the Village of Victor and make a right onto Brace Rd. Look for the course on your right.

WINGED PHEASANT GOLF LINKS
1475 Sandhill Rd., Shortsville, NY 14548 / (716) 289-8846

BASIC INFORMATION

Course Type: Semi-private
Year Built: 1963
Architect: R. Furfare
Local Pro: Joe Diego

Course: N/A
Holes: 18 / Par 70

Back : 6,370 yds. Rating: 69.0 Slope: 120
Middle: N/A   Rating: N/A   Slope: N/A
Ladies: 5,835 yds. Rating: 72.0 Slope: 119

Tee Time: 7 days in advance.
Price: $12 - $18

Credit Cards:	■	Restaurant:	■
Driving Range:	■	Lounge:	■
Practice Green:	■	Meeting Rooms:	■
Locker Room:		Tennis:	
Rental Clubs:	■	Swimming:	
Walkers:	■	Jogging Trails:	
Snack Bar:	■	Boating:	

COURSE DESCRIPTION

Winged Pheasant Golf Links is traditionally styled and open to unpredictable winds. It's a fun challenge for an average golfer to play through and should serve as a good learning ground to experience how one should approach a hole — under windy conditions — by playing low boring shots below the wind to keep the ball on line towards the pin.

This is not the type of layout a better player will find challenging. But it is a course filled many interesting short game features that will make anyone want to play a round regardless of its length.

DIRECTIONS
Coming west on "80", go north on US-395 and go right off the W. McCarren exit. Make a left on Sullivan Lane to the course.

INDIAN HILLS GOLF CLUB
150 Indian Hills Rd., Painted Post, NY 14870 / (607) 523-7315

BASIC INFORMATION

Course Type: Semi-private
Year Built: 1964
Architect: Jack Marsh
Local Pro: Jim Edmister

Course: N/A
Holes: 18 / Par 72

Back : 6,626 yds. Rating: 71.4 Slope: 121
Middle: 6,300 yds. Rating: 69.9 Slope: 118
Ladies: 5,200 yds. Rating: 69.5 Slope: 113

Tee Time: 7 days in advance.
Price: $10 - $18

Credit Cards:	■	Restaurant:	■
Driving Range:	■	Lounge:	■
Practice Green:	■	Meeting Rooms:	
Locker Room:	■	Tennis:	
Rental Clubs:	■	Swimming:	
Walkers:	■	Jogging Trails:	
Snack Bar:	■	Boating:	

COURSE DESCRIPTION

Indian Hills Golf Club features a flat surface that stretches across a field of Bent grass that extends along the shape of each hole towards the many elevated and sometimes highly demanding greens. It's not the hardest challenge in the world, but it does have some outstanding holes that will excite any golfer — despite your handicap.

You'll need to play a more controlled game on the front nine with its shorter yet tighter fairways. The back-nine is both longer, wider, and features a greater variety of water holes. If your natural shot is a fade, then this is the course you've been searching for.

DIRECTIONS
Heading south on Rt. 15 S, the course will be on your right and is visible from the highway. The course is 7 miles south of Corning, New York.

STEUBEN COUNTY

OTTERKILL COUNTRY CLUB

P.O. Box 117 Otter Rd., Campbell Hall, NY 10916/ (914) 427-2301

BASIC INFORMATION

Course Type: Public
Year Built: 1950's
Architect: N/A
Local Pro: Ron Reed

Course: N/A
Holes: 18 / Par 72

Back : 6,761 yds. Rating: 72.8 Slope: 128
Middle: 6,510 yds. Rating: 71.6 Slope: 125
Ladies: 5,551 yds. Rating: 72.6 Slope: 122

Tee Time: 3-4 days in advance.
Price: $15 - $40

Credit Cards:		Restaurant:	■
Driving Range:	■	Lounge:	
Practice Green:	■	Meeting Rooms:	
Locker Room:	■	Tennis:	■
Rental Clubs:	■	Swimming:	■
Walkers:	■	Jogging Trails:	
Snack Bar:		Boating:	

COURSE DESCRIPTION

Otterkill Country Club plays 6,761 yards from the championship tees and is characterized by flat terrain throughout its entire layout. The front-nine plays a little harder than the back; because of its length, and like the rest of the course, a high floating soft fade will get you to the hole a lot quicker than a low boring draw. You'll find most of the fairways carved between trees, yet they're generously open, allowing aggressive play from the tees.

The greens on this course are spectacular and should serve as a great source of enjoyment for you if your putting game happens to be in its groove.

DIRECTIONS

Take Rt. 84 to Exit 5 and follow that to Rt. 208 S for about four miles. Make a right on Otter Rd. and the course will be on your left.

TWIN HICKORY GOLF CLUB

Turnpike Rd., Hornell, NY 14843 / (607) 324-1441

BASIC INFORMATION

Course Type: Semi-private
Year Built: 1964
Architect: N/A
Local Pro: Liz Sherburne (Manager)

Course: N/A
Holes: 18 / Par 72

Back : 6,287 yds. Rating: 70.5 Slope: 114
Middle: 5,799 yds. Rating: 68.8 Slope: 111
Ladies: 4,970 yds. Rating: 69.5 Slope: 112

Tee Time: 1 day in advance.
Price: $8 - $13

Credit Cards:		Restaurant:	
Driving Range:		Lounge:	■
Practice Green:	■	Meeting Rooms:	
Locker Room:	■	Tennis:	
Rental Clubs:	■	Swimming:	
Walkers:	■	Jogging Trails:	
Snack Bar:	■	Boating:	■

COURSE DESCRIPTION

A walk along the *Twin Hickory Golf Club* will confirm how great it is to play the game the way it was meant to be played. As you walk along the flat terrain, you'll be taken aback by some of the natural beauty of the holes, especially the ones that feature a valley as part of their scenery.

You won't find too much trouble blocking your way to the pins, but do play conservatively, for accuracy is much more important and rewarding than distance when you address the ball before your drives.

DIRECTIONS

Take Rt. 17 to Rt. 36 S heading east on Main St. over the bridge. Make your first right on Turnpike Rd. The course will be on your left.

WAYNE HILLS COUNTRY CLUB
P.O. Box 32, Lyons, NY 14489 / (315) 923-7795

BASIC INFORMATION

Course Type: Semi-private
Year Built: 1959 / 1960
Architect: Packard & Wadworth / Packard
Local Pro: Mark Paliotti

Course: N/A
Holes: 18 / Par 72

Back : 6,854 yds. Rating: 72.1 Slope: 126
Middle: 6,629 yds. Rating: 71.8 Slope: 125
Ladies: 5,556 yds. Rating: N/A   Slope: 118

Tee Time: 3 days in advance.
Price: $44

Credit Cards:		Restaurant:	■
Driving Range:	■	Lounge:	■
Practice Green:	■	Meeting Rooms:	■
Locker Room:	■	Tennis:	
Rental Clubs:		Swimming:	■
Walkers:		Jogging Trails:	
Snack Bar:	■	Boating:	■

COURSE DESCRIPTION

You can be assured that you'll get to play every club in your bag before you step off the 18th green at **Wayne Hills Country Club**. It's a tough layout that puts a lot of emphasis on precise yardage readings. If you haven't taken the time to figure out how far you can hit a ball with each one of your clubs, you'll inevitably end up in trouble – the type of trouble that will make it hard for you to walk away with a par.

The 5th hole, a 442 yard par-4, plays into a prevailing wind, making it very difficult to get the required driving length off approximately 240 yards from the tee. Length and accuracy is a must.

DIRECTIONS

Take the New York State Thruway to Exit 42 and follow that for about 8-miles northbound to Rt. 14. Take that 4-miles east to Gannet Rd. The course will be on your right.

BYRNCLIFF RESORT & CONFERENCE CENTER
Box 504, Rt. 20A, Varyburg, NY 14167 / (716) 535-7300

BASIC INFORMATION

Course Type: Public
Year Built: 1967
Architect: N/A
Local Pro: Keith Buttles

Course: N/A
Holes: 18 / Par 72

Back : 6,800 yds. Rating: N/A   Slope: N/A
Middle: 6,350 yds. Rating: 71.2 Slope: 115
Ladies: 5,600 yds. Rating: 74.0 Slope: 119

Tee Time: 1 day in advance.
Price: $9.50 - $28 (all day **Green Fee / Cart**)

Credit Cards:	■	Restaurant:	■
Driving Range:	■	Lounge:	■
Practice Green:	■	Meeting Rooms:	■
Locker Room:	■	Tennis:	■
Rental Clubs:	■	Swimming:	■
Walkers:	■	Jogging Trails:	■
Snack Bar:	■	Boating:	■

COURSE DESCRIPTION

Byrncliff Resort & Conference Center has rolling fairways, mature trees, exciting water holes, and much more.

Try not to get fooled by the length of the holes and the width of the fairways. If you don't place your shots on the proper landing areas, you'll often be left with a long difficult second shot as your approach to the green. The 17th hole, measuring 480 yards from the back-tees, is a long par-4 that requires a perfect drive to the middle of the fairway to avoid sinking your ball on either side of it. This area is approximately 250 yards away from the tee.

DIRECTIONS

Take the New York State Thruway to Rt. 77 (Exit Pembroke) and follow that to Rt. 20 A. Make a left, and look for the course on your left.

ALTERNATIVE COURSES - WEST

Allegany
9-hole

Allegany Hills Golf Course
9622 Hardy's Corner Rd.
Cuba, NY 14727
(716) 437-2658

Evergreen Golf Course
8212 Halls Rd.
Bolivar, NY 14715
(716) 928-1270

Cattaraugus
9-hole

Birch Run Country Club
Birch Run Rd.
Allegany, NY 14701
(716) 484-1720

Ischua Valley Country Club
R.R. 16, P.O. Box 147
Franklinville, NY 14737
(716) 676-3630

St. Bonaventure
C/O Pro Shop
St. Bonaventure, NY 14778
(716) 372-7692

Chautauqua
Public

Moonbrook Country Club
Rt. 60, P.O. Box 663
Jamestown, NY 14701
(716) 484-1720

Shorewood Country Club
West Lake Rd.
Dunkirk, NY 14048
(716) 366-5197

Chautauqua
9-hole

Bemus Point Golf & Tennis Club
72 Main St.
Bemus Point, NY 14712
(716) 386-2893

Cassadaga Lakes Country Club
55 Frisbee Rd.
Cassadaga, NY 14718
(716) 595-3003

Chautauqua Point Golf Course
P.O. Box, 156 Rt. 430
Mayville, NY 14757
(716) 753-7271

Lakeside Golf Club
Westlake Rd. (Rt. 5)
Ripley, NY 14775
(716) 736-7637

Chautauqua
9-hole / Continued

Pinehurst Golf Course
East Main Rd.
Westfield, NY 14787
(716) 326-4424

Rosebook Golf Course
130 Beebe Rd.
Silver Creek, NY 14136
(716) 934-2825

Willow Run Golf Course
Rt. 394
Mayville, NY 14757
(716) 789-3162

Woodcrest Golf Course
Wall St. Rd.
Stedman, NY 14757
(716) 789-4653

Chautauqua
Executive

Forest Heights Golf Course
Forest Ave.
Jamestown, NY 14701
(716) 386-2893

Sunset Valley Golf Course
724 Hunt Rd.
Lakewood, NY 14750
(716) 644-7508

Chemung
Public

Mark Twain State Park
4229 Middle Rd.
Horseheads, NY 14845
(607) 739-0551

Ouleout Creek Golf Course
HC 87, Box 37
Franklin, NY 13775
(607) 829-2100

Chemung
Private

Elmira Country Club
P.O. Box 606, Church St.
Elmira, NY 14902
(607) 734-7777

Erie
Public

Amhert Audobon Golf Course
500 Maple Rd.
Amherst, NY 14221
(716) 632-2888

Erie
Private

Briarwood Country Club
S. 5324 Rogers Rd.
Hamburg, NY 14075
(716) 648-7034

Brookfield Country Club
5120 Shimerville Rd.
Clarence, NY 14031
(716) 632-2050

Country Club Of Buffalo
250 N. Young's Rd.
Williamsville, NY 14221
(716) 632-1100

Craig Burn Golf Club
1231 N. Davis Rd.
E. Aurora, NY 14052
(716) 655-0000

East Aurora Country Club
300 Girdle Rd.
East Aurora, NY 14052
(716) 652-6803

Gowanda Country Club
2623 Brown Rd.
Collins, NY 14034
(716) 337-2100

Lancaster Country Club
6061 Broadway
Lancaster, NY 14086
(716) 684-3700

Orchard Park Country Club
4777 S. Buffalo St.
Orchard Park, NY 14127
(716) 662-3806

Park Country Club
4949 Sheridan Dr.
Williamsville, NY 14221
(716) 3632-2286

Springville Country Club
P.O. Box 157
Springville, NY 14141
(716) 592-2122

Transit Valley Country Club
8920 Transit Rd.
E. Amherst, NY 14051
(771) 688-7311

Wanakah Country Club
S-5161 Lake Shore
Hamburg, NY 14075
(716) 627-2391

Westwood Country Club
772 N. Forest Rd.
Williamsville, NY 14221
(716) 632-7234

Erie
9-hole

Evergreen Golf Club
168 Tonawanda Creek Rd.
Buffalo, NY 14228
(716) 688-6204

Grandview Golf Course
9211 Lake Shore Rd.
Angola, NY 14006
(716) 549-4930

Erie
9-hole / Continued

Greenwood Golf Course
8499 Northfield Rd.
Clarece Center , NY 14032
(716) 741-3395

Oakwood Golf Course
3575 Tonawanda Creek Rd.
Buffalo, NY 14228
(716) 689-1421

Pine Meadows Golf & Country Club
9820 Greiner Rd.
Clarence, NY 14031
(716) 741-3970

South Park Golf Course
2539 S. Park Ave.
Buffalo, NY 14218
(716) 825-9504

Town of Hamburg Golf Course
Boston State Rd.
Hamburg, NY 14075
(716) 648-4410

Erie
Executive

Dande Farms Golf Course
Camey Rd.
Akront, NY 14001
(716) 542-2027

Delaware Golf Course
Delaware Park
Buffalo, NY 14216
(716) 835-2533

Southshore Country Club
S. 5075 Southwestern Blvd.
Hamberg, NY 14075
(716) 649-6674

Genesee
Private

Stafford Country Club
210 E. Main St.
Batavia, NY 14020
(716) 343-9281

Livingston
Private

Caledonia Country Club
Park Pl.
Caledonia, NY 14423
(716) 538-9956

Livingston
9-hole

Brae Burn Recreation Golf Course
Red Jacket St.
Dansville, NY 14437
(716) 335-3101

Keshqua Golf Club
Box 253
Mt. Morris, NY 14510
(716) 658-4545

Monroe
Private

Brooklea Country Club
891 Pixley Rd.
Rochester, NY 14624
(716) 247-4577

Green Hill Golf Club
226 Mendonionia (Rt. 64)
Mendon, NY 14506
(716) 624-9906

Locust Hill Country Club
Jefferson Rd.
Pittsford, NY 14534
(716) 427-7040

Midvale Golf & Country Club
2387 Baird Rd.
Penfield, NY 14526
(716) 586-7100

Monroe Golf Club
155 Golf Ave.
Pittsford, NY 14534
(716) 586-3608

Penfield Country Club
1784 Jackson Rd.
Penfield, NY 14526
(716) 377-7050

Monroe
9-hole

Perinton Golf & Country Club
1344 Macedon Center Rd.
Fairport, NY 14450
(716) 223-7651

Pinewood Country Club
1189 Ogden Parma Townline
Spencerport, NY 14459
(716) 352-5314

Riverton Golf Club
Scottsville West Henrietta Rd.
West Henrietta, NY 14586
(716) 334-6196

Woodcliff Lodge Resort Center
199 Woodcliff Dr.
Fairport, NY 14450
(716) 381-4000

Monroe
Executive

Arrowhead Golf Club
655 Gallup Rd.
Spencerport, NY 14559
(716) 352-5500

Monroe
9-hole

Perinton Golf & Country Club
1344 Macedon Center Rd.
Fairport, NY 14450
(716) 223-7651

Island Valley Golf Course
1208 Fairport Rd.
Fairport, NY 14450
(716) 586-1300

Shore Acres Golf Course
Greenleaf Rd.
Rochester, NY 14612
(716) 621-1030

Niagara
Public

Willowbrook Golf Course
4200 Lake Ave.
Lockport, NY 14094
(716) 434-1631

Niagara
Private

Lockport Town & Country Club
717 E. Ave.
Lockport, NY 14094
(716) 433-4581

Niagara Falls Country Club
505 Mountain View Dr.
Lewiston, NY 14092
(716) 285-1331

Tan-Tara Country Club
4391 Tonawanda Creek Rd.
n. Tonawanda, NY 14120
(716) 694-0366

Niagara
9-hole

Shawnee Country Club
6020 Townline Rd.
Wheatfield, NY 14304
(716) 731-5177

Ontario
Private

Clifton Springs Country Club
P.O. Box 595 Town Line Rd.
Clifton Springs, NY 14432
(315) 462-9885

Cobblestone Creek Country Club
100 Cobble Creek Rd.
Victor, NY 14564
(716) 924-0620

Cherry Hills Golf Club
Rural Rt. 1
Ridgeway, NY 14213
(716) 856-0029

Geneva Country Club
Box 528
Geneva, NY 14456
(315) 789-8786

Seneca Falls Country Club
Box 413, Rt. 89
Seneca Falls, NY 13148
(315) 568-2676

Shelridge Country Club
Telegraph Rd.
Medina, NY 14103
(716) 798-0955

Ontario
9-hole

Big Oak Public Golf Course
33 Packwood Rd.
Geneva, NY 14456
(315) 789-9419

Orleans
Public

Harbour Pointe Country Club
Rt. 18 & 98
Waterport, NY 14571
(716) 682-3922

Orleans
Executive

Ricci Meadows Golf Course
1939 Oak Orchard Rd.
Waterport, NY 14571
(716) 682-3280

Schuyler
9-hole

Watkins Glen Golf Club
126 Lakeview Ave.
Watkins, NY 14891
(607) 535-2340

Seneca
9-hole

Bonavista Golf Club
P.O. Box 234
Williard, NY 14588
(607) 869-5482

Seneca
Executive

Silver Creek Golf Course
1790 E. River Rd., P.O. Box 627
Waterloo, NY 13165
(315) 539-8046

Steuben
Private

Corning Country Club
17121 E. Corning Rd.
Croning, NY 14836
(607) 962-5985

Steuben
9-hole

Bath Country Club
Box 389
Bath, NY 14810
(607) 776-9919

Hornell Country Club
Seneca Rd.
Hornell, NY 14843
(607) 324-4225

Pinnacle State Park Golf Course
Rd. 1, Box 189
Addison, NY 14801
(607) 359-9205

Wayne
Private

Blue Heron Hills Golf Club
1 Country Club Dr.
Macdon, NY 14502
(315) 986-2007

New Country Club
P.O. Box 28
Newark, NY 14513
(315) 331-2370

Ontario Golf Club
P.O. Box 366
Ontario, NY 14519
(315) 524-7184

Sodus Bay Heights Golf Club
Bay View Dr., P.O. Box 289
Sodus Point, NY 14555
(315) 483-6777

Wyoming
Public

Quiet Times Golf Course
Steman Rd.
Attica, NY 14011
(716) 591-1811

Wyoming
Private

Attica Golf Club
P.O. Box 185, 95 Bunnell St.
Attica, NY 14011
(315) 591-2790

Lakeside Country Club
Box 381,
Pen Yan, NY 14527
(315) 536-7552

Silver Lake Country Club
P.O. Box 94
Perry, NY 14530
(716) 237-9949

Wyoming
9-hole

Fox Run Golf Course
4195 Rt. 14
Rockstream, NY 14878
(607) 535-4413

7. N.J. NORTH / COUNTIES AND CITIES

Bergen
B1 / Franklin Lakes ... 1
B1 / Paramus ... 2
B1 / Rivervale ... 3

Essex
B1 / Shorthills ... 4

B1/

Passaic
B1 / Milton ...12

Somerset
B2 / Franklin Township ... 13

B1/

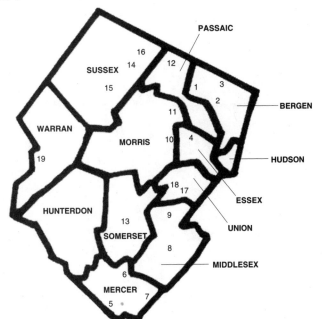

B2 /

B2 /

Mercer
B2 / Trenton ... 5
B2/ Princeton ... 6
B2 / West Windsor ... 7

Middlesex
B2 / East Brunswick ... 8
B2 / Neshanic Station ... 9

Morris
B1 / Parsippany ... 10
B1 / Pompton Plains ... 11

Sussex
B1 / Hamburg ... 14
B1 / Lafayette ... 15
B1 / McAfee ... 16

Union
B2 / Clark ... 17
B2 / Scotch Plains ... 18

Warren
B1 / Belvidere ... 19

HIGH MOUNTAIN GOLF CLUB

8215 Ewins Ave., Franklin Lakes, NJ 07147 / (201) 891-4653

BASIC INFORMATION

Course Type: Semi-private
Year Built: 1968
Architect: N/A
Local Pro: Pat Lawler

Course: N/A
Holes: 18 / Par 72

Back: 6,347 yds. Rating: 69.5 Slope: 118
Middle: 6,101 yds. Rating: 68.6 Slope: 116
Ladies: 5,426 yds. Rating: 70.0 Slope: 117

Tee Time: 7 days in advance.
Price: $16 - $34

Credit Cards:		Restaurant:	■
Driving Range:	■	Lounge:	■
Practice Green:	■	Meeting Rooms:	■
Locker Room:	■	Tennis:	
Rental Clubs:	■	Swimming:	
Walkers:	■	Jogging Trails:	
Snack Bar:		Boating:	

COURSE DESCRIPTION

High Mountain Golf Club is a great little course with many fun holes for the mid-to-high handicapper. Although the course is set up for strategic play, you needn't have to worry about hitting too many errant shots, for the playing field was designed to be forgiving, especially around the wide fairways, from tee-to-green.

The hardest hole on the course is #16, which streches out 587 yards from the back-tees and is a dogleg-left. Hit your tee shot long and straight for proper position. Beware of the creek that sits only 40 yards away from the putting green. Most players will need to lay-up.

DIRECTIONS

From the Garden State Pkwy. or I-287, take Rt. 208 to the Ewling Ave. Exit. Go west to the course. It will be on your left.

PARAMUS GOLF & COUNTRY CLUB

314 Paramus, Paramus, NJ 07652 / (201) 447-6067

BASIC INFORMATION

Course Type: Municipal
Year Built: 1952
Architect: N/A
Local Pro: N/A

Course: N/A
Holes: 18 / Par 71

Back: 6,212 yds. Rating: 67.6 Slope: 109
Middle: 6,086 yds. Rating: 67.2 Slope: 108
Ladies: 5,241 yds. Rating: 72.0 Slope: 117

Tee Time: First come, first serve.
Price: $10 - $32

Credit Cards:	■	Restaurant:	■
Driving Range:		Lounge:	■
Practice Green:	■	Meeting Rooms:	
Locker Room:	■	Tennis:	
Rental Clubs:	■	Swimming:	
Walkers:	■	Jogging Trails:	
Snack Bar:	■	Boating:	

COURSE DESCRIPTION

The course is relatively flat with small elevated greens. There is very little water throughout, which makes the course ideal for quick rounds. It's not unusual for a foursome to complete a game in under 4 1/2 hours. The tees will be expanded for a greater variety of challenges in the near future, but please call to confirm.

The numbers indicate that mid-to-high handicappers will get the most enjoyment out of the course, because of its relative ease. Low handicappers will tear this course apart.

DIRECTIONS

Take Rt. 17 north or south to Century Rd. and go west for approximately 2 1/2 miles until you get to Paramus Rd. Make a right at Paramus Rd. and you'll find the course a half-mile further on your right.

PASCACK BROOK GOLF & COUNTRY CLUB
15 Rivervale Rd., Rivervale, NJ 07675 / (201) 664-5886

BASIC INFORMATION
Course Type: Public
Year Built: 1962
Architect: Handwerg
Local Pro: Yaz Consalvo

Course: N/A
Holes: 18 / Par 69

Back : 6,287 yds. Rating: 70.9 Slope: 121
Middle: 5,991 yds. Rating: 69.0 Slope: 119
Ladies: 5,067 yds. Rating: 69.0 Slope: 116

Tee Time: 7 days in advance.
Price: $25 - $50

Credit Cards:	Restaurant:	■
Driving Range:	Lounge:	■
Practice Green: ■	Meeting Rooms:	■
Locker Room: ■	Tennis:	
Rental Clubs: ■	Swimming:	
Walkers: ■	Jogging Trails:	
Snack Bar: ■	Boating:	

COURSE DESCRIPTION
Pascack Brook Golf & Country Club plays fairly easy, allowing a wide spectrum of players a chance to shoot a good overall score by the time they step off the 18th-tee. This straightforward layout was built on a fairly flat terrain making the course ideal to experiment on. The hardest hole on the playing field is #2. It's a par-4, dogleg-left design, that stretches 443 yards from the back-tees. You'll have to hit your drive about 230 yards to take the dogleg out of position for a clear approach shot. The safest shot to play would be for the center of the long and narrow, front-to-back sloping green.

DIRECTIONS
Take Riverdale Rd. off Westwood Ave. and make a right. The course will be two-minutes from downtown Westwood on your right.

CITY OF EAST ORANGE GOLF COURSE
Parsonage Hill Rd., Short Hills, NJ 07078 / (201) 379-6775

BASIC INFORMATION
Course Type: Semi-private
Year Built: 1920
Architect: N/A
Local Pro: Bruce Applin

Course: N/A
Holes: 18 / Par 70

Back : 6,120 yds. Rating: 67.6 Slope: N/A
Middle: N/A yds. Rating: N/A Slope: N/A
Ladies: 5,640 yds. Rating: 69.8 Slope: N/A

Tee Time: 1 day in advance.
Price: $20 - $25

Credit Cards:	Restaurant:	■
Driving Range:	Lounge:	■
Practice Green: ■	Meeting Rooms:	
Locker Room: ■	Tennis:	
Rental Clubs:	Swimming:	
Walkers:	Jogging Trails:	
Snack Bar: ■	Boating:	

COURSE DESCRIPTION
The ***City Of East Orange Golf Course*** is a friendly enough course geared for the high-handicapper who is short on distance.
A surprising element of the layout is the fact that it sits on 160 acres of land. This wide expanse of terrain is home to many beautiful wildlife species
The hardest hole on the course is the 14th hole. It's a dogleg-right, par-4, that stretches 344 yards from the back-tees. Hit your drive straight and aim your approach shot to the center of the green.

DIRECTIONS
Take Hwy. 78 east to Rt. 24 until you get to the JFK Pkwy. where you'll need to make a left. When you get to Parsonage Hill Rd., make a left at the sign. The course will be a quarter-mile on your left.

MERCER COUNTY

CRANBURY GOLF CLUB
Southfield Rd., West Windsor, NJ 08512 / (609) 799-0341

BASIC INFORMATION

Course Type: Semi-private
Year Built: 1961
Architect: James Britton
Local Pro: Mike Attari

Course: N/A
Holes: 18 / Par 71

Back : 6,312 yds. Rating: 70.0 Slope: 117
Middle: 6,010 yds. Rating: 69.0 Slope: 114
Ladies: 5,545 yds. Rating: 72.0 Slope: 118

Tee Time: 7 days in advance.
Price: $10 - $30

Credit Cards:	■	Restaurant:	■
Driving Range:	■	Lounge:	■
Practice Green:	■	Meeting Rooms:	■
Locker Room:	■	Tennis:	
Rental Clubs:	■	Swimming:	
Walkers:	■	Jogging Trails:	
Snack Bar:	■	Boating:	■

COURSE DESCRIPTION

You don't have to be an extraordinary golfer to play well here. With an overall distance of only 6,312 yards from the back-tees, the course is obviously geared for high-handicappers and people who are short on distance.

This is truly a great course for the part-time golfer who doesn't have the luxury of playing the game often enough and is simply looking for a fun layout to play.

DIRECTIONS

Take the New Jersey Turnpike south to Exit 8 and take Rt. 33 west to its end. Make a left and your first right onto Rt. 571 which will take you to Southfield Rd. Make a left and look for the course on your right.

MOUNTAIN VIEW GOLF COURSE
Bear Tavern Rd., Trenton, NJ 08628 / (609) 882-4093

BASIC INFORMATION

Course Type: Public
Year Built: 1958
Architect: N/A
Local Pro: Steve Bowers

Course: N/A
Holes: 18 / Par 70

Back: 6,775 yds. Rating: 72.0 Slope: 119
Middle: 6,220 yds. Rating: 69.8 Slope: 114
Ladies: 5,500 yds. Rating: N/A Slope: N/A

Tee Time: First come, first serve.
Price: $12z - $24

Credit Cards:		Restaurant:	■
Driving Range:		Lounge:	■
Practice Green:	■	Meeting Rooms:	■
Locker Room:	■	Tennis:	
Rental Clubs:	■	Swimming:	
Walkers:	■	Jogging Trails:	
Snack Bar:	■	Boating:	

COURSE DESCRIPTION

At 6,775 yards from the back-tees, this course will appeal to many different types of golfers. Don't be discouraged by the distance if you're not able to hit a long ball, for the course does offer plenty of room to cut the distance off of each hole with well-placed accurate drives.

A well-managed game is the secret to making pars and birdies, so study the score card carefully before you play each hole. If you can make it through the front-nine with a good score, the back-nine should play a little bit easier.

DIRECTIONS

Take I-95 south to Exit 2 and make a left. Look for the course about a half-mile further on right side of the road.

PRINCETON COUNTRY CLUB

1 Wheeler Way, Princeton, NJ 08540 / (609) 452-9382

BASIC INFORMATION

Course Type: Public
Year Built: N/A
Architect: N/A
Local Pro: Steve Bowers

Course: N/A
Holes: 18 / Par 71

Back: 6,060 yds. Rating: N/A   Slope: N/A
Middle: 5,845 yds. Rating: N/A   Slope: N/A
Ladies: 5,360 yds. Rating: N/A   Slope: N/A

Tee Time: First come, first serve.
Price: $10 - $24

Credit Cards:		Restaurant:	■
Driving Range:	■	Lounge:	■
Practice Green:	■	Meeting Rooms:	■
Locker Room:	■	Tennis:	
Rental Clubs:	■	Swimming:	
Walkers:	■	Jogging Trails:	
Snack Bar:	■	Boating:	

COURSE DESCRIPTION

As of this writing, **Princeton Country Club** was undergoing a reevaluation of its Ratings and Slopes. If you want to know these numbers, you can simply call the establishment for a complete update.

You'll need to play an accurate game of golf to perform well here. The many mature trees that can be found throughout the course can often wreak havoc on your game if you don't stay clear of them on your drives.

To be a winner on this course, play a good solid short game.

DIRECTIONS

Take Rt. 1 south to Edmond Rd. and make a right, then your first left, to Wheeler Rd. The course will only be a short distance from this point and can be found straight ahead.

HILLSBORO COUNTRY CLUB

Wertsville Rd., Neshanic Station, NJ 08853 / (201) 263-7115

BASIC INFORMATION

Course Type: Semi-private
Year Built: 1960's
Architect: George Fazio
Local Pro: Cindy Cooper

Course: N/A
Holes: 18 / Par 70

Back : 5,850 yds. Rating: 68.2   Slope: 114
Middle: N/A   Rating: N/A   Slope: N/A
Ladies: 5,445 yds. Rating: 74.5   Slope: 119

Tee Time: 7 days in advance.
Price: $33 - $42

Credit Cards:		Restaurant:	■
Driving Range:	■	Lounge:	■
Practice Green:	■	Meeting Rooms:	■
Locker Room:	■	Tennis:	■
Rental Clubs:	■	Swimming:	■
Walkers:	■	Jogging Trails:	■
Snack Bar:	■	Boating:	

COURSE DESCRIPTION

Hillsboro Country Club doesn't demand long drives from each of its tees as much as accuracy, followed by good course management. You'll find many opportunities to shoot par or better, for it only plays 5,850 yards from its farthest point.

The 15th hole is the hardest design on the course. It's a par 5 that plays 515 yards from the back-tees and features two doglegs towards the pin. On your second approach shot, you'll need to consider playing over water or holding back. Either way, you'll need to get close to the pin to make your par on the undulating surface of the green.

DIRECTIONS

The course can be found in Hillsboro Township between Rt. 206 and Rt. 202. Please call for exact directions.

150

TAMARACK GOLF COURSE
97 Hardenburg Lane, East Brunswick, NJ 08816 / (908) 821-8881

BASIC INFORMATION
Course Type: Public
Year Built: 1971
Architect: N/A
Local Pro: Ed Heuser

Course: Red & White (18 / Par 72)
Holes: 36

Back: 7,025 yds. Rating: 73.4 Slope: N/A
Middle: 6,340 yds. Rating: 69.8 Slope: 118
Ladies: 5,810 yds. Rating: 72.5 Slope: N/A

Tee Time: First come, first serve.
Price: $6 - $50

Credit Cards:		Restaurant:	■
Driving Range:	■	Lounge:	■
Practice Green:	■	Meeting Rooms:	■
Locker Room:	■	Tennis:	■
Rental Clubs:	■	Swimming:	■
Walkers:	■	Jogging Trails:	
Snack Bar:	■	Boating:	

COURSE DESCRIPTION
Tamarack Golf Course is a challenge for any type of player who is ready to take on a course of this incredible length. You'll find fascinating holes that will dare you to take chances for high rewards, but if you can't execute them properly, you'll usually end up losing a stroke by the time you sink your ball in the cup.

If you end up hitting a misdirected drive, your ball will inevitably end up in the "hard-to-get-out-of," highly grown rough. The course also features lots of sand and water.

DIRECTIONS
Take the New Jersey Turnpike to Exit 9. Hop onto Rt. 18 and head east to Ruese Riders Lane. At the fourth set of lights, make a left to Dunhams Rd. Follow that for four blocks and turn right onto Hardenburg Lane. The course will be one mile on your left.

KNOLL COUNTRY CLUB
Knoll & Green Bank Rd., Parsippany, NJ 07054 / (201) 263-7115

BASIC INFORMATION
Course Type: Public
Year Built: 1938
Architect: Chandler Barks
Local Pro: Steele King

Course: N/A
Holes: 18 / Par 70

Back : 5,884 yds. Rating: N/A Slope: N/A
Middle: N/A Rating: N/A Slope: N/A
Ladies: 5,309 yds. Rating: N/A Slope: N/A

Tee Time: First come, first serve.
Price: $6.50 - $25

Credit Cards:		Restaurant:	■
Driving Range:		Lounge:	■
Practice Green:	■	Meeting Rooms:	
Locker Room:		Tennis:	
Rental Clubs:		Swimming:	
Walkers:	■	Jogging Trails:	
Snack Bar:	■	Boating:	

COURSE DESCRIPTION
Knoll Country Club is a relatively flat course that features a tight playing field geared for mid-to-high handicappers.

The layout is mostly flat with each nine-hole half playing at about the same level of difficulty throughout the course. If you can keep your drives on the fairways (you'll find many opportunities to play your 3-wood from the teeing areas) you'll usually end up being a short distance from the green, which on most occasions will provide you with a good chance to get the ball close enough for a one putt birdie attempt to the hole.

DIRECTIONS
Off Rt. 46, go north to North Beverwick Rd. and make a left. At the end of Knoll Rd, make a right at the second driveway and proceed for about a quarter mile to the course. It will be on your right.

SUNSET VALLEY

Sunset Rd., Pompton Plains, NJ 07044 / (201) 835-515

BASIC INFORMATION

Course Type: Public
Year Built: 1974
Architect: N/A
Local Pro: N/A

Course: N/A
Holes: 18 / Par 70

Back   : 6,483 yds. Rating: 71.7 Slope: 129
Middle: 6,039 yds. Rating: 69.7 Slope: 124
Ladies: 5,274 yds. Rating: 70.8 Slope: 123

Tee Time: 7 days in advance.
Price: $5.25 - $52.50

Credit Cards:		Restaurant:	■
Driving Range:		Lounge:	■
Practice Green:	■	Meeting Rooms:	
Locker Room:	■	Tennis:	
Rental Clubs:	■	Swimming:	
Walkers:	■	Jogging Trails:	
Snack Bar:	■	Boating:	

COURSE DESCRIPTION

Sunset Valley can surprise the best of players into thinking that it's an easy course to conquer. You wouldn't normally think of a course that is only 6,483 yards long as a tough challenge, especially one like this, built in a valley by the side of a mountain. But it's true. With a slope rating of 129 from the back-tees, every player should take this course seriously. You'll find many doglegs, a good variety of traps, and water coming play.

This is also a course that sits in isolation from the hustle and bustle of the city.

DIRECTIONS

Take I-287 to Exit 52A (Rt. 23) to the second set of lights. Make a right going north to the Pompton Turnpike. Make a right onto Sunset Rd. and look for the course on your left.

BOWLING GREEN GOLF & TENNIS CLUB

Schoolhouse Rd., Milton, NJ 07438 / (201) 697-8688

BASIC INFORMATION

Course Type: Semi-private
Year Built: 1966
Architect: Geoffrey Cornish
Local Pro: Tom Staples

Course: N/A
Holes: 18 / Par 72

Back   : 6,689 yds. Rating: 72.9 Slope: 131
Middle: 6,224 yds. Rating: 70.8 Slope: 127
Ladies: 4,966 yds. Rating: 68.5 Slope: 117

Tee Time: 2 days in advance.
Price: $26 - $43

Credit Cards:	■	Restaurant:	■
Driving Range:	■	Lounge:	■
Practice Green:	■	Meeting Rooms:	
Locker Room:	■	Tennis:	■
Rental Clubs:		Swimming:	
Walkers:	■	Jogging Trails:	
Snack Bar:	■	Boating:	

COURSE DESCRIPTION

Bowling Green Golf & Tennis Club is a wonderful establishment that you'll enjoy visiting. You'll find many mature red pine trees lining up the teeing areas and fairways. It's a gorgeous course with many natural chutes.

The front-nine is a little harder than the back-nine, so try to get a feel for the grass on the fairways, the sand density in the traps, and the low-cut grass on the greens. It will help you play a better overall game.

DIRECTIONS

Take Hwy. 23 north to Oak Ridge Rd. Take the Jug Handle across to the first set of traffic lights. Turn right onto Ridge Rd. and go about one mile to the blinking set of lights and make a right onto School House Rd. Look for the course about one mile on your right.

SOMERSET / SUSSEX COUNTIES

QUAIL BROOK GOLF COURSE

New Brunswick Rd., Franklin Township, NJ 08852 / (908) 560-9528

BASIC INFORMATION

Course Type: Public
Year Built: 1982
Architect: Edmond B. Alt
Local Pro: N/A

Course: N/A
Holes: 18 / Par 72

Back : 6,474 yds. Rating: 70.8 Slope: 119
Middle: 5,835 yds. Rating: 67.9 Slope: 113
Ladies: 5,274 yds. Rating: 69.9 Slope: 115

Tee Time: 5 days in advance.
Price: $6 - $35

Credit Cards:		Restaurant:	
Driving Range:	■	Lounge:	
Practice Green:	■	Meeting Rooms:	
Locker Room:	■	Tennis:	
Rental Clubs:	■	Swimming:	
Walkers:	■	Jogging Trails:	
Snack Bar:	■	Boating:	

COURSE DESCRIPTION

Quail Brook Golf Course holds nothing back from a golfer prior to a swing. Each tee offers a clear view of the playing field.

It's not a long course, yet it's not terribly short either. But it's certainly a great place to experiment with your mid-to-low irons. The majority of the course features a flat playing surface which should serve to eliminate your ball from rolling onto an uneven lie. Most players will enjoy the fact that the course was designed to complement a fade over a draw.

DIRECTIONS

Take Hwy. 287 north to Exit 6 and follow the signs to New Brunswick. At the second set of lights, make a right onto Cedar Grove Lane. When you finally see New Brunswick Rd., make a right and follow the signs.

CRYSTAL SPRINGS COUNTRY CLUB

123 Crystal Springs Rd., Hamburg, NJ 07419 / (201) 827-1444

BASIC INFORMATION

Course Type: Public
Year Built: 1990
Architect: Semi-private
Local Pro: David Glenz

Course: N/A
Holes: 18 / Par 72

Back : 6,887 yds. Rating: 73.3 Slope: 132
Middle: 6,451 yds. Rating: 71.3 Slope: 130
Ladies: 5,955 yds. Rating: 70.5 Slope: 123

Tee Time: 5 days in advance.
Price: $46 - $61

Credit Cards:	■	Restaurant:	■
Driving Range:	■	Lounge:	
Practice Green:	■	Meeting Rooms:	
Locker Room:		Tennis:	
Rental Clubs:	■	Swimming:	
Walkers:		Jogging Trails:	
Snack Bar:		Boating:	

COURSE DESCRIPTION

Crystal Springs Country Club offers an awesome challenge for single-digit handicappers. With its slope rating of 132, it is by far one of the hardest courses in New Jersey and should be played from the middle tees by mid-to-high handicappers.

One of the most interesting holes on the course, and perhaps the hardest, is the 10th, which plays 178 yards from back-tees. You'll need to hit your ball over a 100 ft. drop quarry that sits between the tee and the huge "dog-bone" shaped green. It's a very demanding surface.

DIRECTIONS

Take Rt. 80 west to Rt. 23 and go north to Rt. 517 and continue north until you get to Crystal Springs Rd. The course will be on your left.

SUSSEX COUNTY

FARMSTEAD GOLF CLUB

Rt. 3, Box 2300, Lafayette, NJ 87848 / (201) 383-1666

BASIC INFORMATION

Course Type: Public
Year Built: 1963
Architect: Bryan Phoebus
Local Pro: Leslie Van Sickle

Course: Lakeview & Clubview (18 / Par 72)
Holes: 27

Back : 6,680 yds. Rating: 71.2 Slope: 120
Middle: 6,033 yds. Rating: 68.2 Slope: 114
Ladies: 5,900 yds. Rating: 66.3 Slope: 111

Tee Time: 7 days in advance.
Price: $18 - $46

Credit Cards:	■	Restaurant:	■
Driving Range:		Lounge:	■
Practice Green:	■	Meeting Rooms:	■
Locker Room:	■	Tennis:	
Rental Clubs:	■	Swimming:	
Walkers:	■	Jogging Trails:	
Snack Bar:	■	Boating:	■

COURSE DESCRIPTION

With 27 holes of golf to choose from, you won't need to worry about getting a tee-time at this wonderful location.

The course preferred by better players is the Lakeview-nine and the Clubview-nine combination. The holes have been beautifully designed for the average player to get up and down and make par on most occasions. Distance holds second place to accuracy throughout most of the holes. A clear exception would be the par-3, 9th hole, which measures 210 yards from the back-tees, which happens to be the furthest allowable distance for a par-3 hole according to the United States Golf Association. Good luck!

DIRECTIONS

Take Rt. 80 west to Exit 34B. Go north to Rt. 94 and make a left on Course Rd 623. Look for the course 3-miles on your left.

GREAT GORGE'S COUNTRY CLUB

Rt. 517, McAfee, NJ 07428 / (201) 827-6000

BASIC INFORMATION

Course Type: Public (Resort)
Year Built: 1970
Architect: George Fazio
Local Pro: Thomas P. Manziano

Course: Lake / Quarry (18 / Par 72)
Holes: 27

Back : 6,810 yds. Rating: 73.3 Slope: 131
Middle: 6,392 yds. Rating: 70.7 Slope: 126
Ladies: 5,390 yds. Rating: 72.0 Slope: 125

Tee Time: 30 days in advance.
Price: $20 - $69

Credit Cards:	■	Restaurant:	■
Driving Range:	■	Lounge:	■
Practice Green:	■	Meeting Rooms:	■
Locker Room:	■	Tennis:	■
Rental Clubs:	■	Swimming:	■
Walkers:		Jogging Trails:	■
Snack Bar:	■	Boating:	■

COURSE DESCRIPTION

Any golfer who takes the time visit New Jersey and doesn't play at **Great Gorge's Country Club** is missing out on one of the best kept secrets in America.

The natural scenery will astound you, especially during the spring and fall when the leaves change colors on the thousands of trees. All 27 holes of golf have been expertly designed by George Fazio, and are all well-thought out and challenging. With four sets of tees for every hole, you'll enjoy the great excitement that this beautiful resort has to offer.

DIRECTIONS

From New York, take the Lincoln Tunnel to Rt. 3 west, to Rt. 46 west, to Rt. 23 north, to Rt. 94 north (turn right at light at Hamburg), and finally to Rt. 517 north.

ASH BROOK GOLF CLUB

Raritan Rd., Scotch Plains, NJ 07076 / (908) 756-0414

BASIC INFORMATION

Course Type: Public
Year Built: 1953
Architect: N/A
Local Pro: Ron Regooer

Course: N/A
Holes: 18 / Par 72

Back   : 6,960 yds. Rating: 73.4 Slope: 121
Middle: 6,402 yds. Rating: 70.7 Slope: 115
Ladies: 5,710 yds. Rating: 72.8 Slope: 118

Tee Time: 7 days in advance.
Price: $7 - $50

Credit Cards:	Restaurant:	■
Driving Range:	Lounge:	■
Practice Green: ■	Meeting Rooms:	
Locker Room: ■	Tennis:	
Rental Clubs: ■	Swimming:	
Walkers: ■	Jogging Trails:	
Snack Bar: ■	Boating:	

COURSE DESCRIPTION

Ash Brook Golf Club is a delightful course that's challenging and unique. The terrain varies from flat to undulating but never overly rolling. Driving accurately is a must to stay clear from the out-of-bounds areas that are placed on most of the holes.

The 16th hole, a par-4 configuration that measures 466 yards from the back-tees is the hardest hole on the course. Your tee shot has to land between trees on the right and out-of-bounds on the left. A creek runs across the middle of the fairway about 170 yards away from the undulating green.

DIRECTIONS

Take Rt. 22 to Terrill Rd. and continue about 3 miles further and make a right onto Raritan Rd. The course will be about half-a-mile away on your left.

OAK RIDGE GOLF CLUB

136 Oak Ridge Rd., Clark, NJ 07066 / (908) 574-0139

BASIC INFORMATION

Course Type: Public
Year Built: 1928
Architect: Robert Wilkerson
Local Pro: Dan Billy

Course: N/A
Holes: 18 / Par 70

Back   : 6,388 yds. Rating: 69.2 Slope: 104
Middle: 6,001 yds. Rating: 68.2 Slope: 102
Ladies: 5,261 yds. Rating: 69.7 Slope: N/A

Tee Time: First come, first serve.
Price: $7 - $26

Credit Cards:	Restaurant:	■
Driving Range:	Lounge:	■
Practice Green: ■	Meeting Rooms:	■
Locker Room: ■	Tennis:	
Rental Clubs: ■	Swimming:	
Walkers: ■	Jogging Trails:	
Snack Bar: ■	Boating:	

COURSE DESCRIPTION

In a day when it is common for a new development to build a course that extends over 7,000 yards in length, it's nice to know that golf still has a rich history that reflects how the game was once perceived, and how those thoughts have been transferred into the architecture of the late 1920's. Modern equipment has given us unheard of distance, and, because of this, better single digit handicappers will not find much of a challenge on this relatively short course. But if you're new to the game, and distance happens to be a problem, you can use this layout to build your self-confidence, for it's entirely forgiving from tee-to-green.

DIRECTIONS

Take the New Jersey State Pkwy. to Exit 135 and make a left at the first set of lights. The course will be approximately 3 miles further on your right side.

APPLE MOUNTAIN

Rd. 2, Box 24, Belvidere, NJ 07823 / (908) 453-3023

BASIC INFORMATION

Course Type: Public
Year Built: 1973
Architect: Andrew Kiszonak
Local Pro: N/A

Course: N/A
Holes: 18 / Par 71

Back   : 6,593 yds. Rating: 71.8 Slope: 122
Middle: 6,291 yds. Rating: 70.3 Slope: 120
Ladies: 5,214 yds. Rating: 69.8 Slope: 123

Tee Time: 14 days in advance.
Price: $17 - $45

Credit Cards:	■	Restaurant:	■
Driving Range:	■	Lounge:	■
Practice Green:	■	Meeting Rooms:	■
Locker Room:	■	Tennis:	
Rental Clubs:	■	Swimming:	
Walkers:	■	Jogging Trails:	
Snack Bar:	■	Boating:	■

COURSE DESCRIPTION

Apple Mountain offers great golf for the mid-to-high handicappers. It's a fun course that draws a great senior clientele during the week. Future plans are in the works for an exceptional championship-caliber golf course, with the first 9-holes due to open in a couple of years. The course is filled with interesting forms of hazards, such as deep ponds, unique doglegs, trees, sand bunkers, and more! It's an evenly set course, both front and back, that neither favors a draw nor a fade. You'll also see exceptional views of the Delaware Valley.

DIRECTIONS

Take Rt. 78 west to Clinton (town) and take Rt. 31 north to oxford. Make a left at the second set of lights and go two miles further up the mountain. The course will be on your left.

ALTERNATIVE COURSES - NORTH

Bergen
Public

Emerson Country Club
99 Pallisade
Emerson, NJ 07630
(201) 261-8872

Haworth Golf Club
Lakeshore Dr.
Haworth, NJ 07641
(201) 384-7300

Riverdale Country Club
660 Rivervale Rd.
Rivervale, NJ 07675
(201) 391-2300

Rockleigh Golf Course
15 Paris Ave.
Rockleigh, NJ 07647
(201) 768-6353

Bergen
Private

Alpine Country Club
80 Anderson Ave.
Demarest, NJ 07627
(201) 768-2121

Apple Ridge Country Club
269 E. Cresent Ave.
Mahwah, NJ 07430
(201) 843-3990

Arcola Golf Club
Rt. 4 Paramus
Paramus, NJ 07653
(201) 843-9800

Edgewood Country Club
449 River Vale Rd.
River Vale, NJ 07675
(201) 666-6509

Hackensack Golf Course
Soldier Hill Rd.
Oradell, NJ 07649
(201) 261-5505

Knickerbocker Country Club
188 Knickerbocker Rd.
Tenafly, NJ 07670
(201) 568-4034

Montammy Golf Club
Rt. 9 W
Alpine, NJ 07620
(201) 768-9016

Old Tappen Golf Club
Dewolf Rd.
Old Tappen, NJ 07675
(201) 767-1199

Ramsey Golf & Country Club
105 Lakeside
Ramsey, NV 07446
(702) 327-3877

Ridgewood Country Club
Box 598
Ridgewood, NJ 07451
(201) 599-3927

Tamcrest Country Club
Rt. 9 W. & Montammy Dr.
Alpine, NJ 07620
(201) 767-4610

White Beaches Golf Club
70 Howorth Dr.
Howorth, NJ 07641
(201) 385-3100

Bergen
Private - Continued

Orchad Hills Golf Club
Paramus Rd.
Paramus, NJ 07653
(201) 447-3778

ESSEX
Public

Francis Byrne Golf Club
Pleasant Valley Way
West Orange, NJ 07052
(201) 736-2306

Hendrick's Field Golf Course
1 Showboat Circle Dr.
Henderson, NJ 89014
(702) 434-9000

Weeguahic Park Golf Course
Elizabeth Ave.
Newark, NJ 07107
(201) 923-1838

ESSEX
Private

Baltusrol Golf Club
Sunpike Rd.
Springfield, NJ 07081
(201) 376-1900

Cedar Hill Country Club
100 Wallnut St.
Livingston, NJ 07039
(201) 992-4700

Crestmont Country Club
750 Eagle Rock Ave.
West Orange, NJ 07052
(201) 731-0833

Essex County Country Club
350 Mount Pleasant Ave.
West Orange, NJ 07052
(201) 731-1400

Essex Fells Country Club
219 Devon Rd.
Essex Fells, NJ 07021
(201) 226-9850

Forest Hills Field Club
Belleville Ave.
Bloomfield, NJ 07003
(201) 743-1255

Glen Ridge Country Club
555 Ridgewood Ave.
Glen Ridge, NJ 07028
(201) 744-7800

Green Brook Country Club
Green Brook Rd.
North Caldwell, NJ 07006
(201) 228-1800

Maplewood Country Club
28 Baker St.
Maplewood, NJ 07040
(201) 763-4070

Millburn Township
White Oak Ridge Road Park
Short Hills, NJ 07078
(201) 379-4156

Montclair Golf Club
25 Prospect Ave.
West Orange, NJ 07502
(201) 239-1800

Mountain Ridge Country Club
Passaic Ave.
West Caldwell, NJ 07006
(201)575-8200

Rock Spring Golf Club
Rock Spring Rd.
West Orange, NJ 07052
(201) 923-1838

ESSEX
9-hole

Fernwood Country Club
Fernwood Ave.
Roseland, NJ 07068
(201) 226-3200

HUNTERDON
Private

Beaver Brook Golf Club
Alton Place
Clifton, NJ 08809
(908) 735-4022

Cooper Hill Golf Club
Rt. 31-202
Flemington, NJ 08822
(908) 782-4455

Oak Hill Golf Club
Spring Mills
Milford, NJ 08848
(908) 995-2285

MERCER
Private

Bedons Brook Golf Club
Rolling Hill Rd.
Skillman, NJ 08558
(609) 466-3063

Cherry Valley Country Club
1544 The Great Rd.
Skillman, NJ 08558
(609) 466-4464

Hopewell Valley Golf Club
114 Pennington
Hopewell, NJ 08525
(609) 466-9070

Lawrenceville School Course
Rt. 206
Lawrenceville, NJ 08648
(609) 896-1481

Peddre School Golf Course
Highstown Rd.
Highstown, NJ 08520
(609) 490-7542

MERCER
Private - Continued

Skyview Country Club
Sharon Rd.
Robbinsonville, NJ 08691
(609) 259-0905

Springdale Golf Club
26 College Rd. West
Princeton, NJ 08540
(609) 924-3198

Stony Brook Golf Coure
Stony Brook Rd.
Hopewell, NJ 08525
(609) 466-2215

Trenton Country Club
Sullivan Way
Trenton, NJ 08628
(609) 883-3566

MIDDLESEX
Public

Cranbury Golf Course
49 Southfield Rd.
Cranbury, NJ 08512
(609) 799-0341

Rutgers Golf Course
Hopes Lane
Piscataway, NJ 08854
(908) 932-2631

Spooky Brook Golf Course
Elizabeth Ave.
East Milestone, NJ 08873
(908) 873-2241

MIDDLESEX
Private

Clearbrook Golf Club
Belmar Rd.
Cranbury, NJ 08512
(609) 655-3443

Colonia Country Club
Colonia Blvd.
Colonia, NJ 07067
(908) 574-8711

Communities of Concordia G.C.
Rt. 4, Box 266
Cranbury, NJ 08512
(609) 655-5631

Forsgate Country Club
Forsgate Dr.
Tamesboro, NJ 08831
(908) 521-0070

Glenwood Country Club
U.S. Hwy. 90
Old Bridge, NJ 08857
(908) 607-2582

Metuchen Golf & Country Club
Plainfield Rd.
Edison, NJ 08820
(908) 548-3003

Princeton Meadows Country Club
70 Hunters Glen Dr.
Plainsboro, NJ 08536
(609) 799-4000

Rossmoor Golf Course
Rossmoor Dr.
Jamesburg, NJ 08831
(609) 655-3182

MIDDLESEX
9-hole

Plainsfield Country Club West
Woodland & Maple Ave.
Edison, NJ 08817
(908) 769-3672

Tara Green Golf Club
Rt. 27
Somerset, NJ 08873
(908) 247-8284

MORRIS
Public

Flanders Valley Golf Course
Pleasant HIll Rd.
Flanders, NJ 87836
(201) 584-8964

Knoll Country Club
Knoll & Green Bank Rd.
Parsippany, NJ 07054
(201) 263-7115

Meadows Golf Course
79 Two Bridges Rd.
Lincoln Park, NJ 07053
(201) 692-7212

MORRIS
Private

Coakly Russo Memorial G.C.
Lyons UMAC
Lyons, NJ 07939
(908) 647-0180

Fairmont Country Club
Southern Blvd.
Chatham, NJ 07928
(201) 377-8901

Madison Golf Club
Green Ave.
Madison, NJ 07940
(201) 377-5264

Menham Golf & Tennis Club
Golf Lane
Mendham, NJ 07945
(201) 543-7297

Morris Country Golf Club
Punch Bowl Rd.
Convent Station, NJ 07961
(201) 539-1188

Mount Tabor Country Club
Ridgewood Ave. & Country Club Rd.
Mount Tabor, NJ 07878
(201) 627-5995

Peace Pipe Golf Club
Lee Rd.
Denville, NJ 07834
(201) 625-4593

Picatinny Golf & Country Club
Picatinny Aresenal
Dover, NJ 07806
(201) 989-2466

MORRIS
Private - Continued

Rockaway River Country Club
Pocono Rd.
Denville, NJ 07834
(201) 627-4461

Roxiticus Golf Club
Bliss Rd.
Mendham, NJ 07945
(201) 543-4071

Shackamaxon Golf & Country Club
P.O. Box 656
Westfield, NJ 07091
(908) 233-3989

Society Hill Club at Morris
1 Gettysburg Way
Lincoln, NJ 07035
(201) 694-3134

Somerset Hills Country Club
Mine Mount Rd.
Bernardsville, NJ 07924
(908) 766-0044

Spring Brook Country Club
9 Spring Brook Rd.
Morristown, NJ 07960
(201) 539-6660

Twin Brooks Country Club
600 Mountain Blvd.
Watchung, NJ 07060
(908) 561-8858

MORRIS
9-hole

Green Pond Golf Club
Green Pond Rd.
Rockaway, NJ 07866
(201) 983-9494

MORRIS
Executive

Pinch Brook Golf Course
234 Ridgedale Ave.
Floorham Park, NJ 87932
(201) 377-2039

PASSAIC
Public

Passaic County Golf Course
209 Totowa Rd.
Wayne, NJ 07470
(201) 694-6105

PASSAIC
Private

North Jersey Country Club
Hamburg Turnpike
Wayne, NJ 07470
(201) 595-5150

Packanack Golf Club
7 West Asborne Terrace
Wayne, NJ 07470
(201) 694-9754

Preakness Hills Country Club
1050 Ratzer Rd.
Wayne, NJ 07470
(201) 694-2910

Upper Montclair Country Club
177 Hepburn Rd.
Clifton, NJ 08318
(201) 777-5178

SOMERSET
Public

Basking Ridge Country Club
185 Madisonville Rd.
Basking Ridge, NJ 07920
(908) 766-8210

Green Knoll Golf Course
Garretson Rd.
Bridgewater, NJ 08807
(908) 722-1300

SOMERSET
Private

Fiddlers Elbow Country Club
Rattlesnake Bridge Rd.
Bedminister, NJ 07931
(908) 439-2123

Fox Hollow Golf Course
59 Fox Chase Run
Sommerville, NJ 08876
(908) 526-0010

Raritan Valley Country Club
Rt. 28
Bridgewater, NJ 08876
(908) 722-2000

SUSSEX
Public

Lake Mohawk Golf Club
West Shore Trail
Sparta, NJ 07081
(201) 729-6466

High Point Country Club
Clove Rd.
Montague, NJ 08800
(201) 293-3282

Lake Lacawanna Golf Course
Lake Dr.
Lake Lacawanna, NJ 07874
(201) 347-9701

Rockview Club
River Rd.
Montague, NJ 08800
(201) 293-9891

Rolling Green Golf Club
214 Newton-Sparta Rd.
Newtony, NJ 07860
(201) 383-3082

SUSSEX
Private

Lake Mohawk Golf Club
West Shore Trail
Sparta, NJ 07081
(201) 729-6466

Newton Country Club
25 Club Rd.
Newton, NJ 07860
(201) 383-2290

Walkill Country Club
Maple Rd.
Franklin, NJ 07416
(201) 827-9620

SUSSEX
9-hole

Culver lake Golf Course
East Shore Rd.
Culver, NJ 07826
(201) 948-5610

Hidden Acres Golf Course
Box 94, Layton Ayers Rd.
Hainsville, NJ 07851
(201) 948-9804

UNION
Public

Galloping Hill Golf Club
Union & Kenilworth Blvd.
Union, NJ 07083
(908) 686-1556

UNION
Private

Canoe Brook Country Club
1108 Morris Turnpike
Summit, NJ 07901
(908) 277-2683

Echo Lake Country Club
Springfield Ave.
Westfield, NJ 07090
(908) 232-4141

Roselle Golf Club
417 Raritan Rd.
Roselle, NJ 07203
(908) 245-9671

Suburban Golf Club
1730 Morris Ave.
Summit, NJ 07083
(908) 686-0444

UNION
9-hole

Scotch Hills Golf Club
Jerusalem Rd.
Scotch Plains, NJ 07076
(201) 232-9748

WARREN
Public

Blair Academy Golf Course
Blair Academy Rd.
Clark, NJ 07825
(908) 362-6218

WARREN
Private

Harkers Hollow Golf Club
950 Union Town Rd.
Phillipsburg, NJ 08864
(908) 859-0977

Panter Valley Golf & Country Club
Rt. 517
Hackettstown, NJ 07840
(908) 852-6120

WARREN
9-hole

Fairway Village Golf Club
Mine Hill Rd.
Wahington, NJ 07882
(908) 689-1530

8. N.J. SOUTH / COUNTIES AND CITIES

Atlantic

B2 / Absecon ... 1
B2 / Brigantine ... 2
B2 / Buena ... 3
B2 / Gallaway Township ... 4
B2 / Mays Landing ... 5
B2 / McKee ... 6
B2 / Somers Point ... 7

Burlington

B1 / Medford ... 8
B1 / Marlton ... 9
B1 / Moorestown ... 10
B1 / Mt. Laurel ... 11
B1 / Willingboro ... 12

Gloucester

B1 / Sewell ... 18
B1 / Turnersville ... 19
B1 / Woodbury ... 20

Monmouth

B1 / Colts Neck ... 21
B1 / Eatontown ... 22
B1 / Farmingdale ... 23
B1 / Neptune ... 24

Camden

B1 / Blackwood ... 13
B1 / Pennsauken ... 14
B1 / Winslow Township ... 15

Cape May

B2 / Cape May Court House ... 16

Cumberland

B2 / Bridgeton ... 17

Ocean

B1 / Bayville ... 25
B1 / Cream Ridge ... 26
B1 / Lakewood ... 27
B1 / Manahawkin ... 28
B1 / Tuckerton ... 29

Salem

B2 / Alloway Township ... 30
B2 / Elmer ... 31
B2 / Salem ... 32

ATLANTIC COUNTY

BRIGANTINE COUNTRY CLUB

Roosevelt Blvd. & East Shore Dr., Brigantine, NJ 08203 / (609) 266-1388

BASIC INFORMATION

Course Type: Public
Year Built: 1926
Architect: N/A
Local Pro: Pat Vanderstein

Course: N/A
Holes: 18 / 72

Back : 6,600 yds. Rating: 71.3 Slope: 123
Middle: 6,300 yds. Rating: 69.5 Slope: 120
Ladies: 5,600 yds. Rating: 68.3 Slope: 117

Tee Time: 7 days in advance.
Price: $42.50 - $25.00

Credit Cards:	■	Restaurant:	
Driving Range:		Lounge:	■
Practice Green:	■	Meeting Rooms:	■
Locker Room:		Tennis:	
Rental Clubs:	■	Swimming:	
Walkers:	■	Jogging Trails:	
Snack Bar:	■	Boating:	■

COURSE DESCRIPTION

Brigantine Country Club offers a playing platform that features water coming into play on 16 holes. It's not your typical layout, but despite the large amount of water, the course is exciting and fun to play.

Like most of the courses in New Jersey, the terrain is mostly flat with subtle undulations. The majority of the fairways are wide and allow a good amount of room to shape your tee-shots in both directions. The overall design of the course plays well for players of all levels. All you have to do is choose the right tee markers for your level of play.

DIRECTIONS

Take Rt. 30 east to Huron Ave. At the Trump Castle Hotel and Casino, make a left until you get to Brigantine Blvd. Go over the bridge and make a left at Roosevelt Blvd., and follow that street straight to the clubhouse.

BUENA VISTA COUNTRY CLUB

Country Club Lane, Buena, NJ 08310 / (602) 697-3733

BASIC INFORMATION

Course Type: Public
Year Built: 1957
Architect: William Gordon & Son
Local Pro: Dennis Henderson

Course: N/A
Holes: 18 / Par 72

Back : 6,869 yds. Rating: 73.5 Slope: 131
Middle: 6,422 yds. Rating: 71.5 Slope: 127
Ladies: 5,651 yds. Rating: 69.6 Slope: 123

Tee Time: 6 days in advance.
Price: $15 - $22

Credit Cards:		Restaurant:	■
Driving Range:	■	Lounge:	■
Practice Green:	■	Meeting Rooms:	■
Locker Room:	■	Tennis:	
Rental Clubs:	■	Swimming:	
Walkers:	■	Jogging Trails:	
Snack Bar:	■	Boating:	

COURSE DESCRIPTION

In 1957, this course was opened by the great Gene Sarazen, Skee Riegel, Bruce Coltar, and Ed Carmen, who was the club pro at the time. New Jersey Governor Robert B. Meyner delivered the dedication address. Later, in 1961, the course hosted a memorable professional golf event called the Philadelphia PGA championship.

This remarkable test of golf is cut right out of the New Jersey Pinelands. Always kept in the best condition possible, you'll remember this course for a long time to come.

DIRECTIONS

From Atlantic City, take the Atlantic City Expressway to Exit 12 (Rt. 40 east). It should take you about twenty minutes to get to the course from here. Look for it on your right.

GREATE BAY RESORT & COUNTRY CLUB

901 Mays Landing Rd., Somers Point, NJ 08244 / (609) 927-0066

BASIC INFORMATION

Course Type: Semi-private
Year Built: 1920's / 1972
Architect: William Parks / Tom Fazio
Local Pro: Tom Carpus

Course: N/A
Holes: 18 / Par 71

Back : 6,750 yds. Rating: 72.3 Slope: 130
Middle: 6,370 yds. Rating: 70.6 Slope: 127
Ladies: 5,495 yds. Rating: 72.2 Slope: 126

Tee Time: 3-8 days in advance.
Price: $35 - $60

Credit Cards:	■	Restaurant:	■
Driving Range:	■	Lounge:	■
Practice Green:	■	Meeting Rooms:	■
Locker Room:	■	Tennis:	
Rental Clubs:	■	Swimming:	■
Walkers:		Jogging Trails:	
Snack Bar:	■	Boating:	■

COURSE DESCRIPTION

The *Greate Bay Resort and Country Club* is a true shot-makers test of golf. You'll find over 70 bunkers lurking in the distance around the many treacherous fairways. On your way to par, you'll often have to take a step back and ask yourself which position would be best to place your ball on the big, and often severely sloped, putting greens.

Unlike many of the courses that can be found in New Jersey, this one features a wide variety of elevation changes that bring forth the element of playing shots out of uneven lies.

DIRECTIONS

Take the Atlantic City Expressway to the Garden State Pkwy. going south to Exit 7S. Go to Exit 30 (Somers Point / Ocean City) and go to the first stop sign. Make a right, then go to the first traffic light. Make a left and look for the course on your left, too.

GREEN TREE COUNTRY CLUB

Sommers Point & Rd., Mays Landing, NJ 08330 / (609) 625-9131

BASIC INFORMATION

Course Type: Public
Year Built: N/A
Architect: N/A
Local Pro: N/A

Course: N/A
Holes: 18 / Par 72

Back : 5,709 yds. Rating: 67.7 Slope: 111
Middle: 5,349 yds. Rating: 66.6 Slope: 110
Ladies: 4,804 yds. Rating: 65.5 Slope: 109

Tee Time: 7 days in advance.
Price: $8 - $22

Credit Cards:		Restaurant:	■
Driving Range:	■	Lounge:	
Practice Green:	■	Meeting Rooms:	
Locker Room:	■	Tennis:	
Rental Clubs:	■	Swimming:	
Walkers:	■	Jogging Trails:	
Snack Bar:	■	Boating:	■

COURSE DESCRIPTION

Situated in a beautiful Pinelands setting along the Great Egg Harbor river, this county-operated golf course is relatively flat, nestled amid pine and oak trees.

Quite a few water hazards and tight driving areas make this a challenging course to play. Hazards come into play on thirteen holes. The #8 hole is a par-4 that stretches 401 yards, and demands that you navigate your ball over a strategically-placed water hazard directly in front of the green.

This is not a terribly difficult course to play, as you can see by the numbers posted, and as such will appeal mostly to high-handicap players.

DIRECTIONS

Take Rt. 9 to Rt. 559 north approximately 10 miles to the golf course. It will be located on your right.

ATLANTIC COUNTY

MARRIOTT COUNTRY CLUB

401 Rt. 9 South New York Rd., Gallaway Township, NJ 08201 / (609) 652-1800

BASIC INFORMATION

Course Type: Public / Resort
Year Built: 1957
Architect: Tommy & Flynn
Local Pro: Darren Helfrick

Course: Pines / Bay (18 / Par 72)
Holes: 36

Back : 6,885 yds. Rating: 73.0 Slope: 132
Middle: 6,394 yds. Rating: 70.7 Slope: 128
Ladies: 5,837 yds. Rating: 73.2 Slope: 128

Tee Time: 1 - 30 days in advance.
Price: $40 - $75

Credit Cards:	■	Restaurant:	■
Driving Range:	■	Lounge:	■
Practice Green:	■	Meeting Rooms:	■
Locker Room:	■	Tennis:	■
Rental Clubs:	■	Swimming:	■
Walkers:	■	Jogging Trails:	■
Snack Bar:	■	Boating:	■

COURSE DESCRIPTION

The **Marriott Country Club** is one of the most sought-after golfing locations in New Jersey. The Pines course happens to be the one that better players prefer playing, despite the fact that the other course (Bay) was designed by the late Donald Ross.

You'll find plenty of bunkering along the wide variety of hole designs. It's a tough course from the tees, yet it offers plenty of comfort along the greens by giving you the option to roll the ball through the front of the putting surface towards the pin. Oddly enough, that's a feature that many people identify with Donald Ross.

DIRECTIONS

Take Garden State Pkwy. north to Exit 48 (Rt. 9). Go about 7.4 miles further to the hotel. You'll see the course on your right.

MARRIOTT'S SEAVIEW RESORT ON REEDS BAY

401 South New York Rd., Absecon, NJ 08201 / (609) 748-7680

BASIC INFORMATION

Course Type: Resort
Year Built: 1915
Architect: William Flynn & Howard Toomey
Local Pro: Darrin Helfrick

Course: Pines Course (18 / Par 72)
Holes: 36

Back : 6,885 yds. Rating: 73.0 Slope: 132
Middle: 6,394 yds. Rating: 70.7 Slope: 128
Ladies: 5,837 yds. Rating: 73.2 Slope: 128

Tee Time: 1 - 30 days in advance.
Price: $45 - $75

Credit Cards:	■	Restaurant:	■
Driving Range:	■	Lounge:	■
Practice Green:	■	Meeting Rooms:	■
Locker Room:	■	Tennis:	■
Rental Clubs:	■	Swimming:	■
Walkers:		Jogging Trails:	■
Snack Bar:	■	Boating:	

COURSE DESCRIPTION

The Pines course was built through a heavily wooded area. It's a long course that demands strong driving skills, accuracy from the fairways, and a gentle putting stroke on its undulating greens. The Bay course was built by the late Donald Ross. His characteristic small greens, guarded by steep faced bunkers, make up the majority of the hole designs. In 1942, the course hosted the PGA championship with a stellar combination of golfing pro's — despite the fact that America was at war. Sam Snead came out victorious against the likes of Ben Hogan, Byron Nelson, Gene Sarazen, and even Walter Hagen.

DIRECTIONS

Take the Garden State Pkwy. south to Exit 48. At Rt. 9 go south for about six miles and look for the resort on your right.

MAYS LANDING COUNTRY CLUB
Cates Rd., McKee, NJ 08232 / (602) 641-4411

BASIC INFORMATION

Course Type: Public
Year Built: N/A
Architect: N/A
Local Pro: Bob Herman

Course: N/A
Holes: 18 / Par 72

Back : 6,662 yds. Rating: 71.1 Slope: 116
Middle: 6,296 yds. Rating: 69.5 Slope: 112
Ladies: 5,433 yds. Rating: 70.3 Slope: 114

Tee Time: 7 days in advance.
Price: $12 - $25

Credit Cards:	■	Restaurant:	■
Driving Range:	■	Lounge:	■
Practice Green:	■	Meeting Rooms:	■
Locker Room:	■	Tennis:	
Rental Clubs:	■	Swimming:	
Walkers:	■	Jogging Trails:	
Snack Bar:	■	Boating:	■

COURSE DESCRIPTION

The *Mays Landing Country Club* offers an attractive golfing venue for new players and high-handicappers. It's rating and slope is slightly harder than the numbers indicated. You'll need to hit accurate drives to stay clear of the many bunkers that come into play. It's a tight, traditional course, that features many water hazards too.

The 18th hole is the hardest on the course. It's a par-4, dogleg-left, that measures 412 yards from the back-tees. You'll have to hit your drive a minimum of 200 yards to make the turn safely, followed by a well-placed approach shot to the heavily bunkered green.

DIRECTIONS

Go west from Atlantic City to Exit 9 and make a left. At Rt. 40 make a right, and follow that road to the course. Look for it on your left.

GOLDEN PHEASANT GOLF COURSE
141 Country Club Dr, Medford, NJ 08055 / (609) 267-4276

BASIC INFORMATION

Course Type: Public
Year Built: 1953
Architect: N/A
Local Pro: N/A

Course: N/A
Holes: 18 / Par 72

Back : 6,273 yds. Rating: 68.1 Slope: 119
Middle: 6,002 yds. Rating: 67.0 Slope: 116
Ladies: 5,105 yds. Rating: 68.4 Slope: 114

Tee Time: 7 days in advance.
Price: $16.50 - $25

Credit Cards:	■	Restaurant:	■
Driving Range:		Lounge:	
Practice Green:	■	Meeting Rooms:	
Locker Room:		Tennis:	
Rental Clubs:		Swimming:	
Walkers:	■	Jogging Trails:	
Snack Bar:	■	Boating:	

COURSE DESCRIPTION

The *Golden Pheasant Golf Course* will appeal to the not-so-strong golfer who is looking for a short course that features a limited amount of hard play through 18 holes of golf.

This course, among many others like it, offers golfers a chance to work on their short games, despite their individual handicaps. It's a straightforward layout that offers simple golf, for people who prefer to play for the sheer joy of playing, rather than the pure challenge of a highly selected alternative course.

DIRECTIONS

Take Rt. 70 east and go a mile past Medford Circle until you get to Eayrestown Rd. Make a left and follow the street to the course. Look for it on your left.

BURLINGTON COUNTY

INDIAN SPRING GOLF CLUB

Elmwood Rd. & Main St., Marlton, NJ 08035 / (609) 983-0222

BASIC INFORMATION

Course Type: Public
Year Built: 1976
Architect: N/A
Local Pro: N/A

Course: N/A
Holes: 18 / Par 70

Back : 6,299 yds. Rating: 67.9 Slope: 107
Middle: 6,018 yds. Rating: N/A Slope: N/A
Ladies: 5,639 yds. Rating: 71.3 Slope: 115

Tee Time: 7 days with credit-card.
Price: $17 - $20

Credit Cards:		Restaurant:	■
Driving Range:	■	Lounge:	■
Practice Green:	■	Meeting Rooms:	
Locker Room:	■	Tennis:	
Rental Clubs:	■	Swimming:	
Walkers:	■	Jogging Trails:	
Snack Bar:	■	Boating:	

COURSE DESCRIPTION

This scenic course offers simple golf in a comfortable setting. If you're not serious about your game, and you enjoy playing golf as a source of relaxation, you may want to consider playing this course, despite the fact that it's only 6,299 yards in length from the back tees with a below-average slope rating.

DIRECTIONS

Take Marlton Circle to Olga's Diner until you get to Hwy. 70. Proceed east and watch for two passing shopping centers on your right. When the road turns into a single lane, make your first right at the next set of lights. That will be Elmwood Rd by Main St. which will lead you to the course.

RAMBLEWOOD COUNTRY CLUB

200 Country Club Parkway, Mt. Laurel, NJ 08054 / (609) 235-2118

BASIC INFORMATION

Course Type: Public
Year Built: 1962
Architect: N/A
Local Pro: Sean Cooke

Course: Red / Blue (18 / Par 72)
Holes: 27

Back : 6,723 yds. Rating: 72.1 Slope: 130
Middle: 6,289 yds. Rating: 70.3 Slope: 126
Ladies: 5,499 yds. Rating: 71.4 Slope: 126

Tee Time: 7 days in advance.
Price: $13 - $46.50

Credit Cards:	■	Restaurant:	■
Driving Range:		Lounge:	■
Practice Green:	■	Meeting Rooms:	■
Locker Room:	■	Tennis:	■
Rental Clubs:	■	Swimming:	■
Walkers:	■	Jogging Trails:	
Snack Bar:	■	Boating:	■

COURSE DESCRIPTION

This is a well thought out golf course with a great combination of holes. In fact, all three combinations are beautifully appointed.

The Red / Blue combination seems to be the one that better players tend to gravitate to. It's a fantastic layout with many demading holes. You'll need to drive the ball long and accurately, hit your approach shots with finesse, and follow through with a deft putting stroke on the many difficult-to-read greens. The course is set up to accommadate players of all skill levels.

DIRECTIONS

From the New Jersey Turnpike, get off at Exit 4 and go south to the second set of lights. Make a left at Church Rd., followed by another left at the upcoming third road at Corner Club Pkwy. Look for the course on your left.

RANCOCAS GOLF COURSE

Clubhouse Dr., Willingboro, NJ 08046 / (609) 877-5344

BASIC INFORMATION

Course Type: Public
Year Built: 1964
Architect: Robert Trent Jones, Sr.
Local Pro: Position is open

Course: N/A
Holes: 18 / Par 71

Back : 6,634 yds. Rating: 73.0 Slope: 130
Middle: 6,429 yds. Rating: 70.3 Slope: 125
Ladies: 5,284 yds. Rating: 73.0 Slope: 127

Tee Time: 14 days in advance.
Price: $15 - $28

Credit Cards: ■	Restaurant: ■
Driving Range: ■	Lounge:
Practice Green: ■	Meeting Rooms:
Locker Room:	Tennis:
Rental Clubs: ■	Swimming:
Walkers: ■	Jogging Trails:
Snack Bar: ■	Boating:

COURSE DESCRIPTION

The **Rancocas Golf Course** is a championship layout that is truly vintage R.T. Jones, Sr. The front-nine was expertly carved out of a mature hardwood forest and features some of the most competitive tree-lined par-4's you'll ever find.

By contrast, the back-nine is generally open and gently rolling. Extensive sand bunkering and large undulating greens compensate for its openness.

The finishing two holes are absolutely spectacular.

DIRECTIONS

Take the New Jersey Pkwy. to Exit 5 (Rt. 541, Mount Holly Rd.). Take Rt. 541 west to I-295 to the Rt. 626 Exit (Rancocas By Pass). Take Rt 626 west through the town of WIllingboro and turn left onto Country Club Rd.

WILLOWBROOK COUNTRY CLUB

Bridgeboro Rd., Moorestown, NJ 08057 / (609) 461-0131

BASIC INFORMATION

Course Type: Municipal
Year Built: 1967
Architect: Bill Gordon
Local Pro: Brian Feld

Course: N/A
Holes: 18 / Par 72

Back : 6,457 yds. Rating: 71.2 Slope: 125
Middle: 6,204 yds. Rating: 69.9 Slope: 118
Ladies: 5,028 yds. Rating: 68.3 Slope: 110

Tee Time: 7 days in advance.
Price: $13.50 - $38

Credit Cards: ■	Restaurant: ■
Driving Range: ■	Lounge: ■
Practice Green: ■	Meeting Rooms: ■
Locker Room: ■	Tennis:
Rental Clubs: ■	Swimming:
Walkers: ■	Jogging Trails:
Snack Bar: ■	Boating:

COURSE DESCRIPTION

Willowbrook Country Club offers competitive golf that is not overly demanding in any one area. It's an enjoyable layout that mostly appeals to high-handicappers because of its short length.

You can make the most of every hole by playing your 3-wood off most of the tees instead of uslng your driver. Good course management, coupled with accurate play, will put you in position for par or better on many of the holes.

Better players will appreciate the course as an exploratory venue to practice their short games.

DIRECTIONS

Take Hwy. 295 south to Exit 43 an make a right. When you reach the second set of lights, make a left and proceed to the course about a mile further down the road.

PENNSAUKEN COUNTRY CLUB

3800 Haddonfield, Pennsauken, NJ 08109 / (609) 662-4961

BASIC INFORMATION

Course Type: Public
Year Built: 1931
Architect: N/A
Local Pro: Quinton Griffith

Course: N/A
Holes: 18 / Par 70

Back: 6,000 yds. Rating: N/A   Slope: N/A
Middle: 5,700 yds. Rating: 67.9 Slope: 111
Ladies: 4,860 yds. Rating: N/A   Slope: N/A

Tee Time: 7 day in advance.
Price: $22 - $35

Credit Cards: Restaurant: ■
Driving Range: Lounge: ■
Practice Green: ■   Meeting Rooms: ■
Locker Room: Tennis:
Rental Clubs: ■   Swimming:
Walkers: ■   Jogging Trails:
Snack Bar: ■   Boating: ■

COURSE DESCRIPTION

Pennsauken Country Club is very much a senior citizen designed course. It's short on distance, and offers a friendly playing field, surrounded by trees and well placed traps. The small greens are a bit tough to hit if you're not approaching them with a wedge in your hand. Other than that, you'll often have an opportunity to roll your ball between an opening and onto the green towards the pin.

The hardest hole on the course is the #7, par-3, that stretches 276 yards from the back-tees. The "postage-stamp" green slopes from top-to-bottom and features bunkers front left and right. Play the ball to the back-center.

DIRECTIONS

Take the Betsy Ross Bridge to Rt. 90 and get off at Cherry Hill Exit. The course will be about a half-mile further on your left.

PINELAND GOLF CLUB

Rt. 561 Spur, Winslow Township, NJ 08037 / (609) 561-6110

BASIC INFORMATION

Course Type: Public
Year Built: 1963
Architect: N/A
Local Pro: Bill Papa

Course: N/A
Holes: 18 / Par 72

Back : 6,350 yds. Rating: 69.2 Slope: 114
Middle: 6,100 yds. Rating: 68.9 Slope: 113
Ladies: 5,400 yds. Rating: N/A   Slope: N/A

Tee Time: 7 days in advance.
Price: $16 - $21

Credit Cards: ■   Restaurant: ■
Driving Range: ■   Lounge: ■
Practice Green: ■   Meeting Rooms:
Locker Room: ■   Tennis:
Rental Clubs: ■   Swimming:
Walkers: ■   Jogging Trails:
Snack Bar: ■   Boating:

COURSE DESCRIPTION

The **Pineland Golf Club** is centered around a relatively easy course design that allows high-handicap golfers a chance to shoot close to par and have a great time doing it. If you're a single digit handicapper, you won't find much of a challenge awaiting you, unless you're prepared to work on your short game. The course features many tree-lined fairways that extend to mostly small-sized greens. You'll often be driving your ball onto tight landing areas for good second shot positions. The front nine is both longer and tighter than the back and thus demands the most amount of concentration.

DIRECTIONS

Take the Atlantic City Expressway to Exit 33 and make a left. At the first set of lights, make a right and the course will be 2 miles further on your right.

VALLEYBROOK GOLF CLUB

1 Golf View Dr., Blackwood, NJ 08012 / (609) 227-3171

BASIC INFORMATION

Course Type: Public
Year Built: 1960 / 1990
Architect: Howell Purdy ('90)
Local Pro: Kevin Cotter

Course:N/A
Holes: 18 / par 72

Back : 6,123 yds. Rating: 70.6 Slope: 125
Middle: 6,010 yds. Rating: 70.0 Slope: 124
Ladies: 5,319 yds. Rating: 68.1 Slope: 120

Tee Time: 7 days in advance.
Price: $12 - $16

Credit Cards:	Restaurant:	
Driving Range:	■	Lounge:
Practice Green:	■	Meeting Rooms: ■
Locker Room:	■	Tennis:
Rental Clubs:	■	Swimming:
Walkers:	■	Jogging Trails:
Snack Bar:	■	Boating:

COURSE DESCRIPTION

You'll find plenty of back-woods throughout the playing field for errant shots to fall into, a small creek comes into play more than once, and many of the fairways and greens feature tricky slopes. The hardest hole on the course is the 16th. It's a par-4, dogleg-left, that measures 347 yards from the back-tees. Hit your tee shot about 170 yards straight for position. You'll find a creek going along the left of the fairway and in front of the green. Trees also come into play on the right and around the putting surface. Play your approach to the middle of the green.

DIRECTIONS

Take I-295 to Rt. 42 and go south to the Blackwood Clementon Rd. exit. Go right for about a half-mile to the first stoplight. Make a left at Gloucester Rd. and look for the course about a quarter-mile on your left.

AVALON GOLF CLUB

1510 Rt. 9 North Swanton, Cape May Court House, NJ 08210 / (609) 465-4389

BASIC INFORMATION

Course Type: Semi-private
Year Built: 1971
Architect: Bob Hendricks
Local Pro: ted Wenner

Course: N/A
Holes: 18 / Par 71

Back : 6,325 yds. Rating: 70.3 Slope: 122
Middle: 5,896 yds. Rating: 68.4 Slope: 117
Ladies: 4,924 yds. Rating: 70.7 Slope: 122

Tee Time: 7 days in advance.
Price: $31 - $55

Credit Cards:	■	Restaurant:	■
Driving Range:	■	Lounge:	■
Practice Green:	■	Meeting Rooms:	■
Locker Room:	■	Tennis:	
Rental Clubs:	■	Swimming:	
Walkers:	■	Jogging Trails:	
Snack Bar:	■	Boating:	■

COURSE DESCRIPTION

Avalon Golf Club is located about 2 miles from the Atlantic Ocean. It backs up to the beautiful "Great Sound" Bay. The town of Avalon and Stone Harbor can be seen from the highly-elevated 6th tee which is also the signature hole for the course.

You'll find nine lakes and fifty-four bunkers waiting patiently for that one errant shot. The course is neither long nor very difficult to play. It makes for a great afternoon of thoroughly relaxing "short-distance" golf.

DIRECTIONS

Take the New Jersey Turnpike to Exit 13 and proceed for about 3/4 of a mile to Rt. 9. The course will appear on your left.

CAPE MAY NATIONAL GOLF CLUB

P.O. Box 2069, Cape May, NJ 08204 / (609) 884-1563

BASIC INFORMATION

Course Type: Semi-private
Year Built: 1991
Architect: Karl Litton & Robert Mullock
Local Pro: Russell Davis

Course: N/A
Holes: 18 / Par 71

Back : 6,807 yds. Rating: 72.9 Slope: 136
Middle: 6,083 yds. Rating: 69.4 Slope: 123
Ladies: 4,696 yds. Rating: 68.8 Slope: 115

Tee Time: 7 days in advance.
Price: $15 - $46.50

Credit Cards: ■	Restaurant:
Driving Range: ■	Lounge:
Practice Green: ■	Meeting Rooms:
Locker Room:	Tennis:
Rental Clubs:	Swimming:
Walkers: ■	Jogging Trails:
Snack Bar: ■	Boating: ■

COURSE DESCRIPTION

Cape May National is a golf course built in the classic tradition of half a century ago, with major emphasis on shotmaking values! Each hole is designed to fit the particular setting and its appropriate position in relation to the other 17 holes.

To enhance the playability of the holes, the tees, greens and fairways are all the finest Bent Grass. The greens are generally large and undulating and built to USGA specifications. The multiple tees allow you to adjust the challenge to the level of your game, including golf at the championship level.

DIRECTIONS

Take the Garden State Pkwy. south to Exit 4A. Go to the second traffic light (Rt. 9) and turn left. The course will be about 2.2 miles down on the left.

WILDWOOD GOLF & COUNTRY CLUB

Rt. 2 Golf Club Rd., Cape May Courthouse, NJ 08210 / (609) 455-2127

BASIC INFORMATION

Course Type: Semi-private
Year Built: 1939
Architect: N/A
Local Pro: John Stafford

Course: N/A
Holes: 18 / Par 71

Back : 6,285 yds. Rating: 70.2 Slope: 123
Middle: 6,009 yds. Rating: 69.1 Slope: 120
Ladies: 5,470 yds. Rating: 70.3 Slope: 120

Tee Time: 6 days in advance.
Price: $20 - $22

Credit Cards:	Restaurant: ■
Driving Range:	Lounge: ■
Practice Green: ■	Meeting Rooms: ■
Locker Room: ■	Tennis:
Rental Clubs: ■	Swimming:
Walkers: ■	Jogging Trails:
Snack Bar:	Boating: ■

COURSE DESCRIPTION

The *Wildwood Golf & Country Club* offers a friendly atmosphere and an equally friendly golf course that you'll enjoy playing if your a high-handicap player.

The most notorious hole on the course is the 17th hole. This par-4 stretches out to 416 yards from the back-tees. You'll be facing a blind tee-shot towards a rising fairway in the distance. Keep the ball straight and you should do well. Your approach will most likely be played with a mid-to-high iron towards a back-to-front sloping two-tier green that features a bunker back-left and another front-right. You can bailout towards the front-left.

DIRECTIONS

Take Hwy. 49 west to Rt. 553 and go south for about 5-miles to the course. Look for it on your left.

COHNAZICK COUNTRY CLUB
P.O. Box 149 Fairton, Bridgeton, NJ 08320 / (609) 455-2127

BASIC INFORMATION
Course Type: Semi-private
Year Built: N/A
Architect: N/A
Local Pro: John Stafford

Course: N/A
Holes: 18 / Par 71

Back : 6,285 yds. Rating: 70.2 Slope: 123
Middle: 6,058 yds. Rating: 69.1 Slope: 120
Ladies: 5,470 yds. Rating: 70.5 Slope: 120

Tee Time: 6 days in advance.
Price: $10 - $12

Credit Cards:		Restaurant:	■
Driving Range:		Lounge:	■
Practice Green:	■	Meeting Rooms:	■
Locker Room:	■	Tennis:	
Rental Clubs:	■	Swimming:	
Walkers:	■	Jogging Trails:	
Snack Bar:	■	Boating:	■

COURSE DESCRIPTION
It doesn't matter that this course features a playing field of only 6,285 yards from the back-tees, it's still a respectable challenge for mid-to-high handicappers, indicated by its slope rating of 123.

Many of the holes are of the dogleg variety and are well guarded by neighboring trees. You'll need to hit your drives accurately to cut off the corners and get yourself into good position on your following approach shots.

DIRECTIONS
Take Hwy. 49 to the Delaware Memorial Bridge going east. When you finally arrive at Bridgeton, make a right on Hwy. 77 going south. The course will be approximately 5.5 miles further. It will appear on your right.

FREEWAY GOLF COURSE
Siklerville Rd. 11858, Turnersville, NJ 08081 / (908) 227-1115

BASIC INFORMATION
Course Type: Public
Year Built: 1978
Architect: N/A
Local Pro: Bill Bishop

Course: N/A
Holes: 18 / Par 72

Back : 6,536 yds. Rating: 73.6 Slope: 111
Middle: 6,151 yds. Rating: 70.3 Slope: 107
Ladies: 5,395 yds. Rating: 73.4 Slope: 115

Tee Time: 7 days in advance.
Price: $10 - $17

Credit Cards:	■	Restaurant:	■
Driving Range:	■	Lounge:	■
Practice Green:	■	Meeting Rooms:	
Locker Room:	■	Tennis:	
Rental Clubs:		Swimming:	
Walkers:	■	Jogging Trails:	
Snack Bar:	■	Boating:	

COURSE DESCRIPTION
The *Freeway Golf Course* features an easy layout that shouldn't cause too much trouble for even high-handicap players. It's a flat course with very few hazards along its path. Surprisingly enough, the number one handicap hole could have easily come from a much harder layout. This par-3 hole measures 232 yards from the back-tees and is very demanding. You'll need to hit your shot over the big bunker that lies directly in front of the green. The green itself slopes from front to back.

DIRECTIONS
Take Rt. 42 south towards the Atlantic City Expressway. Right before the Expressway, take the Sickerville Exit and make a right. At the first set of lights, make another right to Sickerville, and the course will be on your left.

GLOUCESTER COUNTY

RON JAWORSKI'S EAGLE NEST COUNTRY CLUB
Woodbury, Sewell, NJ 08080 / (908) 464-0535

BASIC INFORMATION

Course Type: Public
Year Built: 1959 / 1962
Architect: William & Dave Gordon (Dave: '62)
Local Pro: Joe Callahan

Course:N/A
Holes: 18 / Par 71

Back : 6,376 yds. Rating: 71.3 Slope: 130
Middle: 6,001 yds. Rating: 70.0 Slope: 128
Ladies: 5,210 yds. Rating: 71.2 Slope: 125

Tee Time: 7 days in advance.
Price: $15 - $25

Credit Cards:	■	Restaurant:	■
Driving Range:		Lounge:	■
Practice Green:	■	Meeting Rooms:	■
Locker Room:	■	Tennis:	
Rental Clubs:	■	Swimming:	
Walkers:	■	Jogging Trails:	
Snack Bar:	■	Boating:	

COURSE DESCRIPTION

This is a good platform for better-than-average golfers to enjoy. You can't judge this course by its distance alone; after all, take a look at its slope rating. At 130, this course can play some mean tricks on your eyes, if you're not prepared for them. You'll need to drive the ball accurately through the many narrow fairways that are featured.

The appropriately numbered 13th hole is the toughest one on the course. This par-4 measures 408 yards from the back-tees. Hit your drive straight down the middle and you'll be left with a mid-to-long iron to a two-tiered green that slopes from back-to-front. Keep your eyes open for the two bunkers that come into play left and front.

DIRECTIONS

Exit the Walt Whitman Bridge to Rt. 42 and go south to Exit 33B. Look for the course about a quarter-mile on your left.

WESTWOOD GOLF CLUB
850 Kings Hwy., Woodbury, NJ 08096 / (908) 845-2000

BASIC INFORMATION

Course Type: Public
Year Built: 1962
Architect: N/A
Local Pro: N/A

Course: N/A
Holes: 18 / Par 71

Back : 5,931 yds. Rating: 68.2 Slope: 116
Middle: N/A yds. Rating: N/A Slope: N/A
Ladies: 5,251 yds. Rating: 69.1 Slope: 114

Tee Time: Monday at noon for the weekend.
Price: $15 - $20

Credit Cards:		Restaurant:	
Driving Range:		Lounge:	
Practice Green:	■	Meeting Rooms:	
Locker Room:	■	Tennis:	
Rental Clubs:	■	Swimming:	
Walkers:	■	Jogging Trails:	
Snack Bar:	■	Boating:	

COURSE DESCRIPTION

The course is kept in excellent shape and offers fun for senior citizens and golfers short on distance. It's not the most difficult course, but it does offer an interesting string of holes that will test your short game quite often. It's also surprisingly hilly for a south Jersey course. You'll find water coming into play on four holes. The course is especially pretty during the spring when it's adorned with daffodils, dogwood trees, and so much more!

DIRECTIONS

Take Rt. 295 to Exit 21. Make a right at the lights and a following right at the next set of lights onto Grove Rd. Bear left and go under the over pass and make a left at the stop sign to Jessup Rd. At the first traffic light, make a left onto Kings Hwy. Look for the course on your right.

MONMOUTH COUNTY

HOMINY HILL GOLF CLUB

Rt. 537 Mercer Rd., Colts Neck, NJ 07722 / (908) 462-9222

BASIC INFORMATION

Course Type: Public
Year Built: Between the '50's and the '60's
Architect: Robert Trent Jones, Sr.
Local Pro: N/A

Course:N/A
Holes: 18 / Par 72

Back : 7,059 yds. Rating: 74.4 Slope: 132
Middle: 6,470 yds. Rating: 71.7 Slope: 127
Ladies: 5,794 yds. Rating: 73.9 Slope: 128

Tee Time: 7 days in advance.
Price: $16 - $34

Credit Cards:
Driving Range: ■
Practice Green: ■
Locker Room: ■
Rental Clubs: ■
Walkers: ■
Snack Bar: ■

Restaurant: ■
Lounge: ■
Meeting Rooms:
Tennis:
Swimming:
Jogging Trails:
Boating: ■

COURSE DESCRIPTION

If you're a serious low-handicap golfer, you're going to greatly enjoy this course.

It's a tough challenge that demands long accurate drives off the tees to avoid the high rough. Your approach shots will need to be precisely executed onto the heavily bunkered large greens. The 17th hole on the course is rated the hardest. It's a par-5 that measures 537 yards from the back-tees. You'll need to hit your drive long and straight to get into position. Set yourself up for a high-lofted alternate wedge on your first approach. Your second approach shot will have to land softly onto the right side of the wide and narrow green.

DIRECTIONS

Take Hwy. 537 east and just west of Rt. 18 exchange (Hwy 537). Follow the signs to the course.

HOWELL PARK GOLF COURSE

Yellow Brook & Preventoriuim Rd., Farmingdale, NJ 07727 / (908) 938-4771

BASIC INFORMATION

Course Type: Public
Year Built: 1967
Architect: Robert Trent Jones, Sr.
Local Pro: Alan Roberts

Course: N/A
Holes: 18 / Par 72

Back : 6,885 yds. Rating: 70.0 Slope: 126
Middle: 6,276 yds. Rating: 70.2 Slope: 120
Ladies: 5,693 yds. Rating: 72.5 Slope: 125

Tee Time: 7 days in advance.
Price: $15.50 - $33

Credit Cards:
Driving Range: ■
Practice Green: ■
Locker Room:
Rental Clubs: ■
Walkers: ■
Snack Bar: ■

Restaurant:
Lounge:
Meeting Rooms: ■
Tennis:
Swimming:
Jogging Trails:
Boating: ■

COURSE DESCRIPTION

The *Howell Park Golf Course* offers a competitive game on a very imaginative layout. You'll be driving off long demanding tee shots.

The most treacherous hole on the course is the par-4, number 8 hole, that measures approximately 455 yards. If you can hit a docent drive straight, you'll only be about 170 yards from the green. It's a long, narrow green, featuring a small bunker on its front right, and a large bunker on its top left. Try to play your approach shot to the bottom right of the green.

DIRECTIONS

Take the Garden State Pkwy. to Exit 98 . Take that to Hwy 195 and go west to Exit 31B. At the first set of lights, make a left and proceed for about 2 1/2 miles. Make a left turn before Howell High School. The course will be on your left.

JUMPING BROOK COUNTRY CLUB

Jumping Brook Rd., Neptune, NJ 07753 / (908) 922-6140

BASIC INFORMATION

Course Type: Semi-private
Year Built: 1925
Architect: Willard Wilkenson
Local Pro: Don Hollis

Course: N/A
Holes: 18 / Par 72

Back : 6,610 yds. Rating: 71.4 Slope: 122
Middle: 6,276 yds. Rating: 69.6 Slope: 118
Ladies: 5,316 yds. Rating: 71.2 Slope: 118

Tee Time: 1- 3 days in advance.
Price: $22 - $29

Credit Cards: ■	Restaurant:	■
Driving Range: ■	Lounge:	■
Practice Green: ■	Meeting Rooms: ■	
Locker Room: ■	Tennis:	
Rental Clubs: ■	Swimming:	
Walkers: ■	Jogging Trails:	
Snack Bar: ■	Boating:	

COURSE DESCRIPTION

Jumping Brook Country Club is an old course with rolling hills and small, elevated greens protected by deep bunkers. It has a variety of short and long, tight and open holes. The front side is both longer and harder than the back. Get to the driving range early to warm up your muscles and get your mind prepared.

The course hosted the 1934 New Jersey Open and the 1951 New Jersey PGA. It's a shot-makers course that favors a good all-around short game.

DIRECTIONS

Take Exit 100 A (Rt. 66 East), from the Garden State Pkwy., and go to the first light. Make a right on Jumping Brook Rd. and proceed directly to the course.

OLD ORCHARD COUNTRY CLUB

54 Monmouth Rd., Eatontown, NJ 07724 / (908) 542-9139

BASIC INFORMATION

Course Type: Public
Year Built: 1929
Architect: N/A
Local Pro: George Craig

Course: N/A
Holes: 18 / Par 72

Back : 6,588 yds. Rating: 70.5 Slope: 116
Middle: 6,183 yds. Rating: 68.6 Slope: 112
Ladies: 5,575 yds. Rating: 70.0 Slope: 115

Tee Time: 30 days in advance.
Price: $21 - $26

Credit Cards:	Restaurant:	■
Driving Range:	Lounge:	■
Practice Green:	Meeting Rooms: ■	
Locker Room: ■	Tennis:	
Rental Clubs: ■	Swimming:	
Walkers: ■	Jogging Trails:	
Snack Bar: ■	Boating:	■

COURSE DESCRIPTION

The **Old Orchard Country Club** offers a formidable challenge to many different types of golfers. It's a wonderful course, because it offers many options from the teeing areas.

The 11th hole is the hardest rated hole on the course. The par-4 stretches 433 yards from the back tees. From the tees, you'll need to hit your drive along the right side of the fairway, away from the huge waste bunkers on your left. Approach shots are typically about 160-180 yards away from the green. You'll need to navigate your ball with a high-fade towards the left side of the putting surface, the only side without a bunker sitting directly in front of it.

DIRECTIONS

Take the Garden State Pkwy. north to Hwy. 105 and pay the toll ($.35). Go east on Hwy. 36 to Hwy. 71 going north. The course will be 1/4 mile on your left.

SHARK RIVER GOLF COURSE

320 Old Corlies Ave., Neptune, NJ 07753 / (908) 922-4141

BASIC INFORMATION

Course Type: Public
Year Built: 1916
Architect: Scotty Iason
Local Pro: Howard Cahoun

Course: N/A
Holes: 18 / Par 71

Back : 6,220 yds. Rating: 68.9 Slope: 112
Middle: 5,530 yds. Rating: 67.8 Slope: 110
Ladies: 5,987 yds. Rating: 71.3 Slope: 116

Tee Time: 5 days in advance.
Price: $14.25 - $30.50

Credit Cards:	■	Restaurant:	■
Driving Range:	■	Lounge:	■
Practice Green:	■	Meeting Rooms:	
Locker Room:		Tennis:	
Rental Clubs:	■	Swimming:	
Walkers:	■	Jogging Trails:	
Snack Bar:	■	Boating:	

COURSE DESCRIPTION

This course is based on an old links design concept. Deep bunkers are scattered in the distance to gobble up your errant tee shots. If this isn't enough, the course also features high rising "elephant grass" that will hide your ball for a lifetime.

Number 9 is an important hole to be prepared for. This par-5 measures 586 yards from the back-tees. You'll need to hit your drive about 240 yards for postion. Both your second and third shots will be played uphill.

The green on this hole is both small and demanding. Play your ball to its front left.

DIRECTIONS

Take Rt. 33 & Rt. 18 to Neptune and follow the signs to the course.

SPRING MEADOW GOLF COURSE

4181 Atlantic Ave., Farmingdale, NJ 07727 / (908) 449-0806

BASIC INFORMATION

Course Type: Public
Year Built: 1954
Architect: N/A
Local Pro: N/A

Course:N/A
Holes: 18 / Par 72

Back : 5,953 yds. Rating: 68.1 Slope: 113
Middle: N/A   Rating: N/A   Slope: N/A
Ladies: 5,310 yds. Rating: 69.7 Slope: 114

Tee Time: First come basis.
Price: $13 - $16

Credit Cards:		Restaurant:	
Driving Range:	■	Lounge:	■
Practice Green:	■	Meeting Rooms:	
Locker Room:	■	Tennis:	
Rental Clubs:	■	Swimming:	
Walkers:	■	Jogging Trails:	
Snack Bar:	■	Boating:	

COURSE DESCRIPTION

This course offers a simple layout for beginners and senior citizens alike. You'll need to place your ball in good position off the tee to get par and birdie opportunities. Good course management will direct you through the many water hazards, sand traps, and trees throughout the course.

All eighteen holes are continuously easy to play. It's a course that will mostly appeal to high-handicappers and all other players who are short on distance.

You shouldn't have much trouble with this one!

DIRECTIONS

Take the Garden State Pkwy. north to Exit 98 to Rt. 34 south. Go right onto Alanwood rd and take that to the end. Make a right at Rt. 524 and look for the course on your left.

OCEAN COUNTY

GAMBLER RIDGE

Burlington Path Rd., Cream Ridge, NJ 08514 / (609) 758-3588

BASIC INFORMATION

Course Type: Public
Year Built: 1983
Architect: Ed Rockhill & Ed Nicholson
Local Pro: Brian Rockhill or Jason Nicholson

Course: N/A
Holes: 18 / Par 71

Back : 6,370 yds. Rating: 70.0 Slope: 111
Middle: 6,102 yds. Rating: 68.8 Slope: 109
Ladies: 5,125 yds. Rating: 68.6 Slope: 108

Tee Time: 7 days in advance.
Price: $10 - $39.50

Credit Cards:	■	Restaurant:	
Driving Range:	■	Lounge:	■
Practice Green:	■	Meeting Rooms:	■
Locker Room:		Tennis:	
Rental Clubs:	■	Swimming:	
Walkers:	■	Jogging Trails:	
Snack Bar:	■	Boating:	■

COURSE DESCRIPTION

Gamble Ridge is not the most difficult course in New Jersey, but it is a good solid design that will put a smile on a high-handicappers' face. This may also be one of the last places on our planet where you can play a round just under 4 1/2 hours. The number one handicap hole on the course is the 8th. This short par-4 stretches 390 yards from the back-tees. You'll be hitting your drive straight uphill to a blind landing area. From that point, you'll need to hit your approach shot to a large two-tiered green that features three bunkers along its right side.

DIRECTIONS

Take the New Jersey Turnpike to Exit 7A and go east to Rt. 537. Make a right at Rt. 539 going north for 2-miles. Make a right at Burlington Rd. and look for the course on your right.

LAKEWOOD COUNTRY CLUB

West County Line Rd., Lakewood, NJ 08701 / (908) 363-8124

BASIC INFORMATION

Course Type: Public
Year Built: 1894 / 1902
Architect: N/A
Local Pro: Todd Toohey

Course: N/A
Holes: 18 / Par 72

Back : 6,182 yds. Rating: 67.9 Slope: 107
Middle: N/A Rating: N/A Slope: N/A
Ladies: 5,764 yds. Rating: 68.7 Slope: 111

Tee Time: 7 days in advance.
Price: $16 - $20

Credit Cards:		Restaurant:	■
Driving Range:	■	Lounge:	■
Practice Green:	■	Meeting Rooms:	■
Locker Room:	■	Tennis:	
Rental Clubs:	■	Swimming:	
Walkers:	■	Jogging Trails:	
Snack Bar:	■	Boating:	■

COURSE DESCRIPTION

You won't find much trouble lurking along the boundaries of this 6,182 yard layout. It's the type of course that will allow better players a chance at birdie on almost every single hole, but the challenge is really focused on the high-handicap player who is not confident enough to play the many tougher courses in New Jersey.

The toughest hole on the course is unquestionably a hard hole for *any* type of player. It's the 15th hole, which measures a staggering 220 yards from the back-tees. Play for the middle of the green and try to block out the three large bunkers that hug the front of it.

DIRECTIONS

Take the Garden State Pkwy. to Exit 91 and follow that road for about a 1/2 mile to Rt. 526. Make a right to the course.

OCEAN ACRES COUNTRY CLUB

Buccaneer Lane, Manahawkin, NJ 08050 / (609) 597-9393

BASIC INFORMATION

Course Type: Public
Year Built: 1963
Architect: N/A
Local Pro: N/A

Course: N/A
Holes: 18 / Par 72

Back : 6,548 yds. Rating: 70.5 Slope: 120
Middle: 6,238 yds. Rating: 69.1 Slope: 118
Ladies: 5,412 yds. Rating: 70.0 Slope: 118

Tee Time: 5 days in advance.
Price: $12 - $20

Credit Cards:	■	Restaurant:	■
Driving Range:		Lounge:	■
Practice Green:	■	Meeting Rooms:	
Locker Room:		Tennis:	
Rental Clubs:	■	Swimming:	■
Walkers:		Jogging Trails:	
Snack Bar:	■	Boating:	

COURSE DESCRIPTION

You'll find many opportunities to shoot par or better on this 18-hole layout. The course is relatively open on the front-nine and plays much tighter along the tree-lined fairways that make up the back-nine.

One of the most exciting holes on the course is the par-3, island green 10th hole, that stretches 183 yards from the back-tees. You'll need to carry the water that sits between the tee-box and the putting area and further along over the large bunker that guards the front of the green.

DIRECTIONS

Take Rt. 22 west for about a block past the G.S. Pkwy. Make a left at Lighthouse Dr. and the course will be about a 1/2 mile further. Look for it on your right.

OCEAN COUNTY GOLF COURSE AT ATLANTIS

Country Club Rd., Tuckerton, NJ 08087 / (609) 296-2444

BASIC INFORMATION

Course Type: Public
Year Built: 1962
Architect: George Fazio
Local Pro: N/A

Course: N/A
Holes: 18 / Par 72

Back : 6,848 yds Rating: 73.6 Slope: 134
Middle: 6,432 yds. Rating: 71.3 Slope: 129
Ladies: 5,579 yds. Rating: 71.8 Slope: 129

Tee Time: 8 days in advance.
Price: $10 - $25

Credit Cards:		Restaurant:	■
Driving Range:	■	Lounge:	■
Practice Green:	■	Meeting Rooms:	
Locker Room:		Tennis:	
Rental Clubs:	■	Swimming:	
Walkers:		Jogging Trails:	
Snack Bar:	■	Boating:	

COURSE DESCRIPTION

The *Ocean Golf Course At Atlantis* is truly a course to be reckoned with. If you can par this baby, design playing extremely good golf. The layout stretches to 6,848 yards from the back-tees. It's not a terribly long course, but it will force you to play accurate finesse shots all day long. This challenging flat course is partial to fades if you can keep your shots away from the many trees that seem to find their way into play. You'll find many difficult traps to contend with along the majority of the small "postage stamp" greens. Bring along your best putting stroke for good results.

DIRECTIONS

Take Hwy. 539 east on Rt. 9 for a half-mile. Bear left on Great Bay Blvd. and go right on Radio Rd. Make a left on Country Club Blvd. The course will be on your right.

SALEM COUNTY

CENTERTON GOLF CLUB

Rt. 540, Elmer, NJ 08318 / (609) 358-2220

BASIC INFORMATION

Course Type: Public
Year Built: 1962
Architect: Ed Carman
Local Pro: Bill Torcucci

Course: N/A
Holes: 18 / Par 71

Back : 6,725 yds. Rating: 69.2 Slope: 120
Middle: 6,305 yds. Rating: 67.8 Slope: 117
Ladies: 5,525 yds. Rating: 71.5 Slope: 120

Tee Time: 6 days in advance.
Price: $16 - $21

Credit Cards:	■	Restaurant:	■
Driving Range:	■	Lounge:	■
Practice Green:	■	Meeting Rooms:	■
Locker Room:	■	Tennis:	
Rental Clubs:	■	Swimming:	
Walkers:	■	Jogging Trails:	
Snack Bar:	■	Boating:	

COURSE DESCRIPTION

The *Centerton Golf Club* offers an excellent combination of beautiful holes to play in a quiet and remote area far away from the hustle-and-bustle of city life. If you enjoy the serenity of playing golf in a remote and secluded area, this course will undoubtedly make your day a memorable one.

The course is relatively flat and easy to walk. It's not a terribly difficult design, but it is an enjoyable one for the mid-to-high handicapper. Golfers enjoy hitting their approach shots to the big greens that offer plenty of roll and excitement.

DIRECTIONS

Take Rt. 55 north or south to Rt. 540 and Almond Rd. Follow the signs to the course.

HOLLYHILLS GOLF CLUB

Friesburg Rd., Alloway Township, NJ 08001 / (609) 935-2412

BASIC INFORMATION

Course Type: Public
Year Built: 1965
Architect: Horace Smith
Local Pro: Steve Keatings

Course: N/A
Holes: 18 / Par 72

Back : 6,376 yds. Rating: 70.8 Slope: 120
Middle: 6,113 yds. Rating: 69.6 Slope: 118
Ladies: 5,056 yds. Rating: 68.0 Slope: 114

Tee Time: 7 days in advance.
Price: $18 - $34

Credit Cards:	■	Restaurant:	■
Driving Range:	■	Lounge:	■
Practice Green:	■	Meeting Rooms:	
Locker Room:	■	Tennis:	
Rental Clubs:		Swimming:	
Walkers:	■	Jogging Trails:	
Snack Bar:	■	Boating:	

COURSE DESCRIPTION

This course is carved out of the hills and woods of New Jersey. It's a fascinating course situated in the middle of nowhere. You'll find an abundance of wildlife throughout this hilly and demanding layout.

The front-nine is both shorter and much easier than the back-nine, so get your birdies while you can. The quiet and serene atmosphere makes playing a round of golf so much better than having to play through a crowded city course that features homes and loud kids on every dogleg. You'll have the opportunity to concentrate on every shot without interruptions.

DIRECTIONS

Take Rt. 40 to Pole Tavern Circle at Rt. 77. In the circle, take 635 west for exactly 7 miles. Turn right on Alloway-Friesburg Rd. The course will be about a mile on your right.

RON JAWORSKI'S WILD OAKS COUNTRY CLUB
75 Wild Oaks Dr., Salem, NJ 08079 / (609) 935-0707

BASIC INFORMATION

Course Type: Public
Year Built: 1972
Architect: Joe Hassler
Local Pro: Mike Nicholosi

Course: Willow Oaks & Ten Oaks (18 / Par 72)
Holes: 27

Back   : 6,633 yds. Rating: 71.8 Slope: 122
Middle: 6,396 yds. Rating: 70.7 Slope: 120
Ladies: 5,360 yds. Rating: 71.1 Slope: 119

Tee Time: First come, first serve.
Price: $18 - $30

Credit Cards: ■   Restaurant:
Driving Range: Lounge: ■
Practice Green: ■   Meeting Rooms: ■
Locker Room: ■   Tennis:
Rental Clubs: ■   Swimming:
Walkers: ■   Jogging Trails:
Snack Bar: ■   Boating: ■

COURSE DESCRIPTION

The **Ron Jaworski's Wild Oaks Country Club** offers a great design with many challenging holes. The course will play best for mid-to-high handicap players. It's not a long course, but you will occasionally find yourself making difficult approach shots to the many small and contoured greens.

The #5 hole is the most difficult design on the course. It's a par-3 that stretches 210 yards from the back-tees. That's a lot of real-estate to cover for any type of golfer. Aim your shot towards the back-middle portion of the green. It should make its way back to the middle because of its back-to-front sloping angle.

DIRECTIONS

Take Rt. 295 to Exit 1C. Make a left at Rt. 49 and another right at Sickler St. The course will be about a mile on your right.

184

ALTERNATIVE COURSES - SOUTH

ATLANTIC
Private

Atlantic City Country Club
1 Leo Frazier Rd.
Northfield, NJ 08225
(609) 641-6688

Frog-Rock Golf & Country Club
420 Boyer Ave.
Hammonton, NJ 08037
(609) 561-5504

Linwood Country Club
Shore Rd.
Linwood, NJ 08221
(609) 927-6124

ATLANTIC
9-hole

Hamilton Trail Country Club
Ocean Heights & Harbor Ave.
Mckee, NJ 08232
(609) 641-6824

Latona Country Club
Oak & Cumberland Rd.
Buena, NJ 08310
(609) 692-8149

Pomona Golf Course
40 W. Massmill Rd.
Pomona Township, NJ 08240
(609) 965-3232

Burlington
Private

Brook Lake Country Club
Brook Lake Rd.
Florham, NJ 07932
(201) 377-2235

Laurel Creek Country Club
651 Centerton Rd.
Moorestown, NJ 08057
(609) 234-7663

Links Golf Club
Crown Royal Pkwy.
Marlton, NJ 08053
(609) 983-2000

Little Mill Country Club
Hopewell Rd.
Marlton, NJ 08053
(609) 767-0559

Medford Lakes Country Club
Oak Dr.
Medford Lakes, NJ 08055
(609) 654-5108

Medford Village Resort & C.C.
Golf View Dr.
Medford, NJ 08055
(609) 654-8211

Moorestown Field Club
629 Chester Avenue
Moorestown, NJ 08057
(609) 235-2326

Riverton Country Club
Highland Ave.
Cinnaminson, NJ 08077
(609) 829-1919

Burlington
Military

McGuire AFB Golf Course
438 Support Group McGuire AFB
Birlington Co, NJ 08601
(201) 377-2235

CAMDEN
Private

Merchantville Country Club
Hampton Rd. & Chapel Ave.
Cherry Hill, NJ 08034
(609) 662-9773

Pine Valley Golf Club
East Atlantic Ave.
Clementon, NJ 08021
(609) 783-9735

Tavistock Country Club
Boro of Tavistock
Haddenfield, NJ 08033
(609) 795-3839

Stone Harbor Golf Club
Rt. 9
Cape May, NJ 08210
(609) 465-9270

CAMDEN
9-hole

Ocean City Golf Course
Bay Ave. (between 22nd & 28th)
Ocean City, NJ 08226
(609) 399-1315

CAMDEN
Executive

Kresson Golf Course
298 Kresson Gibbsboro Rd.
Vorhees, NJ 08043
(609) 424-1212

Cumberland
9-hole

Latona Country Club
Oak Rd. & Cumberland Rd.
Vineland, NJ 08360
(609) 692-8149

CUMBERLAND
Executive

Eastlyn Golf Course
4049 Italia Ave.
Vineland, NJ 08360
(609) 691-5558

186

GLOUCESTER
Private

Woodbury Country Club
467 Cooper St.
Woodbury, NJ 08096
(609) 845-9882

GLOUCESTER
9-hole

Washington TWP Municipal G.C.
P.O. Box 1106
Turnersville, NJ 08012
(609) 227-1435

GLOUCESTER
Executive

Beckett Golf Club
Kings Hwy.
Swedesboro, NJ 08085
(609) 467-4700

Monmouth
Private

Bamm Hollow Country Club
Sunnyside Rd.
Lincroft, NJ 07738
(908) 741-4131

Battleground Country Club
Millhurst Rd.
Tennent, NJ 07763
(908) 462-7575

Beacon Hill Country Club
Beacon Hill Rd.
Atlantic Highlands, NJ 07716
(908) 291-3344

Ft. Monmouth Golf Course
Tinton Ave.
Eatontown, NJ 07703
(908) 532-4307

Hollywood Golf Club
Rosfeld Ave.
Deal, NJ 07723
(908) 531-8950

Manasquan River Golf Club
Riverview Dr.
Brielle, NJ 08730
(908) 528-9678

Navesink Country Club
Navesink River Rd.
Middletown, NJ 07748
(908) 842-3111

Rumson Country Club
Rumson Rd.
Rumson, NJ 07760
(908) 842-2885

Shore Oaks Golf Club
20 Shore Oaks Dr.
Farmingdale, NJ 07727
(908) 938-9696

Springlake Golf Club
Warren Ave.
Spring Lake Heights, NJ 07762
(908) 449-7185

MONMOUTH
9-hole

Colonial Terrace Golf Course
Wicapecko Dr.
Wanamassa NJ 07712
(908) 775-3636

MONMOUTH
Executive

Bel Aire Golf Club
Allaire Rd.
Allenwood, NJ 08720
(908) 449-6024

Pinebrook Golf Club
1 Covered Bridge Blvd.
Englishtwon, NJ 07726
(908) 536-7272

OCEAN
Private

Ocean County Golf Course
Country Club Rd.
Lillle Egg Harbor, NJ 08087
(609) 294-2444

Metedeconk National Golf Club
P.O. Box 1257
Jackson, NJ 08527
(908) 928-4639

Tams River Country Club
419 Washington St.
Jackson, NJ 08753
(908) 349-8867

OCEAN
Executive

Forge Pond Country Club
301 Chambersbridge Rd.
Bricktown, NJ 08723
(908) 920-8899

OCEAN
Military

Lakehurst Golf Club
Navel Air Station
Lake Hurst, NJ 08733
(908) 323-7483

NORTH

Alexandria Bay
Jefferson County

1,000 Island Skydeck
(613) 659-2335

This 395 foot skydeck offers fantastic views of the Thousand Islands.

Hours: *Daily / 8:30-9:00*
Labor Day / 9:00-6:00
Day After Labor Day
to October / 8:30-Dusk

Uncle Sam Boat Tours
(800) ALEX-BAY or (315) 482-2611

Hop aboard one of Uncle Sam's Mississippi styled paddlewheelers' and take a tour around the Thousand Islands. Dinner and luncheon cruises are available and, when season permits, you'll get a chance to visit one of the areas most popular attractions: Boldt Castle. In the early part of the 1900's, Boldt Castle was under construction but due to strange circumstances, construction was ceased, the castle was abandoned, and no one ever lived in it.

(800) 8-ISLAND / Boldt Castle
Hours: *Daily / 10:00-6:00*

Ferry hours can vary, so please call for a complete listing and confirmation.

Amsterdam
Montgomery County

Walter Elwood Museum
And Art Gallery
(518) 843-5151

This museum features changing displays that deal with American culture and history. Permanent displays feature an Eskimo exhibit, a blacksmith shop, a Cherokee Indian teepee, and an Iroquois Indian habitat.

Hours: *Monday-Friday / 8:30-3:30*

Ballston-Spa
Saratoga County

National Bottle Museum
(518) 885-7589

This museum promotes the study and appreciation of antique glass in the hope of preserving the future of this art form. You'll find a huge selection of glassworks on display in the form of bottles, containers, and the tools and machinery used to make them. Interactive displays and video tapes will further enhance your understanding of this interesting art form.

Hours: *Monday-Friday / 10:00-4:00*

Burke
Franklin County

Wilder Farm
(518) 483-1207

Laura Ingalls Wilder used this house as the setting for her novel *Farmer Boy*. You can bring along sandwiches and any other food that you may want to eat during the day for a picnic.

Hours: Monday-Saturday / 11:00-4:00
Sunday / 1:00-4:00

Canajohaire
Montgomery County

Canajohaire Library And Art Gallery
(518) 673-2314

This museum features oil and water color paintings by great American painters like Winslow Homer, John Singleton Copley, etc. You'll also find local historical displays; a look at American industry (such as the Life Saver company); and a genealogy section. Guided tours are available by appointment only.

Hours: Monday-Wed. / 10:00-4:30
Thursday / 1:30-8:30
Friday / 1:30-4:30
Saturday / 10:00-1:30

Canton
St. Lawrence County

St. Lawrence County Museum
(315) 386-8133

This was the home of New York governor and senator Silas Wright. It has been restored and furnished with pieces dating between the 1830's and 1850's. Most of the exhibits relate to the St. Lawrence county area. The museum also houses a fine library.

Hours: Tuesday-Saturday / 10:00-4:00

Chateaugay
Franklin County

High Falls Park
(518) 497-3156
This is a wonderful area for your family to explore as you'll walk through dense nature trails en route to the 120' foot tall waterfall. Many signs along the way identify each of the numerous plants throughout the park. Bring along sandwiches and drinks for a picnic area.

Hours: All Week / 9:00-9:00

Chazy
Clinton County

**The Alice T. Minor
Colonial Collection
(518) 846-7336**

This gorgeous stone home was built in 1824 and features beautiful period pieces. All of the furnishings are original, such as the carpets, glassworks, metalwork, porcelains, and fine furniture. When you're done, you can take a serene walk through the enchanting gardens that are featured on the premises.

Hours: Tuesday-Saturday / 10:00-4:00

Lake Lucerne
Warren County

**Hudson River Rafting Co.
(518) 696-2964**

White water rafting trips are available down the Sacandaga River. These trips run along a 3 1/2 mile stretch of water and typically last about 2 1/2 hours. The trips are broken down into class II and class III designations. A much easier third trip is available, which will allow you to take a dip in the water at certain points.

Hours: All Week / Please call

Massena
St. Lawrence County

**Moses-Saunders Power Dam
(800) 262-6972**

Owned by both Ontario Hydro in Canada and the New York Power Authority, the dam generates approximately 2 million kilowatts of power. The visitor's room is filled with maps of the project, films, and computerized exhibits. You'll learn how electricity is generated and used in many different areas of life.

Hours: All Week / 9:30-6:00

Milton
Saratoga County

**Kedem Royal Winery
(914) 236-4281**

Learn how wine is made and how a vineyard is preserved and farmed by watching the video tape presented at this winery. When you're done, you can visit the converted 19th-century railroad station and barn for a wine tasting session.

Hours: Sunday-Friday / 10:00-4:00

Ogdensburg
St. Lawrence County

Frederic Remington Art Museum
(315) 393-2425

Frederic Remington is known for his depictions of the American frontier. Featured here are some of his works of bronze, oil paintings, watercolors, and sketches done in pen and ink. A short video chronicles his wax method of casting.

Hours: Monday-Saturday / 10:00-5:00
Sunday / 1:00-5:00

Queensbury
Warran County

The Great Escape Fun Park
(518) 792-6568

Rides and shows are presented through the duration of the day in this fun-filled park. It's a terrific location to bring your kids.

Hours: All week / 9:30-6:00

Saratoga Springs
Saratoga County

National Museum Of Racing And Hall Of Fame
(518) 584-0400

Every aspect of thoroughbred horse racing in America is covered in this charismatic museum. Its Hall of Fame honors great trainers, jockeys, and horses. The importance of selective breeding is showcased in the form of photographs and video tapes. You'll even get to play with a simulated racing track that features video tapes of well known trainers and jockeys, each explaining their own techniques and training methods.

Hours: All week / 9:00-5:00

Yaddo
(518) 584-0746

This private estate is made available to all types of artists, from painters to writers, dancers, poets and composers. The estate also features beautiful rose gardens that are open to the public.

Hours: All week / Dawn-Dusk

Utica
Oneida County

Munson-Williams-Proctor Institute
(315) 797-0000

This art center is devoted to the teachings of both visual and performing arts. The school bends slightly towards American Colonial art.

Hours: *Tuesday-Saturday / 10:00-5:00*
Sunday / 1:00-5:00

Albany
Albany County

Albany Institute Of History & Art
(518) 463-4478

Albany's art, culture, and history are on display in the form of creative artifacts and collectibles. Gorgeous paintings, silver works, 18th- and 19th-century furniture, sculptures, and ceramics are points of interest. You'll also find a brilliant array of Egyptian art, another extensive collection of artifacts depicting the Hudson Valley region, and a widespread collection of books in the famous McKinney Library.

Hours: *Tuesday-Friday / 10:00-5:00*
Saturday-Sunday / 12:00-5:00

Cathedral Of All Saints
(518) 463-4478

The Cathedral will have you standing aback the moment you step through its large double door entryway. Designed and built in 1884, this Gothic Revival Episcopal church, features breathtaking works of stained glass, stone carvings, beautiful mosaics, imported 17th century choir stalls that were hand-carved in Belgium, and a unique collection of historical artifacts. Guided tours are available by appointment only.

Hours: *Monday-Friday / 7:30-3:30*
Saturday / 8:00-11:00
Sunday / 12:00-5:00

Governor Nelson A. Rockefeller Empire State Plaza
(518) 473-7521 / Art

Here you'll find a stunning collection of modern American art, a large government building, and a gorgeous performing arts center that hosts both festivals and concerts annually. Another attraction is the observation deck that sits atop the 44-story Corning Tower Building.

(518) 474-4712 / Concerts
(518) 474-2418 / Observation Deck

Tower Building
Hours: *Monday-Saturday / 9:00-4:00*

Auburn
Cayuga County

Cayuga Museum / Case Research Lab Museum
(518) 463-4478

You'll find both changing and permanent displays of historical artifacts that center around the Cayuga County area. A 19th century furnishing display makes up part of the permanent collection. The site of the invention of early motion pictures can be found here too, by the Case Research Laboratory, which is open to the public.

Hours: *Tuesday-Sunday / 12:00-5:00*

Baldwinsville
Onondaga County

Anheuser-Busch Brewery Tour
(315) 635-4114

Anheuser-Busch is the most successful brewery in the history of beer making. An icon among its peers, this tour will take you through the companies brewing process, its packaging department, and a stop at their hospitality room.

Hours: Tuesday-Saturday / 9:00-4:00

Binghamton
Broome County

Ross Park Zoo
(607) 724-5454

You'll see some exciting wildlife in this zoo that encompasses 25 acres of land. Descriptions of each animal's diet, social structure, and habits are clearly displayed. The park also houses a petting zoo.

Hours: All week / 10:00 and 5:00

Catskill
Greene County

Catskill Game Farm
(518) 678-9595

This farm features a great variety of wildlife from all different parts of the world, including rare and endangered species. You'll also find a fun petting zoo for your children and an animal show.

Hours: All week / 9:00 and 6:00

Cazenovia
Madison County

Lorenzo State Historic Site
(315) 655-3200

This historical 1807 mansion houses original furnishings and has a wide collection of horse carriages on display.

Hours: Wed.-Sat. / 10:00 and 5:00
Sunday / 1:00-5:00

Cherry Valley
Otsego County

Cherry Valley Museum
(607) 264-3060

Civil war memorabilia, Indian relics, books, documents, and other items are on display.

Hours: All week / 10:00-5:00

Cooperstown
Otsego County

Corvette Americana Hall Of Fame
(607) 547-4135

Corvettes have been the quintessential American sports car ever since they hit the market in the 1950's. This museum is dedicated to preserving the magic that has made this car the most beloved sports vehicle in the country. You'll see over 40 corvettes dating back to the original of 1953. Multimedia kiosks are set up for interactive information, memorabilia seems to be everywhere, and anything ever associated with the car from commercials, magazine adds, Indy cars, and more are on display.

Hours: All week / 10:00-8:00

National Baseball Hall Of Fame And Museum
(607) 547-9988

If you're like millions of Americans, you'll want to take the time to visit this master-piece museum that honors the game, the players, and the people that have brought it to us over the years. You'll learn about the development of the game and its equipment, you can search through hundreds of photographs, find your favorite superstar's honorary plaque, visit the Great Moments Room, the World Series Room, and leaf through hundreds of books at the National Base-ball Library. This is without question the most informative place to learn about the game of baseball.

Hours: All week / 9:00-9:00

Cortland
Cortland County

The 1890 House Museum
(607) 756-7551

This Victorian Mansion features exten-sive furnishings, beautifully decorated walls, hand-carved furniture, and stained glass windows. Slide shows and other changing exhibits are presented through-out the day.

Hours: Tuesday-Sunday / 1:00-4:00

Ithica
Tompkins County

Cornell University
(607) 254-INFO

Cornell University isone of the finest institutions of higher learning in the U.S. Tours of the campus and its many interesting locations are available daily.

Hours: *Monday-Friday / 9, 11, 1, & 3*
Saturday / 9:00 & 1:00
Sunday / 1:00

Taughannock Falls State Park
(607) 254-INFO

This park will take you through a mile-long valley that features rock formations rising upwards of 400 feet. Trails will guide you around its gorge and to some of the park's more interesting locations. Swimming and camping are allowed during certain parts of the season. You'll need to call for a confirmation of dates.

Hours: *All week / 8:30-Dusk*

Kinderhook
Columbia County

Martin Van Buren
National Historic Site
(518) 758-9689

Martin Van Buren was the eighth President of the United States, and this was his 22 acre estate. His 1797 mansion still remains, with all of its original furnishings.

Hours: *All week / 9:00-4:30*

Sherburne
Chenango County

Rogers Environmental Education Center
(607) 674-4017

The center covers about 580 acres of land that you can hike and explore. It's a wonderful environment filled with beautiful wildlife and plants. Each Saturday, the museum showcases an educational program that deals with the environment and its indigenous forms. Other programs are available for kids during the summer months. All of the trails are open to the public each day from dawn to dusk.

Hours: *Monday-Friday / 8:30-4:45*
Saturday-Sunday / 1:00-4:45

Syracuse
Onondago County

**Milton J. Rubenstein Museum Of
Science And Technology
(315) 425-9068**

Ever wanted to know the inner workings
of a microchip? This museum deals with
scientific phenomena and presents it in
a general format that most people will
be able to easily comprehend. Everything from color, light, gravity, comput-
ers, chemistry, stars, and even animals
are exhibited. Some of the displays have
been specifically developed for hands-
on, interactive experiences. In addition,
you can visit the Silverman Planetarium
which offers terrific sky shows. Please
call for a confirmation of all showings.

Hours: *Tuesday-Saturday / 10:00-5:00*

Albertson
Nassau County

Clark Botanic Garden
(516) 484-8600

This wonderful botanic garden features a widespread collection of rose flowers, wildflowers, a vegetable and herb garden, and some interesting woodlands. You won't need more than a couple of hours to enjoy all of the displays. Tours are available each Sunday beginning at 2:00 or 3:00.

Amenia
Dutchess County

Cascade Mountain Winery
(914) 373-9021

Is there anything better to complement a splendid meal than a fine glass of wine? Tastings and tours are offered each day. Please call to confirm.

Hours: All week / 10:00-6:00

Buchanan
Westchester County

Indian Point Energy Education Center
(914) 737-8174

Watch operators being trained on a nuclear reactor simulator machine.

Hours: Monday-Friday / 8:30-4:30

Centerport
Franklin County

Vanderbilt Mansion, Marine Museum, Planetarium and Park
(516) 262-7800

This mansion is a stunning example of Spanish Revival architecture. All of the furnishings are original, including its beautiful antiques and period pieces. Oddly enough, you'll see some wildlife and marine animals, too. A nearby planetarium features astronomy and science exhibits that are informative and fun to observe. On display are different types of telescopes, the observatory itself, and an incredible 60-foot-diameter dome that features original movies.

Hours: Tuesday-Sunday / 10:00-4:00

Planetarium: (516) 262-7827
Sky Shows: Saturday / 11, 1, 2:30
Sunday / 1, 2:30, 4

East Hampton
Suffolk County

Guild Hall Museum
(516) 324-0713

A unique cultural center with changing exhibits and presentations.

Hours: Monday-Saturday / 10:00-4:00

Cold Spring Harbor
Suffolk County

Whaling Museum
(516) 367-3418

Everything you ever wanted to know about the whaling industry can be found in this interesting museum. A fully equipped whaling boat with various forms of whaling equipment is on display, as well as marine paintings, a diorama of Cold Spring Harbor in 1850, and hundreds of scimshaws (whale bone carvings).

Hours: All week / 11:00-5:00

Hyde Park
Dutchess County

Franklin D. Roosevelt Museum
And Library
(914) 229-8114

This museum is dedicated to both the late President and his wife. You'll see rare photographs, artifacts, letters, official documents, written speeches, and more.

Hours: All week / 9:00-5:00

Home of Franklin D. Roosevelt
National Historic Site
(914) 229-9115

This 1826 house sits atop 200 plus acres of undisturbed land. It includes the graves of both the President and Mrs. Roosevelt, and has been kept in its original condition since the passing of the President in 1945.

Hours: All week / 9:00-5:00

Kings Point
Nassau County

Senate House State Historic Site
(914) 338-2786

The first New York State Senate was held here. You'll learn about its history and how the New York State Government came into being. Additional attractions include art works by prominent Hudson Valley artists.

Hours: Wed.,-Saturday / 10:00-5:00
       Sunday / 1:00-5:00

Newburgh
Orange County

Washington's Headquarters State Historic Site
(914) 561-1765

Between April of 1782 and August of 1783, General Washington resided here. It was the place from where he sent out his order to end the Revolutionary War. A 6-acre park adjacent to the home features an 1887 Tower Of Victory monument. A secondary museum sits close by and features items from the Continental Army.

Hours: Wed.,-Saturday / 10:00-5:00
Sunday / 1:00-5:00

New York
New York County

Ellis Island
(212) 264-8711

Ellis Island was the main point of entry for millions of immigrants, mostly from Europe, between the years 1892 and 1924. Exhibits showcase its history.

Hours: All week / 9:00-5:30

New York Stock Exchange
(212) 656-5167

Take a look at the inner workings of the Exchange by taking a self-guided tour. The visitors' gallery will allow you to peer down at the traders as they negotiate huge blocks of stocks amid the hoopla on the floor.

Hours: Monday-Friday / 9:15-4:00

Statue Of Liberty
National Monument
(212) 269-5755 / (202) 363-3200

In 1884, the statue was given to the United States by France in commemoration of the historic alliance during the American Revolution. It is believed to be the tallest statue of modern times.

Hours: All week / 9:30-5:00

World Trade Center
(212) 435-7397

This has got to be one of the modern architectural wonders of the world. Over 16 acres of space is devoted to offices that join with a beautifully landscaped shopping plaza.

Hours: All week / 9:30-11:30

Empire State Building
(212) 736-3100

The Empire State Building is 1,454 feet tall, making it one of the world's tallest office buildings and free structures throughout the world. The observation deck on the 102nd floor attracts thousands of people annually, because of its breathtaking views of the entire city.

Hours: All week / 9:30-Midnight

Hayden Planetarium
(212) 769-5100

This planetarium, a section of the of the American Museum of Natural History, showcases astronomy exhibits and presents 3D laser light shows. Many of the lectures presented here are interesting and fun to watch.

Hours: Monday-Friday / 12:30-4:45
Saturday / 10:00-5:45
Sunday / 12:00-5:45

Metropolitan Museum Of Art
(212) 535-7710

This museum is considered to be one of the great ones of the world. You'll find Greek, Roman, and Egyptian art; Eastern artifacts and antiquities; Oriental and European paintings with sculptures; musical instruments; ancient glassworks; and many other works of art by American and European artists.

Hours: Tuesday-Sunday / 9:30-5:15
* Friday-Saturday / 5:15-8:45

St. Patrick's Cathedral
(212) 753-2261

As a structure, this is one of the largest cathedrals in the country. It has a seating capacity of 2,500, and features a rose window that stretches 26 feet across. The pipe organ has a total of 7,380 extensions, and twin spiral staircases extend upwards to a height of 330 feet. The Cathedral is a 13th-century Gothic structure and its practicing religion is Catholicism.

Hours: All week / 6:30-8:45

Temple Emanu-El
(212) 744-1400

This is one of the largest Jewish houses of worship around the world. The current sanctuary was built in 1927 yet the structure itself goes back to the year 1845. It's a gorgeous architectural achievement adorned with stain glass windows and wonderfully set mosaics.

Hours: Sunday-Thursday / 10:00-5:00
Friday / 10:00-4:00

United Nations Headquarters
(212) 963-1234 / (212) 963-4440

Each building in the United Nations Headquarters was designed by well known architects admired by their peers. The names of these buildings are as follows: Secretariat, the domed General Assembly, Conference, and the Hammarskjold Library. During the third week of September, the General Assembly meets here for about 14 weeks. Tours are available.

Hours: All week / 9:00-4:45

Old Westbury
Nassau County

Old Westbury Gardens
(516) 333-0048

This 1906 Westbury house is furnished with antiques and paintings. Some of the paintings are by John Singer Sergeant, Henry Rayburn, Sir Joshua Reynolds, and Richard Wilson. But your visit won't be complete unless you take the time to stroll through the lushly landscaped gardens that are styled after the "Great Parks" of England during 18th century.

Hours: Wed.,-Monday / 10:00-5:00

Oyster Bay
Nassau County

Planting Fields Arboretum
(516) 922-9201 or (516) 922-9200

Over 409 acres of land support the numerous greenhouses, natural habitats, and gardens that are featured here. A wide variety of flowers and trees are grown in the arboretum. Another attraction is a beautiful 65-room Tudor Revival mansion that was furnished with 16th- and 17th-century pieces imported from Europe.

Hours: All week / 9:00-5:00

Rye
Westchester County

Playland
(914) 967-2040

This recreational complex offers rides, a beach with a boardwalk, a saltwater lake, river boat rides, an 18-hole miniature golf course, and a children's park. Other attractions include a vintage carousel, their Dragon Coaster, and more!

Hours: Tues., Thurs., Sun. / Noon-11
Fri., Sat., Mon. / Noon-12

Seaford
Nassau County

Tackapausha Museum
And Preserve
(516) 571-7443

Tackapausha Museum is devoted to the study of wildlife and plants on Long Island. You'll learn about their habitats and life cycles and how they interact in their environment. Changing programs and video tapes are at hand to give you a better understanding of the complete picture of their lives. The museum sits on an 80 acre wildlife sanctuary that you can explore afterwards.

Hours: Tuesday-Saturday / 10:00-4:00
Sunday / 1:00-4:00

West Point
Nassau County

United State Military Academy
(914) 938-2203

This is the most respected military academy in the country. Tours are available daily, but only to certain places. Driving is permitted only in designated areas.

Places To Visit at West Point:

Cadet Chapel: Beautiful stained glass windows and one of the country's largest church organs are featured here. (914) 938-2308

Chapel of the Most Holy Trinity: This Catholic church was designed in the Norman Gothic style of architecture and was heavily influenced by the Carthusian abbey church in England. (914) 446-5576

Jewish Chapel: A 1984 addition, this chapel presents a Gothic design used throughout West Point. (914) 938-2710

Old Cadet Chapel: Many beautiful commemoratives can be found on the walls of this 1836 chapel.

Trophy Point: You'll find many artifacts and relics from the American Revolution. (914) 9382638

West Point Museum: Another large collections of artifacts. (914) 938-2203

Alfred
Allegay County

The Museum Of Ceramic Art At Alfred University
(607) 871-2421

Brilliant works of ceramic are featured here. You'll find works from contemporary Americans, ancient pottery from the Southwest, and other works brought over from Europe, Asia, and Africa. Finely crafted sculptures, ceramics, and pottery adorn the premises.

Hours: Tues., Fri., & Sun. / 1:00-4:00

Arcade
Wyoming County

Arcade & Attica Railroad
(716) 496-9877

Take a ride aboard a steam locomotive train with a private guide who will point out historical facts along the areas that you'll be riding through. Other cars are on display too, including the private car that Grover Cleveland used while he was President.

Hours: Wed., Sat., Sun., and Holidays / 12:30 and 3:00 (departures)

Amherst
Erie County

Amherst Museum Colony
(716) 689-1440

Amherst features interesting galleries of one-of-a-kind subjects. If you're a miniature collector, you'll be fascinated by the brilliant works of dioramas that are on display. Other attractions include an art and costume gallery, the Williamsville Lions Gallery of the Senses, and the Michael F. Steffen Technology Center — which houses aviation displays of models and parachutes.

Hours: Tues.-Sat. / 9:30-4:30

Buffalo
Erie County

Albright-Knox Art Gallery
(716) 882-8700

This is truly a spectacular gallery with great works of art by Henri Matisse, Pablo Picasso, William de Kooning, and Jackson Pollock. You'll also see some enchanting historical works that date back to the year 3,000 B.C.

Hours: Tuesday-Saturday / 11:00-5:00 Sunday / 12:00-5:00

Buffalo Zoological Gardens
(716) 837-3900

Both indoor and outdoor displays feature over 200 species of animals and birds. Some of the more sought-after exhibits include the gorilla rain forest exhibit, the lion and tiger outdoor habitat, the World of Wildlife building, and the park's petting zoo. The zoo is also home to rare white tigers and one-horned Indian rhinos.

Hours: All week / 10:00-6:30

Canandaigua
Ontario County

Sonnenberg Gardens
(716) 394-4922

This wondrous 50 acre estate features an 1887 Victorian Mansion that is fully furnished with its original items. Streams, ponds, and fountains accentuate the many beautifully thought-out thematic gardens. A nearby greenhouse complex features an orchid section, a desert house, and a palm house. Don't forget to bring your camera!

Hours: All week / 9:30-5:30

Chautauqua
Chautauqua County

The Chautauqua Institution
(800) 836-ARTS

This institution was founded in 1874 and was used as a Sunday school education center. You'll find many activities for your family to enjoy while learning about the arts, education, religion, theater, dance, and music. The amphitheater presents various lectures and a variety of different forms of entertainment.

Hours: Please call to confirm all attractions.

Corning
Steuben County

Corning Glass Center
(607) 974-8271

Learn the intricacies of glass making in this informative museum. The changing exhibits tackle questions from the past, the present, and the future of the industry. The live lamp-worker demonstrations in the Hall of Science will keep you entertained while you watch them work.

Hours: Monday-Friday / 9:00-7:00
Saturday / 9:00-5:00
Sunday / 12:00-5:00

Elmira
Chemung County

Mark Twain Musical Drama
(800) 395-MARK

Performances of Mark Twain's works are the focal point of this dramatic center.

Hours: Thurs., Sat., Sun., / 2 & 7:30
Tuesday / 7:30
Wednesday / 2:00

Geneseo
Livingston County

National Warplane Museum
(716) 243-0690

This museum is devoted to finding, restoring, and maintaining old World War II aircraft, of which many are on display. The planes bring back a sense of dignity and pride, both for what they stood for and the people that were courageous enough to fly them during the war. You'll also learn how many of the innovations that had been put into these planes were later carried into the manufacturing plants of commercial airlines after the war.

Hours: Monday-Friday / 9:00-5:00
Saturday-Sunday / 10:00-5:00

Lackawanna
Erie County

Our Lady Of Victory Basilica And National Shrine
(716) 823-8841

This is the second oldest Basilica in the country. It was built in 1921 and features huge altars, a rare grotto shrine, and many incredible Italian sculptures.

Hours: Please call.

Lewiston
Niagara County

Earl W. Bridges Artpack
(800) 659-PARK

This splendid 200 acre park sits along the Niagara River gorge and features a theater, an art complex, and other recreational facilities. It's a wonderful park that features live musical performances throughout the year.

Hours: All week / 24 hours

Newark
Wayne County

Hoffmann Clock Museum
(315) 331-4370

Antique clocks of all makes and models are on display for public viewing. You'll be amazed by the variety that you'll see.

Hours: Monday-Friday / 9:30-9:00
Saturday / 9:30-5:30

Niagara Falls
Niagara County

Cave Of The Wind Trip
(716) 278-1730

An elevator will guide you down a 177' drop through the Niagara Falls escarpment. When you finally reach the bottom, you'll have an opportunity to view the falls from a bottom-to-top perspective. You'll see just how big this incredable waterfall is.

Hours: All week / 9:15-8:00

Maid Of The Mist
(716) 278-1730

Maid of the Mist boats take passengers one step closer to the falls by actually entering the Horseshoe Basin along its bottom. You needn't worry about having to change your clothes; raincoats are handed out to each passenger before the boat makes it to the front of the basin.

Hours: Monday-Friday / 9:30-9:00
Saturday / 9:30-5:30

North Chili
Monroe County

Victorian Doll Museum And Chili Doll Hospital
(716) 247-0130

This museum is home to over 1,000 types of dolls made from different types of materials.

Hours: Tuesday-Saturday / 10:0-4:30
Sunday / 1:00-4:00

Orchard Park
Erie County

Burgwardt Bicycle Museum
(716) 662-3853

You'll see bikes from every major period of their development, including some from the 1800's – two hundred types in all. If you happen to be one of the thousands of people that have taken up bicycle riding for the second time, this museum is well worth the time.

Hours: *Mon., Fri., & Sat. / 11:00-5:00*
Sunday / 1:30-5:00

Salamanca
Cattaraugus County

Seneca-Iroquois National Museum
(716) 945-1738

If you enjoy learning about other cultures and their ideas, you'll find this museum quite interesting. It portrays the Iroquois Indians with a deep emphasis on their Seneca nation.

Hours: *Monday-Saturday / 9:00-5:00*
Sunday / 10:00-5:00

NEW JERSEY - EXCURSIONS

NORTH

Andover
Sussex County

Persona Farms
Rt. 517, 350 Andover-Sparta Rd.
Andover, NJ 07821
(201) 729-6161

Persona Farms is an enjoyable restaurant and dinner theater.

Asbury
Monmouth County

King's Road Vineyard
Rt. 579, Box 360
Asbury, NJ 08802
(908) 479-6611

Tours are available by appoinment only. You'll participate in wine tasting, tour the grounds, and visit the gift shop.

Basking Ridge
Somerset County

Brick Academy, The
256 S. Maple Ave.
Basking Ridge, NJ 07920
(908) 766-5955

This fine museum features 19th-century artifacts, photos, and more. You'll also get a tour of the town.

Great Swamp National Wildlife Refuge
152 Pleasant Plains Rd., Box 152
Basking Ridge, NJ 07920
(201) 425-1222

If you enjoy bird watching, this is one of the greatest places to visit. You can walk through 10 miles of marked trails, visit one of two observation blinds, and walk down a half-mile boardwalk.

Lord Sterling Stables
256 S. Maple Ave.
Basking Ridge, NJ 07920
(908) 766-5955

This horseback riding stable is an exciting place to learn the fine art of riding. Lessons are available daily.

Bedminster
Somerset County

Somerset Hills Handicapped Riders
Crossroads Farm Larger Cross Rd.
Bedminster, NJ 07422
(908) 234-1907

This is the perfect place for physically-challenged individuals to experience horseback riding.

Belvidere
Warran County

Yellow Rock Horse Farm
Mountain Lake Rd., Rd 1 Box 449
Belvidere, NJ 07823
(908) 475-4732

Another great place to go horseback riding.

Berkeley Heights
Warran County

Drake House Museum
602 Front St.
Berkeley Heights, NJ 07422
(908) 755-5831

In 1777, the Drake House served as George Washington's headquarters.

Bernardsville
Somerset County

**Scherman-Hoffman
Wildlife Sanctuary**
Hardscrabble Rd., P.O. Box 693
Bernardsville, NJ 07924
(908) 766-5787

This is an extraordinary sanctuary that covers 265 acres. Don't forget to bring your camera!

Blairstown
Warren County

Eagle Ridge Soaring Gliders
Blairstone Airport, 36 Lambert Rd.
Blairstown, NJ 07825
(908) 362-8311

For a once-in-a-lifetime experience, you can take a scenic glider ride over the Delaware Water Gap. Lessons are available upon request.

K.D. Helicopters
Hope-Blairstown Rd.
Blairstown, NJ 07825
(908) 362-6277

This adventurous experience will have you flying in a helicopter over the Delaware Water Gap. If you've never been in a helicopter before, I can assure you that there's nothing like it!

Bridgewater
Somerset County

Bridgewater Commons
400 Commons Way, Suite 100
Bridgewater, NJ 08807
(908) 218-1166

This is the only three-level shopping center in the state of New Jersey. You'll find 160 stores and 3 major department stores, several good restaurants, a seven screen cinema, and more!

Budd Lake
Morris County

Pax Amicus Castle Theater
Lake Shore Dr.
Budd Lake, NJ 07828
(201) 691-2100

This beautiful castle-shaped theater books everything from Broadway to off-Broadway plays, musicals, comedies, and more!

Caldwell
Essex County

Grover Cleveland Birthplace
207 Bloomfield Ave.
Caldwell, NJ 07006
(201) 226-1810

Grover Cleveland was the only president of the United States to have served two nonconsecutive terms.

Chester
Morris County

Historic Chester Business Association
57 E. Main St.
Chester, NJ 07930
(908) 879-4814

This is a great place to shop for unique items and antiques. Everything from furniture to children's items can be found.

Clinton
Hunterdon County

Hunterdon Art Center
7 Lower Center St.
Clinton, NJ 08809
(908) 735-8415

Enjoy exhibitions, the theater, an art gallery, or enroll in an art class.

Cranford
Union County

Union County College
207 Bloomfield Ave.
Caldwell, NJ 07006
(201) 226-1810

Enjoy a taste of the dramatic arts, classical and contemporary music, and other entertainment.

East Brunswick
Middlesex County

Brunswick Square Mall
755 Rt. 18
East Brunswick, NJ 08816
(908) 238-3600

You'll find many antique and retail stores.

East Rutherford
Bergen County

Meadowlands Sports Complex
50 Rts. 120 & 3
East Rutherford, NJ 07073
(201) 935-3900

This area is the home to Giant Stadium, Brenden Byrne arena, and the Meadowlands Racetrack. It also serves as the Sports Hall of Fame for New Jersey.

Far Hills
Morris County

U.S.G.A. Golf House
Liberty Corner Rd.
Far Hills, NJ 07931
(908) 234-2300

The U.S.G.A. Golf House is home to one of the greatest collection of golf memorabilia and artifacts in the world. Every golfer should take the time to discover the importance of the game by studying its history.

Flemington
Hunterdon County

Flemington Speedway
Flemington Fairgrounds, Rt. 31
Flemington, NJ 08822
(908) 782-2413

Great Stock-car racing.

Hawthorne
Middlesex County

20th Century Limited
Raritan Plaza One
Edison, NJ 08837
(908) 417-9345

You'll be swept away in a 140-mile long murder mystery train ride. The ride starts at and returns to the historic NYSW Train Station in Hawthorne. Dining is available upon request.

Hope
Warren County

Land Of Make Believe
Rt. 80, Exit 12
Hope, NJ 07844
(908) 459-5100

This is a great location for a family outing. The park is home to 30 acres of rides, attractions, games, and fabulous water rides. Don't forget your bathing suits.

Lafayette
Sussex County

Lafayette Mill Antiques Center
Rt. 15, P.O. Box 350, RD 3
Lafayette, NJ 07848
(908) 459-5100

If you search long enough, you may find that special antique that you've been looking for.

Madison
Morris County

Korn Photography Gallery
(Drew University)
36 Madison Ave.
Madison, NJ 07940
(201) 408-3777

Here you'll find the works of some of America's most respected photographers on display.

Metuchen
Middlesex County

BIL Coffeehouses
491 Middlesex Ave.
Metuchen, NJ 08840
(908) 632-8502

In the spirit of the '60's, you'll find poets, writers, and others types of performers reading and acting out their works.

Netcong
Morris County

Wild West City
50 Lackawanna Dr., Rt. 206
Netcong, NJ 07857
(201) 347-8900

This amusement park will take your kids back in time and allow them to experience gunfights, train rides, pony rides, and more. A nearby saloon offers both food and entertainment.

Old Bridge
Middlesex County

Raceway Park
230 Pension Rd.
Englishtown, NJ 07726
(908) 446-6331

Raceway Park is home to both drag racing and motorcross racing. Jet skiing is also featured on a nearby lake.

Paramus
Bergen County

Van Saun Zoo
216 Forest Ave.
Paramus, NJ 07652 .
(201) 262- 3771

Visit the wild animals and walk through their bird aviary.

Ringoes
Hunterdon County

Harrison Air
258 Wertsville Rd.
Ringoes, NJ 08551
(609) 466-3389

Book a cross country hot-air balloon ride that you will never forget.

Roseland
Hunterdon County

Green Meadows Petting Zoo Farm
Box 206, Eisenhower Pkwy.
at Eagle Rock Ave.
Roseland, NJ 07068
(201) 228-6966

Your kids will have a ball as they pet different types of friendly animals.

Somerville
Somerset County

U.S. Bicycling Hall Of Fame
166 W. Main St.
Somerset, NJ 08876
(908) 722-3620

There is no other location as important as this one for American cyclists. Their memorabilia include historical bikes, photographs, and honorary plaques of great achievements.

Teaneck
Bergen County

American Statge Company
Rt. 4 & River Rd., P.O. Box 336
Teaneck, NJ 07666
(201) 692-7720

The theater that houses this company seats a total of 290 people. Performances include both classical works that have become standards throughout the country, to the current brilliance of up-and-coming American playwrights. Either way, you're bound to have a fun time if you enjoy the live arts.

Upper Montclair
Essex County

Presby Memorial Iris Gardens
474 Upper Mountain Ave.
Upper Montclair, NJ 07043
(201) 783-5974

A stunning array of Iris flowers are on display here. The Garden is home to over 50,000 of these flowers (4,500 different species), ranging all the way down to dwarfs, up to the median varieties, and all the way up to the tall bearded ones. It's an absolutely astonishing view. The best time of the year to see these flowers is at the tail end of May through the end of the first week in June.

Vernon
Sussex County

Vernon Valley Action Park
Box 848, Rt. 94
Vernon, NJ 07426
(201) 827-2000

This amusement park is the largest self-participating center in the world. Enjoy water slides, race cars, and much more.

Weehawken
Hudson County

Port Imperial Ferry
Pershing Rd.
Hudson, NJ 07087
(201) 902-8736

If you're in the area and would like to cross over to Manhatten, this port offers a regular ferry service.

Spirit of New Jersey
1500 Harbor Blvd.
Lincoln Harbor Marina, NJ 07087
(201) 867-5518

There's no better way to enjoy the harbor. Call about their lunch and dinner cruise packages, and ask them about their buffet dining tour of New York Harbor. A live dance band and a Broadway revue is included.

West Orange
Essex County

New Jersey Ballet
270 Pleasant Valley Way
Essex, NJ 07052
(201) 736-5942

The Paper Mill Playhouse in Millburn is home to thier ballet. Performances are booked throughout the tri-state area.

State Parks & Forests

Allamuchy Mount Park
180 Steven's Park Rd.
Hackettstown, NJ 07840
(908) 852-3790

Here at Allumuchy Mount Park, you'll find over 6,094 acres to explore at your leisure with designated natural areas that are both beautiful and fun to scout through. You can enjoy fishing, hunting, and exploring one of many wonderful hiking trails throughout the park.

Bull's Island Section of Delaware & Raritan Canal Park
2185 Daniel Bray Hwy.
Stockton, NJ 08559
(609) 397-2949

You'll find plenty of fun in the 79 acres of land that form this park. Some of the more popular attractions include hiking and canoeing through trails, fishing along a quiet and serene lake, jogging, and, as a grand finale, picnicking at a location that overlooks a great view.

Delaware & Raritan Canal Park
643 Canal Rd.
Somerset, NJ 08873
(908) 873-3050

Here you can take out your camera, focus on your subject, and click until your heart's content. With 3,578 acres of land to choose from, you'd better bring along plenty of film to capture the park's outer beauty. You can rent either a boat or canoe for the duration of the day. Other attractions include fishing, hiking, running, picnicking and walking through some great nature trails.

Hacklebarney Park
119 Hacklebarney Rd.,
Long Valley, NJ 07853
(908) 879-5677

Hacklebarney Park stretches through 890 acres of land. It includes a designated natural area that's beautiful and fun to walk through. If you're a good photographer, you'll want to bring plenty of film to capture the park's finer qualities. It has a surrealistic quality that you'll enjoy photographing.

High Point Park
1480 State Rt. 23
Sussex, NJ 07641
(201) 875-4800

Sometimes, the best form of relaxation happens almost magically, while unwinding at a new location and taking in the view. Here, with 14,109 acres of land to explore, you're likely to experience those feelings once again. Located at the highest point of New Jersey — hence the name High Point, the park fuses together spectacular views of nature that are worth capturingon film. Other attractions include running, fishing, hiking, picnicking and exploring the park's designated natural area.

Jenny Jump Forest
P.O. Box 150,
State Park Rd.
Hope, NJ 07844
(908) 459-4366

Jenny Jump Forest offers camping, camp shelters, fishing, and hiking trails. It's beautiful array of trees makes it an ideal place to pick a shaded spot to read a good book. Between each chapter, you can take a break, stretch, and take in the beautiful views.

Abraham S. Hewitt Forest
Warwick Turnpike
Hewitt, NJ 07421
(201) 853-4462 / Acres: 2,001

Cheesequake Park
Gordon Rd.
Matawan, NJ 07747
(908) 566-2161 / Acres: 1,274

Liberty State Park
Morris Pesin Dr.
Jersey City, NJ 07054
(201) 915-3400 / Acres: 1,114

Longpond Ironworks State Park
C/O Ringwood Park,
P.O. Box 1304, Sloatsburg Rd.
Ringwood, NJ 07456
(201) 962-7031 / Acres: 1,729

Norvin Green Forest
C/O Ringwood Park,
P.O. Box 1304, Sloatsburg Rd.
Ringwood, NJ 07456
(201) 962-7031 / Acres: 2,331

Ringwood Manor
C/O Ringwood Park,
P.O. Box 1304, Sloatsburg Rd.
Ringwood, NJ 07456
(201) 962-7031 / Acres: 1,031

Shepard Lake
C/O Ringwood Park,
P.O. Box 1304, Sloatsburg Rd.
Ringwood, NJ 07456
(201) 962-7031 / Acres: 541

Skyland Section
C/O Ringwood Park,
P.O. Box 1304, Sloatsburg Rd.
Ringwood, NJ 07456
(201) 962-7031 / Acres: 2,331

Round Valley
Box 45 D, Round Valley Rd.,
Lebanon, NJ 08833
(908) 236-6355 / Acres: 3,639

Spruce Run
Box 289 A
Van Syckels Rd.
Clinton, NJ 08809
(908) 638-8572 / Acres: 1,961

Strokes Forest
R.R. 1 Courson Rd.
Branchville, NJ 07826
(201) 948-3820 / Acres: 15,399

Swartswood Park
Box 123, E. Shore Dr.
Swartswood, NJ 07860-0123
(201) 383-5230/ Acres: 1,420

Voorhees Park
R.D. 3, Box 80, Rt. 513
Glen Gardner, NJ 08826
(908) 638-6969 / Acres: 516

Washington Rock Park
16 Rock Rd.
West Greenbrook, NJ 08833
(908) 566-2161 / Acres: 45

Wawayonda Park
Box 198, Warwick Turnpike
Highland Lakes, NJ 07422
(201) 853-4462 / Acres: 11,330

Worthington Forest
HC62, Box 2, Old Mine Rd.,
Columbia, NJ 07832
(908) 841-9575/ Acres: 5,830

Private Campgrounds

Beaver Hill Campground
Big Spring Rd.
P.O. Box 353
Sussex, NJ 07461
(201) 827-0670 / Acres: 180

Brookwood Swim & Tennis Club
1839 Rt. 46,
Parippany, NJ 07054
(201) 226-3200 / Acres: 18

Camp Taylor Campground
85 Mt. Pleasant Rd.
Columbia, NJ 07054
(908) 496-4333 / Acres: 150

Cedar Ridge Campground
Rt. 521, Box 149-R5
Montague, NJ 07827
(201) 293-3512/ Acres: 68

Columbia Valley Campground
3 Ghost Pony Rd.
Andover, NJ 07821
(201) 691-0596 / Acres: 30

Delaware River Campground
Rt. 46, Box 142
Delaware, NJ 07833
(800) 543-0271 / Acres: 39

Fla-Net Park
20 Flanders-Netcong Rd.
Flanders, NJ 07836
(201) 347-4467 / Acres: 16

Green Valley Beach Inc. Campground
68 Phillips Rd.
Newton, NJ 07860
(201) 383-4026 / Acres: 100

Greenwood Lake Campground
271 Lakeside Rd.
Hewitt, NJ 07421
(201) 728-8505 / Acres: 4

Harmony Ridge Farm & Campground
23 Risdon Dr.
Branchville, NJ 07826
(201) 948-4941 / Acres: 160

Jugtown Mountain Campground
279 Rt. 173
West Portal, NJ 08802
(908) 735-5995 / Acres: 55

Kymer Campground
69 Kymer Rd.
Branchville, NJ 07826
(800) 526-CAMP / Acres: 200

Mountain View Campground
Box 130
Little York, NJ 08834
(908) 996-2953 / Acres: 200

New Yorker Trailer City
4901 Tonnelle Ave.
N. Bergen, NJ 07047
(201) 866-0999 / Acres: 8

Panther Lake Campground
6 Panther Lake Rd.
Andover, NJ 07821
(800) 543-2056 / Acres: 165

Pleasant Acres Farm Campground
61 DeWitt Rd.
Sussex, NJ 07461
(201) 875-4166 / Acres: 170

Rabbit Patch Campground
974 Rt. 619
Newton, NJ 07860
(201) 383-7661 / Acres: 100

Rayewood Campgrounds
120 Clove Rd.
Sussex, NJ 07461
(201) 875-4961 / Acres: 130

Shippekonk Campground
Country Rd. 521, R.D. 5 Box 49
Montague, NJ 07827
(201) 293-3383 / Acres: 62

Sun Air Lakeside Campground
Cozy Lake Rd.
Oak Ridge, NJ 07438
(201) 697-3489 / Acres: 100

Rabbit Patch Campground
974 Rt. 619
Newton, NJ 07860
(201) 383-7661 / Acres: 100

Toye's Recreation Campground
RD 5 Box 495, Rt. 565
Vernon Township, NJ 07641
(201) 702-8167 / Acres: 60

Triplebrook
P.O. Box 70, Honey Run Rd.
Blairstown, NJ 07844
(908) 459-4079 / Acres: 250

Walpack Valley Campground
Rt. 615,
Walpack, NJ 07881
(201) 948-4384 / Acres: 61

YMCA Camp Carr
Hamden River Rd. Annandale
(Mail to: 144 W. Woods Church Rd.)
Flemington, NJ 08822
(908) 782-1030 / Acres: 33

Allentown
Monmouth County

The Horse Park Of New Jersey
Rt. 524, P.O. Box 118
Allentown, NJ 08501
(609) 259-0170

This is New Jersey's first major show-horse location. Come and enjoy it for yourself as you walk through its 147-acre facility.

Atco
Camden County

Atco Raceway
Jackson Rd.
Atco, NJ 08004
(609) 935-5640

Enjoy the thrill of auto racing in the form of funny cars and dragsters. Thrill shows included.

Asbury Park
Monmouth County

Convention Hall / Paramount Theatre
1300 Boardwalk
Asbury Park, NJ 07712
(908) 775-4255

All types of shows are featured at this 1,500 seat theater.

Atlantic City
Atlantic County

Atlantic City Boardwalk

No other boardwalk around the world is as famous as this one. Built in 1870 to serve as a wooden sidewalk while keeping sand out of hotel lobbies and railroad cars, it was the first of its kind. As you walk along it, you'll see some of the most respected gambling institutions in the world, a list of fine restaurants to choose from, amusement centers, historical landmarks, and much more.

Atlantic City draws millions of people annually to its state-of-the-art casino facilities. For further information, please call the following number or write to the address provided below:

Greater Atlantic City Regional Tourism Council
C/O ACCVA,
2314 Pacific Ave.
Atlantic City, NJ 08401
(609) 348-7100, ext. 133

Atlantic City Art Center
Garden Pier
Boardwalk at New Jersey Ave.
Atlantic City, NJ 08401
(609) 347-5844

This art gallery / historical museum has something for every age group.

(Continued)

Atlantic City
Atlantic County

Central Fun Pier Theatre
Boardwalk at Tennessee Ave.
Atlantic City, NJ 08401
(609) 345-8271

All the rides and games a child could possibly want.

Showboat Bowling Center
Boardwalk & Delware Ave.
Atlantic City, NJ 08401
(609) 343-4040

This is a bowler's dream. The bowling lanes and facilities are second to none.

Bridgeton
Cumberland County

Cohanzick Zoo
Bridgeton City Park
Cumberland, NJ 08302
(609) 455-3230 / ext. 242

You'll find a great variety of animal life from all parts of the globe on this 1,100-acre park.

Camden
Camden County

Rutgers University
at Camden Fine Arts Theatre
3rd and Linden St.,
Camden, NJ 08102
(609) 225-6176

This is a fine establishment that brings together a variety of shows from contemporary music, jazz, dance, and traditional theater.

Stedman Art Gallery
Fine Arts Building (Rutgers University)
3rd and Linden St.,
Camden, NJ 08102
(609) 225-6245

Beautiful works by contemporary American artists are on display. Paintings and sculpture are featured.

Thomas H. Kean
New Jersey State Aquarium
1 Riverside Dr.
3rd and Linden St.,
Camden, NJ 08103-1060
(609) 225-6245

This huge aquarium is absolutely astonishing. It's a must-see for anyone interested in marine life. Part of the attraction is a 760,000 gallon tank filled with over 40 species of fish. Another attraction is the 170,000 gallon pool for grey and harbor seals. You'll also find a one-of-a-kind trout stream and a 230 seat auditorium.

Cherry Hill
Camden County

**Flea Market At Garden
State Race Track**
Rt. 70 & Haddonfield Rd.
Camden, NJ 08102
(908) 828-9256

The market is open every Sunday and Wednesday. You'll find a large collection of items to sift through.

Clementon
Camden County

Clementon Lake Amusement Park
144 Berlin Rd.
Camden, NJ 08021
(609) 783-0263

This creative family amusement center includes a petting zoo, kiddie rides, roller coasters, a high dive show, and Splash World, an area of about 3 acres filled with the great water rides.

Egg Harbor City
Atlantic County

Renault Glass Museum
72 N. Bremen Ave.
Egg Harbor, NJ 08215
(609) 965-2111

This museum is home to one of the world's most extensive glass collections.

Englishtown
Monmouth County

Englishtown Auction
90 Wilson Ave.
Englishtown, NJ 07726
(908) 446-9644

This incredable flea market features over 1,000 vendors throughout its 50 acres of land.

Farmingdale
Monmouth County

Garret Flight Center
Allaire Airport, Rt. 34
Monmouth, NJ 07727
(908) 938-9333

If you've never experienced the thrill of a single-engine plane ride, you owe it to yourself to try. Flight instructions are available.

Forked River
Ocean County

JCP&L Energy Spectrum
Oyster Creek Power Plant, Gate #2
P.O. Box 592, Rt. 9, S.
Forek River, NJ 08731
(609) 971-2100

This well thought out museum features interactive displays and educational lectures.

Fort Monmouth
Monmouth County

**U.S. Army Communications
Electronics Museum**
Bldg. 275, Kaplan Hall
Monmouth, NJ 07703
(908) 532-4390

This museum is filled with fascinating electronic equipment. You'll see communication devices that date back to the year 1917, unusual spy cameras, and even notes that had been sent by carrier pigeons to strategic locations.

Freehold
Monmouth County

Battleground Art Center
35 W. Main St., Box 678
Monmouth, NJ 07728
(908) 462-8811

Different types of music are featured here throughout the year. Other attractions include art festivals and youth programs.

Glassboro
Gloucester County

Heritage Glass Museum
Center & High Sts
Glassboro, NJ 08028
(609) 881-7468

Heritage Glass Museum is filled with memorabilia from the 18th century. You'll find beautiful works of glassware and the blowing equipment used to make glass.

Green Bank
Atlantic County

Bel Haven Canoe Rentals
Rt. 542
Green Bank, NJ 08215
(800) 445-0953

Bel Haven has over 200 canoes for rent. The area allows you to set off on a new adventure down one of its four popular rivers: Batsto, Mullica, Oswego, and Wading. It makes for a great day of sightseeing, swimming, picnicking, and photography.

Hopewell
Cumberland County

The Off Broadstreet Theatre
5 S. Greenwood Ave.
Cumberland, NJ 08526
(609) 466-2766

Nothing beats a good night of solid entertainment, and that's exactly what you'll receive at the Off Broadstreet Theatre. Their desserts are absolutely incredible!

Mays Landing
Atlantic County

Atlantic Community College
5100 Black Horse Pike
Atlantic, NJ 08330-2699
(609) 343-4900

The Atlantic Community College puts on great shows. Some of the attractions include concerts, dances, drama, film, and lectures. If you happen to be a student of the arts, you'll want to come and view one of the school's open rehearsals and take notes on how the class works with the teacher/director and how they interact among each other as actors and friends.

Oceanville
Atlantic County

The Noyes Museum
Lily Lake Rd.
Atlantic, NJ 08231
(609) 652-8848

The permanent collection of contemporary folk and American art is worth the trip alone, but the museum also features a rotating exhibition for further viewing.

Pomona
Atlantic County

Stockton Performing Arts Center
Stockton State College
Jimmy Leeds Rd.
Atlantic, NJ 08240
(609) 652-9000

A full spectrum of performances and events can be found here. Music, jazz, dance, theater and childrens' plays are performed on a regular basis.

Princeton
Mercer County

Creative Theatre Unlimited
102 Witherspoon St.
Mercer, NJ 08542
(609) 924-3489

This theater is strictly committed to putting on quality plays for children and offering open classes to study the art of acting.

Princeton University
185 Nassau St.
Mercer, NJ 08544
(609) 258-3676

Princeton University is one of the most celebrated Ivy League schools in America. The school aims at a more sophisticated audience that can appreciate the fine and subtle attributes of a classic. But that's not all: their dance shows and film series are just as exciting and entertaining.

Red Bank
Monmouth County

**Monmouth County Arts Council /
Count Basie Theatre**
99 Monmouth St.
Monmouth, NJ 07701
(908) 842-9000

You'll find a healthy assortment of entertainment coming your way at this wonderful theater. Musical performances can be heard from classical, jazz, jazz-rock, and pop. The center also hosts ballet, modern dance groups, and a children's theater.

Toms River
Ocean County

Robert J. Novines Planetarium at Ocean County College
College Dr. off Hoppers Ave.
Ocean, NJ 08745-2001
(908) 255-0342

Watch the stars come out at this terrific planetarium.

Trenton
Mercer County

Boehm Porcelain
25 Fairfax St., P.O. Box 5051
Mercer, NJ 08618
(609) 392-2207

Enjoy a film presentation and the studio's four room gallery display.

Cybis Porcelain Studio
65 Norman Ave.
Mercer, NJ 08618
(609) 392-6074

This studio offers both an art demonstration and a film show. Afterwards, you'll want to tour the grounds.

New Jersey State Museum
CN530, 205 W. State St.
Mercer, NJ 08625
(609) 292-6333

Amazing works of art from the 19th- and 20th-century are on display. World renowned artists and local artists are featured, too. Indian artifacts, films, lectures, dinosaur fossils, a planetarium, a children's theatre, and other special events are provided to keep everyone in your family happy and entertained.

Trenton City Museum Of Ellarslie
Cadwalader Park,
Parkside and Belview
Mercer, NJ 08618
(609) 989-3632

Trenton is famous for its fine works of porcelain art. Boehn, Cybis, or Lenox, you'll see them all. The museum is an 1848 Italianate villa that features exhibits of fine art, history, and decorative crafts.

Wildwood
Cape May County

Long before Atlantic City became a major competitor in the gambling world, Wildwood was one of America's most sought-after vacation spots.

Morey's Pier
25th Ave. & Boardwalk
Schellenger Ave. & Boardwalk
Wildwood, NJ 08260
(609) 729-0586

Your kids are going to love you for this one — if you don't forget to bring yoiur wallet — as you guide them through an amusement park full of rides and several water slides, original in their architecture and on par with some of the larger water parks that can be found across this country.

WHERE TO STAY - NEW YORK

Albany

Marriott Hotel Albany
189 Wolf Rd.
Albany, NY 12205
(518) 458-8444

Mount Vernon Motel
576 Columbia Tpke.
East Greenbush, NY 12061-1612
(518) 477-9352

Omni Albany Hotel
State & Lodge St.
Albany, NY 12207
(518) 462-6611 / (800) THE OMNI

Ramada Inn Albany
1228 Western Ave.
Albany, NY 12203
(518) 489-2981

Red Roof In Albany
188 Wolf Rd.
Albany, NY 12205
(518) 459-1971

Travel Lodge Albany
1230 Western Ave.
Albany, NY 12203
(518) 489-4423

Washington Inn at Albany
1375 Washington Ave.
Albany, NY 12206
(518) 459-3100

Alexandria Bay

Bonnie Castle Resort
Outer Holland St.
Alexandria, NY 13607
(315) 482-4511

Capt Thompson's Resort
James St. (St. Lawrence River)
Alexandria, NY 13607
(315) 482-9961

Edgewood Resort
Edgewood Rd. (St. Lawrence River)
Alexandria, NY 13607
(315) 482-9922

North Star Motel
Rt. 12
Alexandria, NY 13607
(315) 482-9332

Pine Tree Point Resort
Anthony St.
Alexandria, NY 13607
(315) 482-9911

Amsterdam

Holiday Inn
10 Market St.
Amsterdam, NY 12010
(518) 843-5760

Super 8 Motel
NYS Thruway & Rt. 30
Amsterdam, NY 12010
(518) 843-5888

Continued

Windsor Motel
Rt. 30
Amsterdam, NY 12010
(518) 843-0243

Batavia

Days Inn-Batavia
200 Oak St.
Batavia, NY 14020
(716) 343-1440

Sheraton Inn Batavia
8250 Park Rd.
Batavia, NY 14020
(716) 344-2100

Treadway Inn of Batavia
8204 Park Rd.
Batavia, NY 14020
(800) 228-2842 / (800) 873-2392

Bolton Landing

Bonnie View Hotel
Lake Shore Dr.
Bolton Landing, NY 12814
(518) 644-5591

Melody Manor Motel
Lake Shore Dr.
Bolton Landing, NY 12814
(518) 644-9750

Victorian Village Resort Lodge
Lake Shore Dr.
Bolton Landing, NY 12814-0012
(518) 644-9401

Buffalo

Motel 6
4400 Maple Rd.
Buffalo, NY 14226
(716) 834-2231

Best Western in Downtown
510 Delaware Ave.
Buffalo, NY 14202
(716) 886-8333

Buffalo Marriott
1340 Millersport Hwy.
Amherst, NY 14221
(716) 689-6900 / (800) 334-4040

Hampton Inn Buffalo / Amherst
10 Flint Rd.
Amherst, NY 14226
(716) 689-4414 / (800) 426-7866

Holiday Inn Amherst
1881 Niagara Falls Blvd.
Amherst, NY 14228
(716) 691-8181 / (800) HOLIDAY

Holiday Inn Buffalo Downtown
620 Delaware Ave.
Buffalo, NY 14202
(716) 886-2121 / (800) HOLIDAY

Holiday Inn Buffalo Gateway
601 Dingens St.
Buffalo, NY 14206
(716) 896-2900

Hyatt Regency Buffalo Downtown
2 Fountain Plaza
Buffalo, NY 14202
(716) 856-1234 / (800) 233-1234

Hotel Lenox
140 North St.
Buffalo, NY 14201
(716) 884-1700

Lord Amherst
5000 Main St.
Buffalo, NY 14226
(716) 839-2200 (800) 544-2200

Quality Suites by Journey's End
601 Main St.
Buffalo, NY 14203
(716) 854-5500

Ramada Inn Buffalo Airport
6643 Transit Rd.
Buffalo, NY 14221
(716) 634-2700

Red Roof Inn Buffalo - Amherst
42 Flint Rd.
Amherst, NY 14226
(716) 689-7474

Residence Inn Buffalo Amherst
100 Maple Rd.
Williamsville, NY 14221
(716) 632-6622

Super 8 Motel
1 Flint Rd.
Amherst, NY 14226
(716) 688-0811

Towne House Hotel
999 Main St.
Buffalo, NY 14203
(716) 884-2160

University Inn & Conference Center
2401 N. Forest Rd.
Buffalo, NY 14226-0823
(716) 636-7500

Canandaigua

Econo Lodge Muir Lakes
170 Eastern Blvd.
Canandaigua, NY 14424
(716) 394-9000

Inn On The Lake, The
770 S. Main St.
Canandaigua, NY 14424
(716) 394-7800

Chautaqua

Athenaeum Hotel
Lake Dr.
Chautaqua, NY 14722
(716) 357-4444

Clymer

Peek 'N Peak Resort
Ye Olde Rd.
Clymer, NY 14724
(716) 355-4141

Cooperstown

Cooper Inn
Chestnut & Main Sts.
Cooperstown, NY 13326
(607) 547-2567

Deer Run Motel
Rt. 80, Rd. #2, Box 722
Cooperstown, NY 13326
(607) 547-8600

Otesaga Hotel
Lake St., P.O. Box 311
Cooperstown, NY 13326
(607) 547-9931 / (800) 348-6222

Tunnicliff Inn
3436 Pioneer St.
Cooperstown, NY 13326
(607) 547-9611

Corning

Comfort Inn Corning
66 W. Pulteney St.
Corning, NY 14830
(607) 962-1515

Corning Hilton
Denison Pkwy. E.
Corning, NY 14830
(607) 962-5000 / (800) HILTONS

Lodge on the Green
Canada Rd. Rts. 15 & 417
Corning, NY 14870
(607) 962-2456

Super 8 Motel
255 S. Hamilton
Corning, NY 14870
(607) 937-5383

Cortland

Budget Inn
4408 N. Homer Ave.
Cortland, NY 13045
(607) 753-3388

Comfort Inn
2 1/2 Locust Ave.
Cortland, NY 13045
(607) 753-7721

Holiday Inn - Cortland
2 River St.
Cortland, NY 13045
(607) 756-4431

Super 8 Motel
188 Clinton Ave.
Cortland, NY 13045
(607) 756-5622

Geneseo

Days Inn Geneseo
4242 Lakeville Rd.
Geneseo, NY 14454
(716) 243-0500

Geneseo

Motel 6
485 Hamilton St.
Geneseo, NY 14456
(607) 789-4050

Chanticleer Motor Lodge
473 Hamilton St.
Geneseo, NY 14456
(607) 789-7600

Geneva on the Lake
1001 Lochland Rd.
Geneseo, NY 14456
(607) 789-7190

Hamilton

Colgate Inn
1-5 Payne St.
Geneseo, NY 13346
(315) 824-2300

Happauge

Marriotts Windwatch Hotel & Golf
1717 Vanderbilt Motor Pkwy.
Happauge, NY 11788
(516) 232-9800 / (800) 228-9290

Radisson Hotel Islandia
3635 Express Dr. N.
Happauge, NY 11788
(516) 232-3000

Ramada Inn
1515 Veteran's Memorial Hwy.
Happauge, NY 11788
(516) 582-3600

Hornell

Super 8 Motel
Route 36 & 66
Hornell, NY 14843
(607) 324-6222

Horseheads

Motel 6
151 Route 17
Horseheads, NY 14845
(607) 739-2525

Holiday Inn Elmira Horesheads
602 Corning Rd.
Horseheads, NY 14845
(607) 739-3681

Howard Johnson
Rt. 14 & 17
Horseheads, NY 14845
(607) 739-5636

Red Carpet Inn
1122 S. Main St.
Horseheads, NY 14845
(607) 739-3831

Jamestown

Comfort Inn
2800 N. Main St.
Jamestown, NY 14702-3296
(716) 664-5920

Holiday Inn Jamestown
150 W. Fourth St.
Jamestown, NY 14701
(716) 664-3400

Johnstown

Holiday Inn
308 N. Comrie Ave.
Johnstown, NY 12095
(716) 762-4686

Kiamesha Lake

Concord Resort Hotel
Concord Rd.
Kiamesha Lake, NY 12751
(914) 794-4000

Lake George

Alpine Village Resort Hotel
Lake Shore Dr.
Lake George, NY 12845
(518) 668-2193

Antlers Resort Hotel
POB 711
Lake George, NY 12845
(518) 668-5791

Best Western of Lake George
Exit 21 at I-H78
Lake George, NY 12845
(518) 668-5701

Depe Dene Resorts
Rt. 9N, Lake Shore Dr.
Lake George, NY 12845
(518) 688-2788

Fort William Henry Motor Inn
Canada St.
Lake George, NY 12845
(518) 668-3081

Georgian Luxury Resort
384 Canada St.
Lake George, NY 12845
(518) 668-3081

Holiday Inn Turf at Lake George
Rt. 9, Canada St.
Lake George, NY 12845
(518) 668-5781 / (800) HOLIDAY

Howard Johnson Tiki Resort
Canada St.
Lake George, NY 12845
(518) 668-5744

Marine Village Resort
350 Canada St.
Lake George, NY 12845
(518) 668-5478

Omni Sagamore Hotel
Lake George at Bolton Landing
Lake George, NY 12814
(518) 644-9400 / (800) THE-OMNI

Ramada Inn
I-87 at Exit 21 & Rt. 9N
Lake George, NY 12845
(518) 668-3131

Roaring Brook Ranch Tennis Resort
Rt. 9N S.
Lake George, NY 12845
(518) 668-5767

Lake Placid

Adirondack Inn
217 Main St.
Lake Placid, NY 12946
(518) 523-2424

Art Devlin's Olympic Motor Inn
350 Main St.
Lake Placid, NY 12946
(518) 523-3700

Bark Eater Inn
Alstead Hill Rd.
Keene, NY 12942
(518) 576-2221

Best Western Golden Arrow Hotel
150 Main St.
Lake Placid, NY 12946
(518) 523-3353 / (800) 582-5540

Holiday Inn Sunspree Resort
1 Olympic Dr.
Lake Placid, NY 12946
(518) 523-2556 / (800) 874-1980

Howard Johnson Resort Lodge
90 Saranac Ave.
Lake Placid, NY 12946
(518) 523-9555

Lake Placid Hilton Resort
One Mirror Lake Dr.
Lake Placid, NY 12946
(518) 523-4411 / (800) HILTONS

Lake Placid Manor
Whiteface Inn Rd.
Lake Placid, NY 12946
(518) 523-2573

Mirror Lake Inn
5 Mirror Lake Dr.
Lake Placid, NY 12946
(518) 523-2544

Ramada Inn Lake Placid
8-12 Saranac Ave.
Lake Placid, NY 12946
(518) 523-2587

Whiteface Inn Resort & Club
Whiteface Inn Rd.
Lake Placid, NY 12946
(518) 523-2551 / (800) 422-6757

Liberty

Days Inn
Rt. 17, Exit 100
Liberty, NY 12754
(914) 292-7600

Holiday Inn Express
Rts. 17 & 52
Liberty, NY 12754
(914) 292-7171

Liberty Motel
204 S. Main St.
Liberty, NY 12754
(914) 292-7272

New Age Health Spa
Rt. 55
Neversink, NY 12765
(914) 985-7601

Liverpool

Arborgate Inn
430 Electronics Pkwy.
Liverpool, NY 13088
(315) 453-6330

Homewood Suites
275 Elmwood Davis Rd.
Liverpool, NY 13088
(315) 451-3800

Liverpool Motel
7360 Oswego Rd.
Liverpool, NY 13090
(315) 451-8550

Lockport

Best Western Lockport Inn
515 S. Transit St.
Lockport, NY 14094
(716) 434-6151

Montauk

Atlantic Terrace
Ocean View Terrace
Montauk, NY 11954
(516) 668-2050

Beach House Ocean Resort
S. Embassy & S. Elmwood
Montauk, NY 11954
(516) 668-2700

Driftwood on the Ocean
Rt. 27, Box S.
Montauk, NY 11954
(516) 668-5744

Montauk Yacht Club Resort Marina
Star Island Rd.
Montauk, NY 11954
(516) 668-3100 / (800) 832-4200

Oceanside Beach Resort
5 Eton St. & Montauk Hwy.
Montauk, NY 11954
(516) 668-3000

Panaramic View
Old Montauk Hwy.
Montauk, NY 11954
(516) 668-3000

Ruschmeyer's Hotel & Motel
Second House Rd.
Montauk, NY 11954
(516) 668-2877

Wave Crest Resort
Old Montauk Hwy.
Montauk, NY 11954
(516) 668-2864

Montgomery

Super 8 Motel
207 Montgomery Rd.
Montgomery, NY 12549
(914) 457-3143

Niagara Falls

American Motor Inn
9401 Niagara Falls Blvd.
Niagara Falls, NY 14304
(914) 297-2660

Avalon Bed & Breakfast Inn
337 Buffalo Ave.
Niagara Falls, NY 14303
(716) 285-5916 / (800) 455-9555

Beacon Motel
9900 Niagara Falls Blvd.
Niagara Falls, NY 14304
(716) 297-3647

Best Western Red Jacket Inn
7001 Buffalo Ave.
Niagara Falls, NY 14304
(716) 283-7612

Best Western Summit
9500 Niagara Falls Blvd.
Niagara Falls, NY 14304
(716) 297-5050

Castle Motor Inn
9802 Niagara Falls Blvd.
Niagara Falls, NY 14304
(716) 297-3730

Comfort Inn The Point
One Prospect Point
Niagara Falls, NY 14303
(716) 284-6835 / (800) 284-6835

Days Inn - Falls View
20 Rainbow Blvd.
Niagara Falls, NY 14303
(716) 285-9321 / (800) 633-1414

Econo Lodge
7708 Niagara Falls Blvd.
Niagara Falls, NY 14304
(716) 283-0621

Holiday Inn
114 Buffalo Ave.
Niagara Falls, NY 14303
(716) 285-2521

Holiday Inn Convention Center
231 Third St.
Niagara Falls, NY 14303
(716) 282-2211 / (800) 955-2211

Holiday Inn Grand Island / Niagara
100 White Haven Rd.
Niagara Falls, NY 14072
(716) 773-1111 / (800) HOLIDAY

Howard Johnson at the Falls
454 Main St.
Niagara Falls, NY 14305
(716) 285-5261 / (800) 282-5261

Howard Johnson Lodge East
6505 Niagara Falls Blvd.
Niagara Falls, NY 14304
(716) 283-8791

Inn at the Falls Hotel
240 Rainbow Blvd.
Niagara Falls, NY 14303
(716) 282-1212

Manchester House
653 Main St.
Niagara Falls, NY 14301
(716) 285-5717

Quality Inn Rainbow Bridge
443 Main St.
Niagara Falls, NY 14301
(716) 284-8801 / (800) 777-2280

Radisson Hotel Niagara Falls
3rd & Old Falls
Niagara Falls, NY 14303
(716) 285-3361 / (800) 777-7800

Rainbow House Bed & Breakfast
423 Rainbow Blvd. S.
Niagara Falls, NY 14303
(716) 282-1135 / (800) 724-3536

Ramada Inn
219 Fourth St. & Rainbow Blvd.
Niagara Falls, NY 14303
(716) 282-1734 / (800) 333-2557

Ramada Inn Niagara
401 Buffalo Ave.
Niagara Falls, NY 14303
(716) 285-2541

Thruway Motor Inn
6115 Niagara Falls Blvd.
Niagara Falls, NY 14304
(716) 283-3444

Travel Lodge Niagara Falls
200 Rainbow Blvd.
Niagara Falls, NY 14303
(716) 285-7316

Norwich

Howard Johnson Hotel
75 N. Broad St.
Norwich, NY 13815
(607) 334-2200

Pearl River

Pearl River Hilton
500 Veterans Memorial Dr.
Pearl River, NY 10965
(914) 735-9000 / (800) HILTONS

Plattsburgh

Comfort Inn
495 Cornelia St.
Plattsburgh, NY 12901
(518) 562-2730

Days Inn
I-87 & Rt. 3
Plattsburgh, NY 12901
(518) 561-0403

Econo Lodge
610 Upper Cornelia St.
Plattsburgh, NY 12901
(518) 561-1500

Holiday Inn
I-87 & Rt. 3
Plattsburgh, NY 12901
(518) 561-5000

Howard Johnson Motor Lodge
Cornelia St., I-87 at Exit 37
Plattsburgh, NY 12901
(518) 561-7750

Poughkeepsie

Courtyard by Marriott
408 South Rd.
Poughkeepsie, NY 12601
(914) 485-6336

Days Inn-Poughkeepsie
62 Haight Ave.
Poughkeepsie, NY 12603
(914) 454-1010

Econo Lodge
418 South Rd., Rt. 9
Poughkeepsie, NY 12601
(914) 452-6600

Edison Motor Inn
313 Manchester Rd. (Route 55)
Poughkeepsie, NY 12603
(914) 454-3080

Friendship Inn
576 South Rd., Rt. 9
Poughkeepsie, NY 12601
(914) 462-4400

Holiday Inn Express
341 South Rd.
Poughkeepsie, NY 12601
(914) 473-1151

Inn at the Falls
50 Red Oaks Mill Rd.
Poughkeepsie, NY 12603
(914) 462-5770 / (800) 344-1466

Radisson Hotel Poughkeepsie
40 Civic Center Plaza
Poughkeepsie, NY 12601
(914) 485-5300 / (800) 777-7800

Ramada Inn - Poughkeepsie
679 South Rd.
Poughkeepsie, NY 12601
(914) 462-4600

Rochester

Motel 6
155 Buell Rd.
Rochester, NY 14624
(716) 436-2170

Brookwood Inn
800 Pittsford-Victor Rd.
Pittsford, NY 14534
(716) 248-9000

Comfort Inn Airport
395 Buell Rd.
Rochester, NY 14624
(716) 436-4400

Comfort Inn West
1501 Ridge Rd. West
Rochester, NY 14615
(716) 621-5700

Days Inn Downtown
384 East Ave.
Rochester, NY 14607
(716) 325-5010

Depot Inn
41 N. Main St.
Rochester, NY 14534
(716) 381-9900

Downtown Motor Lodge
390 South Ave.
Rochester, NY 14620
(716) 454-3550

Econo Lodge Rochester South
940 Jefferson Rd.
Rochester, NY 14632
(716) 427-2700

Hampton Inn
717 E. Henrietta Rd.
Rochester, NY 14623
(716) 272-7800

Holiday Inn Genesee Plaza
120 Main St. E.
Rochester, NY 14604
(716) 546-6400 / (800) HOLIDAY

Holiday Inn Rochester South
1111 Jefferson Rd.
Rochester, NY 14623
(716) 475-1510

Howard Johnson Lodge
3350 W. Henrietta Rd.
Rochester, NY 14623
(716) 475-1661

Hyatt Regency Rochester Downtown
125 E. Main St.
Rochester, NY 14604
(716) 546-1234 / (800) 233-1234

King James Motel
2835 Monroe Ave.
Rochester, NY 14618
(716) 442-9220

Marketplace Inn
800 Jefferson Rd.
Rochester, NY 14623
(716) 475-9190

Marriott Thruway Hotel
5257 W. Henrietta Rd.
Rochester, NY 14602-0551
(716) 359-1800

Radisson Inn Rochester
175 Jefferson Rd.
Rochester, NY 14623
(716) 475-1910

Red Roof Inn Rochester
4820 W. Henrietta Rd.
Rochester, NY 14467
(716) 359-1100

Residence Inn Rochester
1300 Jefferson Rd.
Rochester, NY 14623
(716) 272-8850

Stouffer Rochester Plaza Hotel
70 State St.
Rochester, NY 14614
(716) 546-3450

Strathallan Hotel
550 East Ave.
Rochester, NY 14607
(716) 461-5010

Super 8 Motel
1000 Lehigh Station Rd.
Rochester, NY 14467
(716) 359-1630

Travelers Motel
2100 Monroe Ave.
Rochester, NY 14618
(716) 244-3700

Wellesley Inn North
1635 W. Ridge Rd.
Rochester, NY 14615
(716) 621-2060

Wellesley Inn South
797 E. Henrietta Rd.
Rochester, NY 14623
(716) 427-0130

Salamanca

Dudley Motor Inn
132 Main St.
Salamanca, NY 14779
(716) 945-3200

Saranac Lake

Comfort Inn Adirondack
148 Lake Flower Ave.
Saranac Lake, NY 12983
(518) 891-1970

Point, The
Star Route, Box 65
Saranac Lake, NY 12983
(518) 891-1152

Hotel Saranac of Paul Smith College
101 Main St.
Saranac Lake, NY 12983
(518) 891-2200

Saratoga Springs

Best Western Playmore Farms
3291 S. Broadway
Saratoga Springs, NY 12866
(518) 584-2350

Gideon Putnam Hotel
Saratoga Spa State Park
Saratoga Springs, NY 12866
(518) 584-3000

Holiday Inn
232 Broadway at Circular
Saratoga Springs, NY 12866
(518) 584-4550

Sheraton Saratoga Springs
534 Broadway
Saratoga Springs, NY 12866
(518) 584-4000 / (800) 325-3535

Westchester House Bed & Breakfast, The
102 Lincoln Ave.
Saratoga Springs, NY 12866
(518) 587-7613

Schenectady

Days In Schenectady
167 Nott Terrace
Schenectady, NY 12308
(518) 370-0851

Holiday Inn Of Schenectady
100 Nott Terrace
Schenectady, NY 12308
(518) 393-4141

Ramada Inn & Convention Center
450 Nott Terrace
Schenectady, NY 12308
(518) 370-7151

Travel Lodge Schenectady
759 State St.
Schenectady, NY 12307
(518) 393-6692

Stamford

Red Carpet Motor Inn
Corner of Routes 10 & 23
Stamford, NY 12167
(607) 652-7394

Syracuse

Best Western Airport Inn
Airport Rd.
Syracuse, NY 13212
(315) 455-7362

Best Western Travelers Motor Inn
6491 Thompson Rd.
Syracuse, NY 13206
(315) 437-0222

Comfort Inn Downtown
454 James St.
Syracuse, NY 13203
(315) 425-0015

Comfort Inn Fairgrounds
7010 Interstate Island Rd.
Syracuse, NY 13209
(315) 453-0045

Courtyard By Marriott
6415 Yorktown Circle
Syracuse, NY 13057
(315) 432-0300

Days Inn at the Dinkler
1100 James St.
Syracuse, NY 13203
(315) 472-6961

Days Inn North
400 Seventh North St.
Syracuse, NY 13088
(315) 451-1511

Embassy Suites
6646 Old Collamer Rd.
Syracuse, NY 13507
(315) 446-3200

Genesee Inn Executive Quarters
1060 E. Genesee St.
Syracuse, NY 13210
(315) 476-4212

Hampton Inn East Syracuse
6605 Old Callamer Rd.
Syracuse, NY 13507
(315) 463-6443

Holiday Inn Carrier Circle
Carrier Circle
Syracuse, NY 13057
(315) 437-2761

Holiday Inn Syracuse
Farrell Rd. & Rt. 690
Syracuse, NY 13209
(315) 457-8700 / (800) HOLIDAY

Holiday Inn Syracuse Airport
6701 Buckly Rd.
Syracuse, NY 13212
(315) 457-4000

Holiday Inn University Area
701 E. Genesee St.
Syracuse, NY 13210
(315) 474-7251

Howard Johnson Motor Lodge
Thompson Rd. at Carrier Circle
Syracuse, NY 13206
(315) 437-2711

Inn at the Circle, The
Exit 35, NYS Thrwy.
Syracuse, NY 13206
(315) 463-6601

Quality Inn North
1308 Buckly Rd.
Syracuse, NY 13212
(315) 451-1212

Quality Inn Riverside
930 South First St.
Fulton, NY 13069
(315) 593-2444

Ramada Inn
1305 Buckley Rd.
Syracuse, NY 13212
(315) 457-8670

Red Carpet Inn
Rt. 11 at Northern Lights
Syracuse, NY 13212
(315) 454-3266

Red Roof Inn - Syracuse
6614 n. Thompson Rd.
Syracuse, NY 13206
(315) 437-3309

Sheraton Inn Syracuse
Electronics Pkwy.
Syracuse, NY 13088
(315) 457-1122

**Sheraton University Inn &
Conference Center**
801 University Ave.
Syracuse, NY 13210-0801
(315) 475-3000

Super 8 Motel
421 7th North St.
Syracuse, NY 13088
(315) 451-8888

Hotel Syracuse
500 South Warren St.
Syracuse, NY 13202
(315) 422-5121

Syracuse Marriott
6302 Carrier Pkwy.
Syracuse, NY 13057
(315) 432-0200 / (800) 782-9847

Utica

Best Western Gateway Motor Inn
175 N. Genesee St.
Utica, NY 13502
(315) 732-4121

Consort Inn
Champion Rd.
New Hartford, NY 13413
(315) 735-3392

Holiday Inn Utica
1777 Burrstone Rd.
New Hartford, NY 13413
(315) 797-2131

Howard Johnson Motor Lodge
302 N. Genesee
Utica, NY 13502
(315) 724-4141

Radisson Hotel
200 Genesee St.
Utica, NY 13502
(315) 797-8010

Red Roof Inn - Utica
20 Weaver St,
Utica, NY 13502
(315) 724-7128

Travel Lodge - Utica
1700 Genesee St.
Utica, NY 13502
(315) 724-2101

Watertown

Holiday Inn
300 Washington St.
Watertown, NY 13601
(315) 782-8000

New Parrot Motel
5795 Washington St.
Watertown, NY 13601
(315) 788-5080

Quality Inn
1190 Arsenal St.
Watertown, NY 13601
(315) 788-6800

Ramada Inn
6300 Arsenal St.
Watertown, NY 13601
(315) 788-0700

Wellsville

Wellsville Motel
Rt. 417 E.
Wellsville, NY 14895
(716) 593-2494

Woodbury

Quality Inn at Woodbury
7758 Jericho Tpke.
Woodbury, NY 11797
(516) 921-6900

Ramada Inn Woodbury
8030 Jericho Tpke.
Woodbury, NY 11797
(516) 921-8500

WHERE TO STAY - NEW JERSEY

Absecon

Comfort Inn
405 E. Absecon Blvd.
Absecon, NJ 08201
(609) 646-5000

Hampton Inn Hotel
240 E. Whitehorse Pike
Absecon, NJ 08201
(609) 652-3344

Asbury Park

Berkeley Carteret Hotel
1401 Ocean Dr.
Asbury, NJ 07712
(908) 776-6700

Atlantic City

Bally's Grand Casino Hotel
Boston & Pacific Aves.
Atlantic City, NJ 08401
(609) 340-7100

Holday Inn Boardwalk
Chelsea Ave. at the Boardwalk
Atlantic City, NJ 08401
(609) 348-2200

Marriott Seaview Hotel
Rte. 9
Atlantic City, NJ 08201
(609) 748-1990 / (800) 932-800

Merv Griffin's Resort Casino Hotel
Boardwalk & North Carolina Ave.
Atlantic City, NJ 08404
(609) 340-6300 / (800) 336-MERV

Sheraton Inn Atlantic City West
6821 Black Horse Pike
Atlantic City, NJ 08232
(609) 272-0200 / (800) 782-9237

Trump Taj Mahal
1000 Boardwalk @ Virgina
Atlantic City, NJ 08401
(609) 449-1000 / (800) TAJ-TRUMP

Berlin

Berlin Motor Lodge
262 Rt. 73
Berlin, NJ 08009
(609) 768-5353

Bernardsville

Old Mill Inn
Rt. 202 & North Maple Ave.
Bernardsville, NJ 07924
(609) 221-1100

Bordentown

Econo Lodge
U.S. 130 & 206
Bordentown, NJ 08505
(609) 298-5000

Continued

Quality Inn Bordentown
1083 Rt. 206
Bordentown, NJ 08505
(609) 298-3200

Bridgeport

Holiday Inn - Bridgport
Pureland Industrial Park
Bridgeport, NJ 08014
(609) 467-3322

Camden

Four Winds Motor Lodge
1950 Admiral Wilson Blvd.
Bridgeport, NJ 08109
(609) 757-0500

Cape May

Grand Hotel of Cape May
Oceanfront at Philadelphia Ave.
Cape May, NJ 08204
(609) 884-5611

Inn of Cape May
601 Beach Dr.
Cape May, NJ 08204
(609) 884-3483

Cardiff

Inn of the Dove Hotel
6665 Black Horse Pike
Cardiff, NJ 08232
(609) 645-1100

Carteret

Holiday Inn
1000 Roosevelt Ave.
Carteret, NJ 08232
(908) 541-9500

Cherry Hill

Days Inn
Rt. 70 & Cuthbert Blvd.
Cherry Hill, NJ 08002
(609) 665-1100

Howard Johnson
832 N. Black Horse Pike
Cherry Hill, NJ 08012
(609) 228-4040

Clark

Howard Johnson Lodge
70 Central Ave.
Clark, NJ 07066
(908) 381-6076

Clifton

Howard Johnson
680 Rt. 3 W
Clifton, NJ 07014
(201) 471-3800

Ramada Hotel
265 Rt. 3 E
Clifton, NJ 07014
(201) 778-6500

Clinton

Holiday Inn Clinton
111 Rt. 173
Clinton, NJ 08809
(908) 735-5111

Stewart Inn
South Main St.
Stewartville, NJ 08886
(908) 479-6060

Cookstown

Days Inn Executive
Writestown-Cookstown Rd.
Cookstown, NJ 08511
(609) 723-6500

Cranford

Days Inn
Exit 136, Garden State Pkwy.
Cranford, NJ 07016
(908) 272-4700

East Brunswick

Sheraton Inn East Brunswick
195 Eggers St.
East Brunswick, NJ 08816
(908) 828-6900

East Hanover

Ramada Hotel
130 Rt. 10 W.
East Hanover, NJ 07926
(201) 386-5622

East Orange

Royel Inn
120 Evergreen Place
East Orange, NJ 07018
(201) 677-3100

East Rutherford

Sheraton Meadowlands
2 Meadowlands Plaza
East Rutherford, NJ 07073
(201) 896-0500

East Windsor

Ramada Inn & National Conference Center
399 Monmouth St.
East Windsor, NJ 08520
(609) 448-7000

Eatontown

Holiday Inn Tinton Falls
700 Hope Rd.
Eatontown, NJ 07724
(908) 544-9300

Edison

Ramada Inn Raritan Center
Raritan Center Pkwy.
Edison, NJ 08837
(908) 225-8300 / (800) HOLIDAY

Wellesley Inn
831 Rt. 1 S.
Edison, NJ 08817
(908) 287-0171

Elizabeth

Newark Airport Hilton
1170 Spring St.
Elizabeth, NJ 07201
(908) 351-3900 / (800) HILTONS

Englewood

Radisson Hotel Englewood
401 Van Brunt St.
Englewood, NJ 07631
(01) 871-2020 / (800) 333-3333

Englishtown

Marlboro Motor Lodge
Hwy. 9
Englishtown, NJ 07726
(908) 536-5150

Fairfield

Radisson Fairfield Hotel
690 Rt. 46 E.
Fairfield, NJ 07004
(201) 227-9200 / (800) 333-3333

Ramada Inn Fairfield
38 Two Bridges Rd.
Fairfield, NJ 07004
(201) 575-1742 / (800) 228-3838

Fanwood

Best Western The Mansion Hotel
295 South Ave.
Fanwood, NJ 07023
(908) 654-5200 / (800) 688-1110

Floorham Park

Hamilton Park Executive Conference Center
175 Park Ave.
Fairfield, NJ 07932
(201) 377-2424

Fort Lee

Comfort Inn
725 River Rd.
Edgewater, NJ 07020
(201) 943-3131

Days Inn of Fort Lee
2339 Rt.4 E.
Fort Lee, NJ 07024
(201) 944-5000

Holiday Inn Fort Lee
2117 Rt. 4 E.
Fort Lee, NJ 07024
(201) 461-3100 / (800) HOLIDAY

Freehold

Freehold Gardens Hotel
50 Gibson Place
Freehold, NJ 07728
(908) 780-3870

Freehold Motor Hotel
4089 Hwy. 9
Freehold, NJ 07728
(908) 462-3450

Great Gorge

Seasons Resort & Conference Center
P.O. Box 637, Rt. 517
McAfee, NJ 07428
(201) 827-6000

Hackensack

Best Western Oritani Hotel
414 Hackensack Ave.
Hackensack, NJ 07601
(201) 488-8900

Hammonton

Lakefront Motel
700 S. Whitehorse Pike
Hammonton, NJ 08037
(609) 561-0932

Hasbrouck Heights

Sheraton Hasbrouck Heights
650 Terrace Ave.
Hackensack, NJ 07604
(201) 288-6100 / (800) 325-3535

Hazlet

Ramada Inn
2870 Hwy. 35
Hazlet, NJ 07730
(908) 624-2400

Wellesley Inn
3215 Hwy. 35
Hazlet, NJ 07730
(908) 888-2800

Hightstown

Town House Motel
Rt. 33 & NJ Turnpike
Hightstown, NJ 08520
(609) 448-2400

Jersey City

Quality Inn
Holland Tunnel Plaza
Jersey City, NJ 07302
(201) 653-0300

Kenilworth

Holiday Inn
S. 31st. St.
Kenilworth, NJ 07033
(908) 241-4100

Lakewood

Best Western Leisure Inn
1600 Rt. 70
Lakewood, NJ 08701
(908) 367-0900

Budget Inn
1000 Madison Ave.
Lakewood, NJ 08701
(908) 364-2020

Ledgewood

Days Inn
1691 Rt. 46
Ledgewood, NJ 07852
(908) 241-4100

Linden

Benedict Motel
401 W. Edger Rd., US Rts. 1 & 9
Linden, NJ 07036
(908) 862-7700

Linden

Benedict Motel
401 W. Edger Rd., US Rts. 1 & 9
Linden, NJ 07036
(908) 862-7700

Livingston

Holiday Inn Livingston
550 W. Mount Pleasant Ave.
Livingston, NJ 07039
(201) 994-3500

Lyndhurst

Quality Inn Sports Complex
10 Polito Ave.
Lyndhurst, NJ 07071
(201) 933-9800

Maple Shade

Landmark Inn
Rts. 73 & 38
Maple Shore, NJ 08052
(609) 235-6400

Marmora

Kings Court Motel
115 South Shore Rd.
Marmora, NJ 08223
(609) 90-3366

Mahwah

Ramada Inn Mahwah
180 Rt. 17 S.
Mahwah, NJ 07430
(201) 529-5880 / (800) 228-3838

Middletown

Howard Johnson Lodge
750 Hwy. 35 South
Middletown, NJ 07748
(908) 671-3400

Millville

Country Inn by Carlson
1125 Village Dr.
Millville, NJ 08332
(609) 825-3100

Montvale

Ramada Inn
100 Chestnut Ridge Rd.
Montvale, NJ 07645
(201) 391-7700

Morristown

Madison Hotel
1 Convent Rd.
Morristown, NJ 07960
(201) 285-1800 / (800) 526-0729

Mount Arlington

Sheraton Inn Mt. Arlington
15 Howard Blvd.
Mount Arlington, NJ 07856
(201) 770-2000

Mount Holly

Best Western Inn
1135 Burlington
Mount Holly, NJ 08060
(609) 261-3800

Howard Johnson
Burlington-Mount Holly Rd.
Mount Holly, NJ 08060
(609) 267-6550

Mount Laural

Clarion Hotel
915 Rt. 73 at I-295
Mount Laural, NJ 08054
(609) 234-7300

Ramada Hotel
555 Fellowship Rd.
Mount Laural, NJ 08054
(609) 273-1900

Travelodge Viscount Hotel
1111 Rt. 73
Mount Laural, NJ 08054
(609) 234-7000

Mount Laural

Clarion Hotel
915 Rt. 73 at I-295
Mount Laural, NJ 08054
(609) 234-7300

Neptune

Ho Jo Inn
Rt. 35, Asbury Park Circle
Neptune, NJ 08054
(609) 235-3939

New Brunswick

Brunswick Hilton & Towers
3 Tower Center Blvd.
E. Brunswick, NJ 08816
(908) 828-2000 / (800) 932-3322

Hyatt Regency
New Brunswick Downtown
2 Albany St.
Brunswick, NJ 08901
(908) 873-1234 / (800) 233-1234

New Providence

Best Western Murry Hill Inn
535 Central Ave.
New Providence, NJ 07974
(908) 665-9200 / (800) 688-7474

Newark

Hilton Gateway
In Gateway Center Raymond Blvd.
Newark, NJ 07102
(201) 622-5000

Ramada Hotel
36 Valley Rd.
Clark, NJ 07114
(908) 574-0100 / (800) 228-3838

Sheraton Newark Airport
901 Spring St., US 1 & 9
Newark, NJ 07102
(908) 527-1600 / (800) 334-8484

North Bergen

Days Inn North Bergen
2750 Tonnelle Ave.
North Bergen, NJ 07047
(201) 348-3600

Ocean City

Beach Club Hotel
1280 Boardwalk at 13th St.
Ocean City, NJ 08226-0929
(609) 399-8555

Days Inn
7th & Boardwalk
Ocean City, NJ 08226
(609) 398-2200

Flanders Hotel
11th St. & Boardwalk
Ocean City, NJ 08226
(609) 399-1000

Santa Barbara Suite Resort Hotel
10th St. at Wesley Ave.
Ocean City, NJ 08226
(609) 398-4700

Paramus

Radisson Inn Paramus
601 From Rd.
Paramus, NJ 07652
(201) 262-6900 / (800) 777-7800

Park Ridge

Marriott Park Ridge
300 Brae Blvd.
Park Ridge, NJ 07656
(201) 307-0800 / (800) 831-1000

Parsippany

Embassy Suites-Parsippany
909 Parsippany Blvd.
Parsippany, NJ 07054
(201) 334-1440

Parsippany Hilton
1 Hilton Court
Parsippany, NJ 07054
(201) 267-7373 / (800) HILTONS

Pequannock

Regency House Hotel
140 Rt. 23 N.
Pequannock, NJ 07444
(201) 696-0900

Penns Grove

Howard Johnson
10 Howard Johnson Lane
Penns Grove, NJ 08069
(609) 299-3800

Phillipsburg

Howard Johnson Lodge
1315 US Hwy. 22
Phillipsburg, NJ 08865
(908) 454-6461

Piscataway

Embassy Suites-Piscataway
121 Centennial Ave.
Piscataway, NJ 08854
(908) 980-0500

Plainfield

Holiday Inn
4701 Stelton Rd.
South Plainfield, NJ 07080
(908) 753-5500

Point Pleasant Beach

Crystal Point Yacht Club & Hotel
River Rd. & Rt. 70
Point Pleasant Beach, NJ 08742
(908) 899-9000

Gull Island Inn
205 Broadway
Point Pleasant Beach, NJ 08742
(908) 295-3440

Harbor Lights Inn
301 N. Broadway
Point Pleasant Beach, NJ 08742
(908) 295-3440

Sheraton Oceanside Inn
1620 Oceanside Ave.
Point Pleasant Beach, NJ 08742
(908) 892-2111

Princeton

Days Inn Princeton
4191 Rt. 1
Princeton, NJ 08052
(908) 329-4555

Howard Johnson
2991 Brunswick Pike
Lawrenceville, NJ 08648
(609) 896-1100

Hyatt Regency Princeton / Carnagie Center
102 Carnagie Center
Princeton, NJ 08540
(609) 987-1234

Mariott Princeton
201Village Blvd.
Princeton, NJ 08540
(609) 452-7900 / (800) 242-8689

Nassau Inn
10 Palmer Square
Princeton, NJ 08542
(609) 921-7500

Ramada Princeton
4355 Rt. 1 on Ridge Rd.
Princeton, NJ 08540
(609) 452-2400 / (800) 228-3838

Rahway

Village Motel
667 E. Milton Ave.
Rahway, NJ 07065
(908) 382-1500

Ramsey

Wellesley Inn
946 Rt. 17 N.
Ramsey, NJ 07446
(201) 934-9250

Red Bank

Oyster Point Hotel
146 Bodman Pl.
Red Bank, NJ 07701
(908) 530-8200 / (800) 345-3484

Ridgefield

Turnpike Motor Hotel
Rt. US 46
Ridgefield, NJ 07657
(201) 943-2500

Rochelle Park

Ramada Hotel Rochelle Park
375 W. Passaic St.
Rochelle Park, NJ 07662
(201) 845-3400 / (800) 228-3838

Rockaway

Howard Johnson Lodge
Greenpond Rd.
Rockaway, NJ 07866
(201) 625-1200

Saddle Brook

Marriott Saddle Brook
Garden State Pkwy., at I-80
Rockaway, NJ 07662
(201) 843-9500 / (800) 831-1000

Secaucus

Embassy Suites Hotel Meadowlands
455 Plaza Dr.
Secaucus, NJ 07094
(201) 864-7300

Continued

Ramada Plaza Suite Hotel
350 Rt. 3 W., Millcreek Dr.
Secaucus, NJ 07094
(201) 863-8700

Seaside Heights

Aztec Motel
901 Boardwalk
Seaside Heights, NJ 08751
(908) 793-3000

Short Hills

Hilton at Short Hills
41 John F. Kennedy Pkwy.
Short Hills, NJ 07078
(201) 379-0100 / (800) 932-3322

Somerset

Radisson Hotel Somerset
200 Atrium Dr.
Somerset, NJ 08873
(908) 469-2600

Ramada Inn of Somerset
Weston Canal Rd. & I-287 (Exit 7)
Somerset, NJ 08873
(908) 560-9880 / (800) 228-3838

Somerville

Best Western Red Bull
1271 Rt. 22 W.
Somerville, NJ 08807
(908) 722-4000

Springfield

Spring Garden Inn
295 Rt. 22 E.
Springfield, NJ 07081
(201) 376-7700

Spring Lake

Chateau
500 Warren Ave.
Spring Lake, NJ 07762
(908) 974-2000

Hewitt Wellington Hotel
200 Monmouth Ave.
Spring Lake, NJ 07762
(908) 974-1212

Warren Hotel
901 Ocean Ave.
Spring Lake, NJ 07762
(908) 449-8800

Stone Harbor

Golden Inn Hotel & Conference Center
Oceanfront at 78th Ave. St.
Avalon, NJ 08202
(609) 368-5155

Summit

Grand Summit Hotel
570 Springfield Ave.
Summit, NJ 07901-4599
(908) 273-3000

Teaneck

Marriott At Glenpointe
100 Frank W. Burr Blvd.
Teaneck, NJ 07666
(201) 836-0600 / (800) 228-9290

Tenafly

Clinton Inn Hotel
145 Dean Dr.
Tenafly, NJ 07670
(201) 871-3200

Tinton Falls

Residence Inn by Marriott
90 Park Rd.
Tinton Falls, NJ 07724
(908) 389-8100

Toms River

Holiday Inn Toms River
290 Hwy. 37 E.
Toms River, NJ 08753
(908) 244-4000

Howard Johnson
Rt. 37 & Hooper Ave.
Toms River, NJ 08753
(908) 244-1000

Quality Inn at Toms River
815 Rt. 37 W.
Toms River, NJ 08755
(908) 341-2400

Ramada Hotel Toms River Lakewood
2373 Hwy. 9
Toms River, NJ 08755
(908) 905-2626

Totowa

Holiday Inn
1 Rt. 46 Westbound
Totowa, NJ 07512
(201) 785-9000

Trenton

Days Inn Bordentown
State Rt. 206, NJ Turnpike Exit 7
Trenton, NJ 08505
(609) 298-6100 / (800) 325-2525

Union

Union Motor Lodge
2735 Rt. 22 W.
Union, NJ 07083
(908) 687-8600

Vineland

Ramada Inn Vineland
2216 W. Landis Ave.
Vineland, NJ 08360
(201) 696-3800

Warren

Sommerset Hills Hotel
200 Liberty Corner Rd.
Warren, NJ 07059
(908) 647-6700 / (800) 688-0700

Wayne

Wayne Motor Inn
535 Rt. 23
Wayne, NJ 07470
(908) 696-2000

Westfield

Best Western Westfield Inn
435 N. Ave. W.
Westfield, NJ 07090
(908) 654-5600 / (800) 688-5454

Wildwood Crest

Madrid Resort Hotel
427 E. Miami Ave.
Wildwood Crest, NJ 08260
(609) 729-1600

Saratoga Inn
7501 Ocean Ave.
Wildwood Crest, NJ 08260
(609) 522-7712

Singapore Hotel
515 E. Orchard Rd.
Wildwood Crest, NJ 08260
(609) 522-6961

Whippany

Marriott Hanover
1401 Rt. 10 E.
Whippany, NJ 07981
(201) 538-8811 / (800) 242-8681

Woodbridge

Woodbridge Hilton
120 Wood Ave.
Woodbridge, NJ 08830
(908) 494-6200 / (800) HILTONS

Woodcliff Lake

Woodcliff Lake Hilton
200 Tice Blvd.
Woodcliff Lake, NJ 07675
(201) 391-3600 / (800) 932-3322

INDEX - NEW YORK COURSES

LEGEND

Public = {P}
Semi Private = {SP}
Private = {Pr.}
Military = {M}
9-hole {9}
Executive = {E}
Par-3= {3}

NEW YORK

Fenway Golf Club {Pr.}, 101
Fillmore Golf Course {E}, 67
Fisher Island Club {Pr.}, 97
Fishkill Golf Course {9}, 91
Forest Heights Golf Course {E}, 137
Forest Park Golf Course {E}, 96
Four-X-Four Golf Club {9}, 48
Fox Run Golf Course {9}, 144
Foxfire Golf & Tennis Club {P}, 61
Foxhill Golf & Country Club {Pr.}, 97
French Hollow Fairways {9}, 65

Galway Golf Club {9}, 48
Garden City Country Club {Pr.}, 92
Gardiner's Bay Country Club {Pr.}, 97
Genegantslet Golf Club {SP}, 56
Genesee Valley Golf Clug {P}, 124
Geneva Country Club {Pr.}, 142
Glen Core Club {E}, 93
Glen Core Golf Club {E}, 94
Glen Head Country Club {Pr.}, 92
Glen Oak Golf Club {M}, 113
Glen Oaks Club {Pr.}, 92
Glens Falls Country Club {Pr.}, 49
Golden Oak Golf Club {E}, 66
Golf Club Of New Port, The {P}, 28
Golf Knolls {9}, 46
Governeur Golf Club {9}, 48
Gowanda Country Club {Pr.}, 138
Grandview Farms {9}, 72
Grandview Golf Course {9}, 138
Granit Hotel & Country Club {R}, 87
Green Hill Golf Club {Pr.}, 140
Green Lakes State Park Club {P}, 62
Green Meadows Golf Club {9}, 49
Green Ridge Golf Course {9}, 95
Greenview Country Club {P}, 37
Greenwood Golf Course {9}, 139
Grossinger Golf Course {P}, 85
Grygiel's Pine Hills Golf {P}, 44

Hampton Hills Golf & Country Club {Pr.}, 97
Hanah Country Club {P}, 58
Harbour Pointe Country Club {P}, 142
Hauppauge Country Club {SP}, 82
Hertage Hills Country Club {Pr.}, 102
Hiawatha Trails {3}, 65

Hidden Valley Country Club {Pr.}, 73
Hidden Valley Golf Club {P}, 33
Highland Park Golf Club {P}, 54
Highlands Country Club {Pr.}, 102
Hiland Golf Club {SP}, 41
Hillandale Golf Course {E} 73
Hillview Golf Course {P}, 108
Holiday Valley Resort {P}, 107
Holland Hills Golf Course {SP}, 78
Holland Meadows Golf Course, {E}, 44
Hollow Hills Golf Course {9}, 90
Homewack Hotel Golf Course {9}, 100
Hornell Country Club {9}, 143
Huntington Crescent Club {Pr.}, 97
Hyde Park Golf Course {P}, 128

IBM Country Club {Pr.}, 66
IBM Country Club {Pr.}, 91
IBM Country Club {Pr.}, 92
Indian Head Golf Course {9}, 73
Indian Hills Golf Club {Pr.}, 98
Indian Hills Golf Club {SP}, 133
Indian Island Golf Course {P}, 97
Inlet Golf Club {P}, 27
Irondequoit Country Club {Pr.}, 100
Ischua Valley Country Club {9}, 136
Island Glenn Country Club {9}, 100
Island Valley Golf Course {9}, 141
Island's End Golf & Country Club {P}, 97
Ithaca City Golf Course {9}, 73
Ives Hill Country Club {Pr.}, 45

James Baird State Park Course {P}, 91

Kanon Valley Country Club {Pr.}, 69
Katsbaan Golf Club {9}, 100
Keshqua Golf Club {Pr.}, 140
Kingsboro Golf Club {9}, 44
Kissena Park Golf Course {E}, 96
Knickerbocker Country Club {9}, 68
Knollwood Country Club {Pr.}, 102
Kutsher's Country Club {P}, 90

Lafayette Country Club {Pr.}, 70
Lake Pleasant Golf {9}, 44
Lake Shore Country Club {SP}, 124
Lake Shore Yacht & Country Club {Pr.}, 70
Lakeside Country Club {Pr.}, 143

Park Country Club {Pr.}, 138
Peek 'N' Peek Recreation {P}, 109
Pehquenakonck Country Club {9}, 103
Pelham Country Club {Pr.}, 102
Pelham Split Rock American Golf Club {P}, 75
Penfield Country Club {Pr.}, 140
Peninsula Golf Club {9}, 94
Perington Golf & Country Club {9}, 140
Phillip J. Rotella Municipal {P}, 81
Pine Brook Golf Club {Pr.}, 43
Pine Grove Country Club {E}, 71
Pine Haven Country Club {Pr.}, 65
Pine Hills Country Club {P}, 97
Pine Hollow Country Club {Pr.}, 93
Pine Meadows Golf & Country Club {9}, 139
Pinehurst Golf Course {9}, 137
Pines Golf Club, The {9}, 47
Pines Hotel & Golf Club {9}, 100
Pinewood Country Club {9}, 140
Pinnicle State Park Golf Course {9}, 143
Piping Rock Club {Pr.}, 93
Plandome Country Club {Pr.}, 93
Plattsburgh AFB Golf Club {M}, 43
Pleasant Knolls Golf Course {9}, 69
Pleasant Valley Golf {9}, 68
Pleasant View Lodge {9}, 68
Pleasantville Country Club {Pr.}, 102
Point East Golf Course {9}, 70
Pompey Club {Pr.}, 70
Port Jefferson Country Club {Pr.}, 98
Port Jervis Country Club {Pr.}, 94
Potdam Town & Country Club {9}, 48
Powelton Club, The {Pr.}, 94
Poxabogue Golf Course {9}, 90

Quaker Ridge Golf Club {Pr.}, 102
Queens Hill Country Club {Pr.}, 91
Queensbury Golf Course {P}, 42
Quiet Times Golf Course {P}, 143
Quogue Field Club {Pr.}, 98

Radisson Greens Golf Course {SP}, 63
Rainbow Country Club {9}, 68
Raymondville Golf & Country Club {P}, 48
Rea Hook Golf Club {9}, 91
Ricci Meadows Golf Course {E}, 142
Richmond County Country Club {Pr.}, 96

Ridgemont Country Club {Pr.}, 100
Ridgeway Country Club {Pr.}, 102
Rip Van Winkle {9}, 68
River Oak Golf Club {SP}, 114
River View Country Club {P}, 47
Riverbend Golf Course {P}, 67
Riverton Golf Club {9}, 140
Robert Van Patten Golf Course {P}, 47
Rockhill Golf & Country Club {P}, 84
Rockland Country Club {Pr.} 96
Rockland Lake Championship G.C. {E}, 96
Rockville Links Course {Pr.}, 93
Rome Country Club {SP}, 34
Rosebook Golf Course {9}, 137
Rothland Golf Course {P}, 114
Roundabout Country Club {P}, 100
Rustic Golf & Country Club {9}, 45
Rye Golf Club {Pr.}, 102

University {P}, 73

Sacandaga Golf Club {9}, 44
Sadaquada Golf Clug {E}, 47
Sadaquada Golf Club {Pr.}, 46
Sag Harbor Golf Course {9}, 90
Sagamore Resort & Golf Club {R}, 42
Salem Golf Club {Pr.}, 102
Salmon Creek Country Club {SP}, 125
Sands Point Golf Club {Pr.}, 93
Saranac Inn Golf & Country Club {SP}, 24
Saranac Lake Golf Club {9}, 43
Saratoga Golf & Polo Club {Pr.}, 47
Saratoga Spa State Park {P}, 39
Sauquoit Knolls Golf Club {9}, 46
Saxon Woods Golf Club {P}, 90
Scarsdale Golf Club {Pr.}, 102
Schenectady Municipal Golf Course {M}, 39
Schuyler Meadows Club {Pr.}, 65
Scott's Corners Golf Course {9}, 95
Seneca Falls Country Club {Pr.}, 142
Seneca Golf Course {9}, 70
Seneca Lake Country Club {SP}, 132
Sewane Club, The {Pr.}, 93
Shadow Lake Golf Club {P}, 125
Shadow Pines Golf Club {P}, 126
Shaker Ridge Country Club {Pr.}, 65
Shawangunk Country Club {Pr.}, 101
Shawnee Country Club {9}, 141

Sheldridge Country Club {Pr.}, 142
Shepard Hills Country Club {Pr.}, 72
Sheridan Park Golf Course {M}, 115
Shinnecock Hills Golf Course {Pr.}, 98
Shore Acres Golf Course {9}, 141
Shorewood Country Club {P}, 136
Sidney Golf & Country Club {Pr.}, 68
Silver Creek Golf Course {E}, 142
Silver Lake Country Club {Pr.}, 144
Silver Lake Golf Course {9}, 95
Siwanoy Country Club {Pr.}, 102
Six-S Country Club {P}, 105
Skaneateles Country Club {Pr.}, 70
Skenandoa Club Of Clinton {Pr.}, 91
Skene Valley Country Club {P}, 42
Skyline Golf & Country Club {P}, 69
Skyridge Chalet & Golf {9}, 69
Sleepy Hollow Golf Club {P}, 45
Smithtown Landing Golf Club {P}, 97
Soaring Eagle Golf Course {P}, 110
Sodus Bay Heights Golf Club {Pr.}, 143
South Fork Country Club {Pr.}, 98
South Hampton Golf Club {Pr.}, 98
South Hills Country Club {P}, 109
South Park Golf Course {9}, 139
Southern Duchess Country Club {Pr.}, 91
Southshore Country Club {E}, 139
Southward Ho Country Club {Pr.}, 98
Spook Rock Golf Course {9}, 96
Spring Lake Golf Course {P}, 97
Springville Country Club {Pr.}, 138
St. Andrews Golf Club {Pr.}, 102
St. Bonaventure {9}, 136
St. George's Golf & Country Club {Pr.}, 98
St. Lawrence State Park G.C. {P}, 48
St. Lawrence University Golf Course {P}, 40
Stadium Golf Club {P}, 40
Stafford Country Club {Pr.}, 139
Stamford Golf Club {SP}, 58
Stonebridge Golf & Country Club {P}, 35
Stonehedges Golf Course {P}, 72
Stony Ford Golf Course {P}, 79
Storm King Golf Club {Pr.}, 94
Sullivan County Golf & C.C. {Pr.}, 90
Sundown Golf & Country Club {9}, 67
Sunken Meadow State Park G.C. {9}, 90
Sunningdale Golf Club {Pr.}, 102
Sunnycrest Golf Course {9}, 70

Sunnyville Resort {E}, 69
Sunset Valley Golf Course {E}, 137
Swan Lake Golf & Country Club {P}, 90
Swan Lake Golf Club {P}, 97
Sycamore Country Club {SP}, 51

Tall Tree Golf Course {E}, 90
Tam O'Shanter Club {Pr.}, 93
Tan-Tara Country Club {Pr.}, 141
Tanner Valley Golf {P}, 69
Tarry Brae Golf Course {P}, 90
Tee Bird Country Club {P}, 49
Tennanah Lake Golf & Tennis Club Inc. {SP}, 86
Terry Hills Golf Course {P}, 117
Teugega Country Club {Pr.}, 46
Thendara Golf Club {SP}, 28
Thomas Carvel Country Club {M}, 77
Thousand Acres Golf Club {P}, 49
Thousand Island Golf Club {R}, 29
Ticonderoga Country Club {SP}, 24
Timber Point Country Club {P}, 97
Tioaga Country Club {P}, 72
Towers Country Club {Pr.}, 93
Town Of Hamburg Golf Course {9}, 139
Town Of Schroon Golf {9}, 43
Towne Isle Golf Club & Range {P}, 69
Top Of The World Golf Course {9}, 49
Transit Valley Country Club {Pr.}, 138
Tri-County Country Club {SP}, 110
Trumansburg Golf Club {9}, 73
Tupper Lake Golf Course {P}, 26
Turrin Highlands Golf Course {P}, 31
Tuscarora Golf Club {Pr.}, 70
Tuxedo Club, The {Pr.}, 95
Twaalfskill Club {Pr.}, 100
Twin Brook 18-hole Course {P}, 48
Twin Hickory Golf Club {SP}, 134
Twin Hills Golf Course {P}, 126
Twin Ponds Golf & Country Club {P}, 35

Vails Grove Golf Course {9}, 95
Vails Grove Golf Course {9}, 103
Valley View Golf Course {M}, 36
Van Cortland {P}, 75
Van Schaick Island Country Club {9}, 65
Vassar Golf Course {9}, 91
Vesperhills Golf Course {9}, 70

NEW YORK EXCURSIONS INDEX

INDEX - NEW JERSEY COURSES

NEW JERSEY EXCURSIONS

WE WANT YOUR INPUT!

It's possible that things may have changed at some of the golf courses I've selected by the time you visit. If changes have occurred, please let me know. And if you disagree with one of my recommendations, I'd like to hear that too. The address is listed below.

Our goal is to provide you with a guide book that is second to none. Things do change, however: phone numbers, prices, addresses, etc. Should you come across any new information, we'd appreciate hearing from you. No item is too small for us, so if you have any recommendations or suggested changes, please write us.

The address is:

Jimmy Shacky
c/o Open Road Publishing
P.O. Box 11249
Cleveland Park Station
Washington, DC 20008

YOUR PASSPORT TO GREAT GOLF!!
FROM OPEN ROAD PUBLISHING

OTHER GREAT GOLF GUIDES
IN THE ACCLAIMED "SHACKY SERIES"
Let Jimmy Shacky guide you to the fairway of your choice!
Ask your bookstore for:

• FLORIDA GOLF GUIDE
by Jimmy Shacky, $14.95

• GOLF COURSES OF THE SOUTHWEST
by Jimmy Shacky, $14.95
Includes accommodations and reviews fun things to do in each state.